The Renaissance in England

The men, the knowledge and the literature

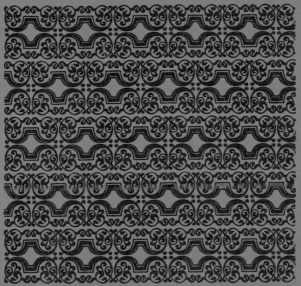

The Renaissance in England

EDITED BY

J. V. CUNNINGHAM

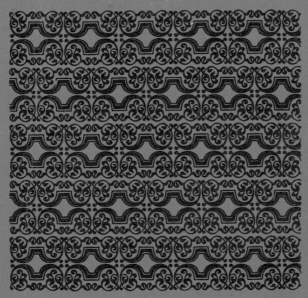

riginal Harbinger Book

1.98

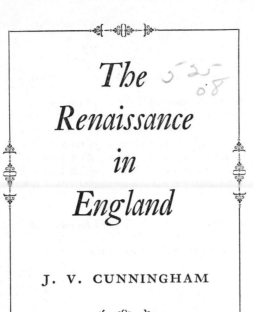

The Renaissance in England

J. V. CUNNINGHAM

An Original Harbinger Book

HARCOURT, BRACE & WORLD, INC.

New York

9235

The poems of John Hoskyns are reprinted, by permission of Louise Brown Osborn, from her book *The Life, Letters, and Writings of John Hoskyns, 1566–1638* (New Haven: Yale University Press [1937]).

Preface

This is a book designed to be read through with pleasure and profit. Nothing is included merely because it is representative; only because it is interesting. And yet the whole is an image of the time, though five-sixths of the selections are not to be found in the standard anthologies. It is, at least, an image of a view of the time, a view less golden than is usual.

The texts have been ruthlessly modernized; *Mr. More* for *Master More*. The punctuation is light, though prose of this period, it must be said, was not written for modern punctuation: just keep on going, it will all come out in the end. For the language is not our language:

> As woods whose change appears
> Still in their leaves throughout the sliding years,
> The first-born dying, so the aged state
> Of words decay, and phrases born but late
> Like tender buds shoot up and freshly grow.
> Ourselves and all that's ours to death we owe.

Yet less needs to be glossed than is often supposed; the context will specify what must be meant. When Elyot speaks of "the bright leam of a torch or candle," how could gloss add anything to understanding, except, possibly, reassurance? And, indeed, this is the way we learned and learn our own language.

Where it seemed absolutely necessary to give gloss or context, it is given in the headnotes.

The greater number of the texts were originally prepared with accuracy and learning by my research assistant, Mrs. Barbara Herrnstein Smith, now of Bennington College.

                                                                        J.V.C.

July 19, 1965
Sudbury, Mass.

WE must not look upon the immense course of times past as men overlook spacious and wide countries from off high mountains, and are never the near to judge of the true nature of the soil, or the particular site and face of those territories they see.

SAMUEL DANIEL [1603]

Contents

[xi]

Introduction

In dealing with the past, as in dealing with our own autobiography, we parcel it out in periods. And these need not be merely arbitrary. What is arbitrary is that we mark off a period in light of some aspect of the times that interests us; in light of other aspects we would mark it off differently. For some, at least, of the authors in this book there was such a thing as the Renaissance in England. It was an event in the history of literature and of learning.

The time is the hundred and some years after the discovery of America, from the youth of Thomas More to the publication of Shakespeare's collected plays in 1623. It is the time of the diffusion of printing, the exploitation of gunpowder, the exploration of the New World. It is the time of the Reformation and of an increasing nationalism in Western Europe: Christianity became regional, and theology an instrument of international affairs.

The place is England, a small northern country on the edge of the great world of that time, and with about the same secondary importance in the international scene of its day as Great Britain has in the larger scene of today. But it was not, at the start, Great Britain. Scotland until 1603 was an independent kingdom and after 1603 had still an independent government

under a common monarch. Moreover, in the preceding century
it was often hostile and for the most part allied with France:
Mary, Queen of Scots, for example, was for a time Queen of
France. Nor was England itself a country unified and homo-
geneous. The North was remote, unruly border country, poor,
feudal, and feuding. It was the world of the border ballads, of
the Percys and the Dacres. Wales, to the west, was at the beginning of this period still thoroughly Celtic, a region where
Owen Glendowers still called "spirits from the vasty deep,"
though toward the end it had been sufficiently assimilated to
the central culture of England. Ireland was an outpost in un-
easy subjection, and the relationship of English and Irish was
precisely that of the English and the American Indian. We are
concerned, in brief, with London and with central, southern,
and eastern England.

And with very few people. There were fewer, indeed, in the
1490's than there had been a century and a half earlier, as a
consequence of the Black Death and the subsequent recurrent
plagues. However, from this time on the population was on
the increase. We do not have, of course, any precise figures
since there was nothing like the modern census, but we can
make informed guesses. The population in 1490 was about equal
to the present population of Connecticut; in 1623, to that of
Florida. The striking increase was in the population of London:
from the size of Portland, Maine, to almost the size of Portland,
Oregon, in a hundred and some years.

At the beginning of this period the literary models in English
were Chaucer, Gower, and Lydgate in verse; there were none
in prose. The only prose work of general reputation in the
world of letters, Thomas More's *Utopia* (1516), was written
in Latin. At the end of this period there were for models
the achievements of Shakespeare and Jonson, Beaumont and
Fletcher, Sidney and Spenser, Bacon and Donne. There was a
literature that, as Jonson said of Shakespeare in the commenda-
tory poem to the first collected edition, could challenge com-

parison with "all that insolent Greece or haughty Rome sent forth." At the beginning is Leonard Cox's simple assumption that "logic"—the old Aristotelian logic—"is a plain and sure way to instruct a man of the truth of anything," and the lore of the four elements; at the end, Gilbert's conception of the earth as a giant lodestone, and Harvey's demonstration of the circulation of the blood.

This, then, was the Renaissance in England. For the Renaissance is a notion properly applicable to the world of letters and of learning. It denotes, of course, a rebirth and referred originally to a revival of interest in the literature of Antiquity and its associated learning after, so it was thought, the monkish barbarism of the intervening centuries. The idea was then extended to the Early Modern rebirth of a special kind of intellectual excitement. So, at least, some of the authors in this book themselves thought. "Learning first flourished in Greece," writes Thomas Campian in 1602, "from thence it was derived unto the Romans . . . Learning, after the declining of the Roman Empire and the pollution of their language through the conquest of the barbarians, lay most pitifully deformed till the time of Erasmus, Reuchlin, Sir Thomas More, and other learned men of that age, who brought the Latin tongue again to light, redeeming it with much labour out of the hands of the illiterate monks and friars."

Francis Bacon a few years later saw the literary and intellectual history of the immediate past in much the same terms, only more explicitly developed, and with dispraise for both parties, as befitted the rhetorician of the New Learning of modern science:

Martin Luther, conducted no doubt by a higher providence, but in discourse of reason finding what a province he had undertaken against the bishop of Rome and the degenerate traditions of the church and finding his own solitude being no ways aided by the opinions of his own time, was enforced to awake all antiquity, and to call former times to his succours to make a party against the present time. So that the ancient authors, both in divinity and in humanity, which had long time slept in libraries, began generally to be read and revolved. This by consequence did draw on a necessity of a more exquisite travail in the languages original, wherein those authors did write, for the better understanding of those authors, and the better advantage of pressing and applying their words. And thereof grew again a delight in their manner of style and phrase, and an admiration of that kind of writing; which was much furthered and precipitated by the enmity and opposition that the propounders of those primitive but seeming new opinions had against the schoolmen; who were generally of the contrary part, and whose writings were altogether in a different style and form; taking liberty to coin and frame new terms of art to express their own sense, and to avoid circuit of speech, without regard to the pureness, pleasantness, and, as I may call it, lawfulness of the phrase or word. And again, because the great labour that then was with the people (of whom the Pharisees were wont to say, *Execrabilis ista turba, quae non novit legem*), for the winning and persuading of them, there grew of necessity in chief price and request eloquence and variety of discourse, as the fittest and forciblest access into the capacity of the vulgar sort: so that these four causes concurring, the admiration of ancient authors, the hate of the schoolmen, the exact study of languages, and the efficacy of preaching, did bring in an affectionate study of eloquence and copy of speech, which then began to flourish. This grew speedily to an excess; for men began to hunt more after words than matter; more after the choiceness of the phrase, and the round and clean composition of the sentence, and the sweet falling of the clauses, and the varying and illustration of their words with tropes and figures, than after the weight of matter, worth of subject, soundness of argument, life of invention, or depth of judgment. Then grew the flowing and watery vein of Osorius, the Portugal bishop, to be in price. Then did Sturmius spend such infinite and curious pains upon Cicero the Orator, and Hermogenes the Rhetorician, besides his own books of Periods and Imitation, and the like. Then did Car of Cambridge, and Ascham with their lectures and writings almost deify

Cicero and Demosthenes, and allure all young men that were studious unto that delicate and polished kind of learning. Then did Erasmus take occasion to make the scoffing Echo: *Decem annos consumpsi in legendo Cicerone;* and the Echo answered in Greek, "*Ove, Asine.*" Then grew the learning of the schoolmen to be utterly despised as barbarous. In sum, the whole inclination and bent of those times was rather towards copy than weight.

For Campian and Bacon, then, there is a clearly distinguished period in the history of literature and of learning beginning around 1500 Erasmus (1465–1536), Reuchlin (1455–1522), More (1478–1535), Luther (1483–1546)—and extending to their own day. The initiators were Northern: German, Dutch, English. Nothing is said of Italy. The culture opposed and displaced is that of the Old Church, the scholasticism of monks and friars. The New Learning is associated with the Reformation.

What did it involve? It involved, first of all, a revolution in style, a rebirth, as they saw it, of the Latin language itself. Not that Latin had ceased to be used in the Middle Ages: there is more medieval Latin in print in a large university library than a man could, or would, read in a lifetime. It was, in fact, the only language of learning and remained the principal language of learning until the nineteenth century. But medieval Latin had shed the idiomatic quirks of the language of Plautus and the stately period of the language of Cicero. It had become a kind of Basic Latin, a clear, dry, precise medium that welcomed and harbored all the technical words, "terms of art," of the medieval sciences. And so the revolution in style was inevitably a revolution in learning, and, since learning was in large part divinity, it was associated with the revolution in religion.

It was first a revolution in Latin and then a revolution in the vernacular. And though the re-realization of classical models and classical experience was only part of the story in the vernacular literatures, it was part of the story. Something of Vergil's descent into Hell had long before been assimilated in the medieval tradition, and is here realized again in Sackville's *Vision of Hell*. But the worlds of ancient dialogue and Horatian satire are first naturalized in English in the early sixteenth century by More and by Wyatt. And the subjective erotic world of Propertius and Ovid is recaptured first by Donne in the Valedictions and Elegies of the 1590's. Indeed, the great stylistic achievement of the period, apart from the inimitable style of the later Shakespeare, the plain style of Jonson and of Donne at his best, is consciously modeled on the classical plain style. It is a consequence of the Renaissance.

This literature, with some glimpses of the men and the thought of the times, is presented in this book, though only, of course, in selection. We have left out the great plays of Shakespeare and of Jonson; a few of these would have taken up all the space, and they are easily available elsewhere. But we have included a scene attributed with much likelihood to Shakespeare which will be unfamiliar to most readers and a selection, also probably unfamiliar, from the masterly and charming court entertainments of Jonson. For the rest, some selections will be familiar to those who have some acquaintance with the period, but others will be fresh, and the whole, we hope, will give a new and more accurate picture of the times.

THE STRUCTURE OF SOCIETY

There were, to be simple about it, but no more simple than the views of the time warrant, two kinds of people in Renaissance England: those that mattered and those that did not. The latter were "the multitude, wherein be contained the base and vulgar inhabitants not advanced to any honor or dignity," as Sir Thomas Elyot puts it. They do not often appear in this book, and when they appear it is scarcely with dignity, except for John Heywood's prisoner. They include the vulgar countrywomen at Dame Elinor's alehouse, figures of fun; the artisan, William Waring, doing ecclesiastical penance; the London rioters on Evil May Day; the gossipy servingmen in *A Yorkshire Tragedy*, and Annis Herd, the supposed witch. They are all minor figures, not of much account in this society.

The group that mattered is fairly easy to define. They were those who lived on the unearned income from inherited land. These were the men "of ancient honor and name," however recently acquired. To fall from this class, to lose one's patrimony and dissipate one's inheritance, as the Yorkshire gentleman did, is the final ruin. It is a disgrace not only to oneself but also to one's ancestors and posterity. It is for this reason that he kills his children:

> My lands showed like a full moon about me, but now the moon's i' th' last quarter, waning, waning. And I am mad to think that moon was mine; mine and my father's and my forefathers'— generations, generations. Down goes the house of us, down, down it sinks. Now is the name a beggar; begs in me that name which hundreds of years has made this shire famous. In me and my posterity runs out.

> My oldest beggar! thou shalt not live to ask an usurer bread, to cry at a great man's gate or follow "good your honor" by a coach. No, nor your brother; 'tis charity to brain you.

The gulf between the two estates was regarded as absolute, though in practice it was not quite. It is the distinction still preserved in the armed forces between the enlisted men and the commissioned officers. The one is governed, the other is the governing class. There were, however, two distinct views on the structure of the governing class, views that are clearly formulated by Fulke Greville in his account of the Queen's intervention in the quarrel between Sir Philip Sidney and the Earl of Oxford in 1579:

> The Queen, who saw that by the loss or disgrace of either she could gain nothing, presently undertakes Sir Philip, and (like

an excellent monarch) lays before him the difference in degree between earls and gentlemen, the respect inferiors owed to their superiors, and the necessity in princes to maintain their own creations as degrees descending between the people's licentiousness and the anointed sovereignty of crowns: how the gentleman's neglect of the nobility taught the peasant to insult both.

The motivating fear in the Queen's position is fear of "the people's licentiousness," of the insulting peasant. If not structured and controlled by order and degree the irrational lower classes would destroy all order. For, says Elyot, when man "hath destroyed that wherewith he doth participate by the order of creation, he himself of necessity must then perish, whereof ensueth universal dissolution." "Imagine," says the character, Thomas More, addressing the London rioters in *Evil May Day:*

> that you sit kings in your desires,
> Authority quite silenced by your brawl,
> And you in ruff of your opinions clothed,
> What had you got? I'll tell you: you had taught
> How insolence and strong hand should prevail,
> How order should be quelled, and by this pattern
> Not one of you should live an aged man:
> For other ruffians, as their fancies wrought,
> With self-same hand, self reasons, and self right,
> Would shark on you, and men, like ravenous fishes,
> Would feed on one another.

It was a plausible fear. There was no police force, no standing army. The London riot is put down by the presence of noblemen and their retainers, and by the eloquence of Thomas More. There was poverty, grievance, and there were too many rootless men, such as those described by Hythloday in More's *Dialogue* and interviewed by Thomas Harman. To deal with this potentially disruptive situation, the means of order were, in the Queen's view, the reverence attached to "the annointed sovereignty of crowns" and the hierarchical stepping down by degrees of power and respect, inviting and compelling awe from inferior to superior. It was a congenial way of thinking, for the universe itself was so ordered, from the lowest element to the highest sphere, as was that celestial society that rose by degrees through all the orders of angels to God.

On the other hand, Sidney's view that there are really only the two classes, ordered by the relationship of master and servant, is perhaps more accurate of his society than the elaborate hierarchical structure that the Queen and Sir Thomas Elyot expound, though both apply. This is Greville's account of Sidney's position:

> Whereunto Sir Philip, with such reverence as became him replied: first, that place was never intended for privilege to wrong: witness herself, who how sovereign soever she were by throne, birth, education and nature, yet was she content to cast her own affections into the same moulds her subjects did, and govern all her rights by their laws. Again, he besought Her Majesty to consider that, although he were a great lord by birth, alliance and grace, yet he was no lord over him: and therefore the difference of degrees between free men could not challenge any other homage than precedency. And by her father's act (to make a princely wisdom become the more familiar) he did instance the government of King Henry the Eighth, who gave the gentry free and safe appeal to his feet against the oppression of the grandees, and found it wisdom by stronger corporation in number to keep down the greater in power, inferring else that if they should unite, the overgrown might be tempted by still coveting more to fall (as the angels did) by affecting equality with their maker.

The motivating fear in Sidney's position is the fear of great magnates, of such "grandees" as had in the preceding century caused the feudal chaos of the Wars of the Roses. Those that matter are the "free men," and, among these, difference in degree is only a matter of ceremony. The particular relationship among the free men is of the same sort as the general relationship between the two classes of the commonweal; it is that of master and servant. All, for example, are servants of the crown. But Oxford, though a great lord, is not to be lord over Sidney, unless there had been, as there was not, some specific feudal obligation on Sidney's part to Oxford. And what obligations do exist do not inhere in the prerogative of degree but are under and by the law. Nor was this doctrine merely of theoretical interest. Mary, Queen of Scots, like the Princes in the selection from Sidney's *Arcadia*, entitled "Law," claimed as an absolute prince not to be answerable to the law of England. The claim was disallowed, though the point was not settled.

This, then, is a world quite different from ours, and the difference is important to the concerns of this book. In our world it is not the wealthy or the great officers of state and their associates who make the principal contributions to literature and learning. We have, at the most, an occasional man of letters somewhere in the government—an Assistant Secretary of State —and a scientific adviser to the President. And we have no millionaire poets. But in the world of Renaissance England literature and learning are produced by and for the wealthy and governing class. A simple enumeration will make this clear.

The highest officer of state in England, in dignity if not necessarily in power, was the Lord Chancellor (or, with lesser prerogatives, the Lord Keeper of the Great Seal). He took precedence. Two of the most important of our authors were Lords Chancellor, Thomas More and Francis Bacon, and Bacon's father had been Lord Keeper. John Donne, until the disgrace of his clandestine marriage, had been secretary to Sir Thomas Egerton, the Lord Keeper.

The next highest officer of state was the Lord Treasurer. Thomas Sackville, cousin to Queen Elizabeth, created Earl of Dorset by James I, was Lord Treasurer. Sir Philip Sidney was the son of a Lord Deputy of Ireland, and the nephew of the Earls of Warwick and of Leicester. At the time of his early death he was Governor of Flushing. Sir Walter Ralegh, of course, was for a long time one of the Queen's favorites, Captain of the Guard, Lord Lieutenant of Cornwall, Lord Warden of the Stannaries, and Governor of Jersey. Sir Fulke Greville, later Lord Brooke, "neither sought for nor obtained any great place or preferment in court during all the time of his attendance, neither did he need it, for he came thither backed with a plentiful fortune, which, as himself was wont to say, was the better held together by a single life, wherein he lived and died a constant courtier of the ladies." Yet he became eventually Chancellor of the Exchequer and a Privy Councillor.

Sir Thomas Wyatt, who was in a position to pursue in vain one of Henry VIII's mistresses, was Ambassador to the court of Charles V, as was also Sir Thomas Elyot. John Skelton and John Palsgrave were tutors, and Gilbert and Harvey were physicians to royalty. John Heywood was court entertainer and servant to three sovereigns, Henry VIII, Edward VI, and Mary. Hooker's great work was commissioned by the government. Even Shakespeare, who had legitimate pretensions to gentility which his success confirmed, was first the Lord Chamberlain's servant and then the King's servant, and wore the King's livery on a state occasion. The popular drama of his day could not exist except by the favor of the great. Even Jonson, the stepson of a master bricklayer, becomes in legal documents "gentleman" and received for many years a handsome pension from the King. And Spenser wrote almost solely for court preferment: the *Prothalamium* celebrates the betrothal of the Earl of Worcester's daughters, and has as a kind of climax a fulsome compliment to the Earl of Essex. The Gascoigne selection is a begging poem to Lord Grey of Wilton, Lord Deputy of Ireland, who was also Spenser's patron.

But it is not only a literature by and for the governing class, it is also a literature in which class distinctions are literary distinctions. Tragedy, for example, is concerned only with the governing class, and usually with heads of states, with Lear, with Claudius and Hamlet, with Julius Caesar. The death of a

salesman was not tragic. Even those few plays which modern
historians of literature distinguish as "domestic tragedies," that
is, as not primarily political, are nevertheless concerned with
men of ancient honor and means, as in *A Yorkshire Tragedy*.

This will seem strange to us, but what is even more strange
is that there were class distinctions in matters of sex and of
love. Whoring and lust may be expected in the lower class.
It is whoring and lust in the upper class, or between nobility
and the citizen's wife, that is particularly the object of satiric
vehemence in Wyatt, Greville, and Jonson. The worst is the
corruption of the best. So it is "my lord" Stallion and his
"court-bred filly," "stretched upon the rack of lust," who are
the special objects of invective. And, conversely, the whole
area of what we call romantic love is the prerogative only of
the upper class. It is an experience open to Lady Hungerford
and Darrell of Littlecote, to Lady Rich and Sir Philip Sidney,
to Argalus and Parthenia and Shakespeare's Viola and Orsino.
In them it may be destructive or amusing; it may even be ridiculous to the calm sight of those not in love, as in Jonson's *Lovers
Made Men;* but it is proper. In their servants it is comic and
ridiculous, with the ridiculousness of impropriety:

> Much ado there was, God wot;
> He would love and she would not.

There are, furthermore, class distinctions in style. By and
large, in the drama the one class speaks in verse, the other in
prose. This is quite clear in the early Shakespeare, and in *A
Midsummer Night's Dream* there are even further refinements.
The heads of state speak a dignified blank verse; the well-born
lovers blank verse and couplets; the rude mechanicals speak
rudely in prose; and the extra-human characters have their class
distinction: they may use lyric measures. The distinction in use
between prose and blank verse is also apparent in the dramatic
selections in this book. But there are distinctions also in prose.

The sustained sentence, the aureate diction, the verbal figures of repetition are proper to, are required by, the heroic world of Argalus and Parthenia, and furnished for a century afterwards the model for courtly speech. There was a consonance between elevation in rank and an elevated style. On the contrary, the lower class character in the *Arcadia* speaks like Mrs. Quickly:

> Oh the good old woman, well may the bones rest of the good old woman! She called me to her into her house. I remember full well it stood in the lane as you go to the barber's shop, all the town knew her, there was great loss of her. She called me to her, and taking first a sup of wine to comfort her heart—it was of the same wine that comes out of Candia which we pay so dear for nowadays, and in that good world was very good cheap—she called me to her, "Minion," said she—indeed I was a pretty one those days though I say it—"I see a number of lads that love you."

In brief, it was not a democratic society.

THE OLD LEARNING AND THE NEW

Shakespeare in the sixty-sixth sonnet, enumerating the upside-downness of things in this world, how captive Good is in the service of Captain Ill, speaks of "art made tongue-tied by authority." It is an odd statement, and odd in its context, even if properly understood. For it is not, of course, as it is often taken to be, a reference to literary and dramatic censorship. His "art" is not our art. It referred, rather, to give a rough translation, to the world of learning. And what is complained of in the phrase is that the constant repetition of the old basic texts prevented the formulation of new propositions. It is as if he had been reading Bacon, or had been listening to Ben Jonson: "I know nothing can conduce more to letters than to examine the writings of the Ancients, and not to rest in their sole authority, or take all upon trust from them . . . For to all the observations of the Ancients, we have our own experience."

There was in Renaissance England what we may call the Old Learning and the New. The New Learning developed slowly and comes into prominence only toward the end of our period. It comprised a hodgepodge of recent concerns and developments, in mathematics and science, in various interests associated with the new classical philology, grammar, for example, and antiquarian research, all with a much clearer history on the continent than in England. But there were accomplishments: Gilbert's speculations, Harvey's demonstration, Bacon's intuition. There was the cold sociological interviewing of Thomas Harman. There were interesting developments in the common law, represented by Coke's *Reports* (1600–1615). There was the new history: Bacon's *Henry VII* (1622) and Lord Herbert's *Henry VIII;* the profound learning of John Selden; and the new antiquarian and topographical discovery of England, of which Camden's *Britannia* (1586) and Stow's *Survey of London* (1598) are best known. But, for the most part, the Old Learning was still dominant.

It was, essentially, the learning of the Middle Ages, and formed the matrix and texture of most of the thought and literature of the time. To understand that, we must relearn it, at least in outline. It was the common possession of everyone of the least education. It was an elementary learning, consisting largely of a series of clear and simple distinctions. There are the three souls, the four elements, the three grammatical genders, the seven deadly sins. These were learned as one learns the Catechism, and repeated again and again as one recites the Catechism. Indeed, the Catechism itself was a good part of the learning, for theology was still the principal science, as judicial astrology was still the principal experimental, that is, predictive science.

Nor was this learning only a school matter. It was matter for well-bred conversation in the houses of the upper class. An Elizabethan musician, onetime "servant and scholar" to John Heywood, tells in his autobiography of the conversation in the household of a woman who had been to court:

> She took pleasure many times to talk and discourse of such things as she by experience had had some knowledge of: as sometimes, of religions, she would argue in matters of controversy in religion; sometimes of profane matters; sometimes she would touch matters of the country, with the good husbandry and housewifery thereof . . . sometimes we should enter into talk of humors, the which of them four, bearing chiefest rule in man, should instinct incline and provoke him to follow those effects whereunto they were inclined. Then should we sometimes wade into communication and talk of the planets and the celestial signs with the constellations, and what their operations and workings were, and what effects they wrought in all things that were subject to them.

It is only to be expected, then, that this system of elementary distinctions should appear everywhere in the literature of the times as allusion, as material, and as structural principle. A simple example of the latter is afforded by Donne's little epigram on Hero and Leander:

> Both robbed of air, we both lie in one ground,
> Both whom one fire had burnt, one water drowned.

The whole story of the lovers is apprehended, summarized and enclosed in the simple scheme of the four elements, in phrases of four and six syllables, in iambic pentameter and rhymed. It is neat, ingenious, and absolute in its own way. But it must not be thought that this is anything peculiar to Donne. Sidney, some years earlier, in one of the *Arcadia* poems has the following two lines:

> Man oft is plagued with air, is burnt with fire,
> In water drowned, in earth his burial is . . .

The two lines do not rhyme—the form is terza rima, not couplets—but otherwise the correspondences technically and in the structural use of the four elements are exact.

The elementary distinctions of this learning were so securely the possession of everyone who counted that a writer could jump from one to another without transition or strain. This is what Donne does in his witty conjugations. If you will turn to his *Valediction: Of my Name in the Window,* you will find in the fifth stanza the doctrine of the three souls: the rational, by which one understands; the sensitive, in common with animals, by which one perceives; the vegetable, in common with plants, the principle of growth and decay:

> as all my souls be
> Imparadised in you—in whom alone
> I understand and grow and see—

He passes in the next stanza to the theological doctrine of the Resurrection of the Body:

> Till my return, repair
> And recompact my scattered body so.

And then the principle of judicial astrology, the influence of the stars:

> As all the virtuous powers which are
> Fixed in the stars are said to flow
> Into such characters as graved be
> When these stars have supremacy . . .

The modern reader who needs notes and patient explanation may think of Donne as ranging in such passages through various fields of learning. To Donne it was, for the exercise of wit, a single field with interchangeable parts. They were all of a piece.

What is new in these passages from Donne is not the learning or the use of learning, though it is a little more on display than was customary. What is new is literary. The monumental quality of Donne's epigram suggests the revived classical tradition of Sannazaro rather than the brutal doggerel tradition of John Heywood. And the world of the *Valediction* is the revived world of Latin erotic elegy, of Propertius and Ovid, where "thy melted maid, Corrupted by the lover's gold, and page," lays "His letter at thy pillow."

DEATH, RELIGION, AND LOVE

People in different times and places are alike and different. If we stress the difference we make them seem unintelligible. If we stress the similarities we encourage ourselves to understand them too readily, and so to misunderstand them. All men are concerned with death and love, and hence with religion, but not all have the same concern.

The Englishman of this period was more at home with death than we are. He lived with it, and sometimes for it. He said much about it, but there is not much to be said about what was said: it is all so simple and direct. There was a preoccupation with the fact of death; not with the subtlety of decay, as in Thomas Mann's *Death in Venice*, but with the bareness of the whitened skull. It was a preoccupation directed to the calm acceptance of death. The principal art of life, in fact, was the art of dying well. So the first literary selection in this book is a meditation on a skull, and a meditation in medieval form. It begins with the traditional syllogism, "All men are mortal," in inverted order: the conclusion, "Die we must," followed by the explicit major premise, "It is general to be mortal." The signs of death are then enumerated, and we conclude with a prayer. Again, in another short poem, Heywood's prisoner, awaiting hanging and quartering, pauses as he searches for worms in his hand, and meditates: in doing this I am only showing myself an enemy to the worm and a friend to the crow who will eat me as I hang on the gibbet. To speak here of acceptance of death is understatement. And so, again and again, sometimes with the assurance of salvation, "When Thou hast done that Thou hast Donne," the simple fact of death is looked at and embraced.

The attitude, of course, is Christian, as was the society. The essence of Christianity was still the incomprehensible mystery of God, the Trinity, and the historical fact that God became man, the Incarnation, so classically stated by Hooker. "The strength of our faith is tried by those things wherein our wits and capacities are not strong." But there were variations in Christianity, some of which are important for our purposes. For a principal fact of England at this time is the change in religion, or rather the successive changes under four monarchs, Henry VIII, Edward VI, Mary, and Elizabeth. The two poles were Rome and Geneva, the Old Religion and the Reformed, with differences of doctrine, of feeling, and with political differences. For religion was politics, and politics religion, and neither was the less sincere for that. Of our authors four were executed for treason, and in each case religion and the question of the succession of the crown were involved: More, the Lady Jane, Tichbourne, and finally Ralegh, though in his case as pretext rather than fact.

Between Rome and Geneva or Germany there was more than a difference in politics, or the differences in doctrine clearly stated in the *Examination of Lady Jane Grey;* there were also differences in feeling. They are apparent in the attitudes of the Lady Jane and Abbot Fecknam. They are apparent in two poems, each of the highest quality, that illustrate as well as anything the emotional difference between Calvinism and Catholicism. As feeling it can only be experienced. But one can say that in Greville's *Down in the Depths* the firm conviction of absolute corruption and the equal conviction of divine election ("Even there appears this saving God of mine") march doggedly through the stanzas with an unsocial and impressive solemnity. It is an experience of simultaneous corruption and salvation; it is not a prayer. Jonson's *To Heaven*, on the other hand, is a prayer, an act of perfect contrition:

> Yet dare I not complain, or wish for death
> With holy Paul, lest it be thought the breath
> Of discontent, or that these prayers be
> For weariness of life, not love of thee.

But Rome and Geneva were not the only possibilities. We can see in Donne's *Satire: On Religion* (the *Third Satire*, line 43 to the end) the possibilities open in the 1590's to a young man in his twenties, of good family, whose patrimony has been partially dissipated. He is ambitious for service in the State, partly for itself and partly to repair his fortunes, but he is also by family, training, and temperament a Roman Catholic. As such he would be debarred from preferment. He enumerates in the satire five positions, each of which he scornfully rejects, phrasing his scorn in similes identifying the quest for the True Church with that of true love. "Seek true religion. O where?" One man seeks her at Rome because he knows she was there a thousand years ago. But this is to worship her old clothes. Another at Geneva. For this Donne has even greater contempt. The passion for Calvinism is compared to a "lecherous humor" for coarse country wenches, "contemptuous yet unhandsome." The next possibility is that true religion is to be found in the English Church. It is good that Donne's *Satires* were not printed in his lifetime; he could not quite have been hanged for what he says. The English Church, he tells us, has changed like fashions in clothes. Whatever some preachers ("vile ambitious bawds") and some laws bid us accept at the moment we are to take as perfect. We are, in fact, to take our religion as a ward in that society must take whatever wife his guardian offers, or pay the forfeit. We must accept the current religion, or pay the fines for recusancy. These three positions, Rome, Geneva, and Canterbury, we may call regional. The next two are philosophical. The skeptic argues from the diversity of churches that there is no true church; his opposite maintains on the same grounds that one is as good as another, and so any one will do.

Donne's own position, which he now proceeds to sketch out, is a curious one but sufficiently clear. He is sure there is a True Church, and only one True Church, and he seems pretty sure that it is not one of the five already enumerated. The problem is to find it. There will be required, first of all, a patient searching of tradition, for though truth and falsehood are near twins, truth is a little older. Secondly, consider that Rome, Geneva, and Canterbury on any point may all be wrong. The example he gives is that the adoration, condemnation, and depreciation of images "may all be bad." Finally, "doubt wisely," for truth is to be found, as Polonius knew, by indirections and "assays of bias." But it is a wise doubting as a means to truth, which can be found and, once found, held to, not a wise doubting as a way of life. For we must find the True Church before old age, "death's twilight," "for none can work in that night." In brief he does not know the True Church, but is certain he will find it in due time by patient and supple inquiry, and he is certain it will not be a church stipulated by the State. What good will it do at the last judgment, he asks, to plead that Philip of Spain or the Pope, Henry VIII or the Puritan Martin Marprelate, taught you your doctrine? The final source of power is God and not the State.

So we come to love. There are in this book several traditions in the depiction of love, and it may be helpful to name them and to make some simple distinctions. There is, of course, love as an Idea, the exemplar being that heavenly love that Spenser hymned, of which the lady of courtly love is sometimes a parody. Then there is the tradition of Christian preaching, of Juvenal's satires and Martial's epigrams, and this is still with us. It is ugly, realistic in detail, brutal with either a vehement or an urbane brutality. Campian's *Epigram*, "Kate can fancy only beardless husbands," illustrates the urbane. Again, there is the tradition of Latin erotic poetry, of Catullus, Tibullus, Propertius, and Ovid. To put it too briefly, for the tradition comprises a wide range of themes and sentiments, it is frankly sexual, however musingly subjective. For this reason it seems realistic to us. Jonson's "You have a husband is the just excuse Of all that can be done him," gives the essence of the matter, and Donne's *Elegy* and Campian's *It Fell on a Summer's Day* illustrate it. Finally, there is the tradition of courtly love, or perhaps one should say of love at Court. This seems to us artificial in comparison with Donne's world, and in this we are right and wrong. It is artificial, but it is an artificiality that had been lived and experienced by a society through many generations, whereas Donne's world was a re-creation from literary Antiquity, though, perhaps, a re-creation that had contemporary validity. The society was a society of people who thought themselves important, and were, and who often had superfluous leisure. How they occupied this Campian tells us in *Now Winter Nights:* "Though love and all his pleasures are but toys, They shorten tedious nights." So courtly love may involve an evening's unserious pastime, a ritual flirtation, the sentimental occupation of years, or it may be the ornate setting of vulgar adultery. But its locale is the Court where it helps pass the time. It helps pass the time as befitted the atmosphere, with formality, compliment, ceremony, with precedent and by rules. Sidney's *Astrophil and Stella* and Ralegh's *Cynthia* illustrate the tradition.

Astrophil and Stella is the earliest sonnet sequence in English, and raises the problem of that literary form, and the allied problem of love at Court. The poet depicts in a sonnet at the beginning of the sequence the slow progress on his part of the relationship, by stages from liking through loving, to an absolute submission to the tyranny of love at a time when he had already lost the opportunity for legitimate fulfillment. His reason argues sophistically against reason in favor of passion, and he sends this clear delineation of the act of mortal sin as a compliment to the lady. (This is curious hyperbole for an earnest Christian.) Then realizing the shame of enduring such tyranny, he meets the lady and tells her, "Go to, unkind, I love you not," though he doesn't mean it. She in turn takes the first step in the dance of love, the look, and admits the lover to a chaste relationship. Then the attempted kiss, the banishment, the denial, the poems in absence, and finally the resolution: that she should authorize him to accept, as in her service, an office of state. This, plausibly, would be the governorship of Flushing, which he accepted in 1585, the year before his death.

The problem of the sonnet sequence is usually conceived in terms of the question, Is this fiction? or memoir? and is sometimes solved by denying there is a problem. The poems "should be read as poems," that is, without locating the field of experience they refer to. But this is to destroy them as poems. To return, by fiction is meant that the situation is invented; the structure, at least in part, planned out in advance; and the work as a whole responsible to the truth of human nature but not to fact. As memoir, on the other hand, the poems are evidence, their genesis private, and the reader eavesdrops. If only the two terms, fiction and memoir, were available and applicable, one would have to say that the sequence is memoir. For this is not the way Sidney thought of fiction or wrote it.

We know from his critical treatise, the *Defence of Poesy*, his conception of fiction, and we know from the *Arcadia* how he wrote it. Fiction was, first of all, ideal, presenting notable images of virtue and vice. What this means we can see in the episode of Argalus and Parthenia. The hopeless and constant lover, offered an exact replica of his love—indeed, it is Parthenia herself, unidentified—courteously declines: "It is only happiness I refuse, since of the only happiness I could and can desire I am refused." He is in love with her identity. This is a notable image of the virtue of constancy. But the images need not be only of virtue and vice. If there is a hunt, let it be the ideal hunt, as one might write an account today of the ideal summer vacation. If one thinks of representing a young girl in love, let it be not this girl or that but the essence of a young girl in love, and then one writes Jonson's *A Nymph's Passion*.

Fiction is also an imitation of an action, that is, an interconnected series of external events of a certain size—something more than a stolen kiss or a disturbance of feeling, something with a plot in the old sense. Something with such striking and notable events as the disfigurement and the cure of Parthenia. The cure, one may remark on the side, is marvelous but not supernatural or impossible, though it was undoubtedly beyond the competence of any physician of the time. It is, in fact, an early instance of science fiction. The plot should also have, as almost necessary ingredients, a final reversal of fortune, usually as in this episode simultaneous with a recognition of identity. *Astrophil and Stella* may be, though I think not, ideal, but there is in it no imitation of an action, no striking event, no reversal of fortune, and no recognition. It is not fiction.

The poems, then, are memoir in that they record an experience in the game of love. But they are not memoir in the sense that the poet attempts to come to terms with that experience, or to delineate it for a reader or for himself. The poems are not private, though intended for a very limited audience, and are not written to be overheard, but are rhetorically addressed to an audience. It is a very small audience of those in the know. The poems are, in fact, actions in the game of love, and their locale is the Court. They are for the most part compliments to the lady, apologies, explanations, entreaties: their aim is to persuade.

The context of such poems is, interestingly enough, clearly pictured in the *Arcadia* as a moment in the larger structure of the story of Pamela and Musidorus. Pamela at one point pities Musidorus in his love despair and shows her pity by a look.

He, presuming, offers to kiss her, and is summarily banished. It is a situation from *Astrophil and Stella*. And then we have this depiction of the lover as poet:

> Then began he only so far to wish his own good, as that Pamela might pardon him the fault, though not the punishment: and the uttermost height he aspired unto, was that after his death she might yet pity his error and know that it proceeded of love, and not of boldness. That conceit found such friendship in his thoughts, that at last he yielded, since he was banished her presence, to seek some means by writing to show his sorrow, and testify his repentance. Therefore getting him the necessary instruments of writing, he thought best to counterfeit his hand (fearing that already as she knew his, she would cast it away as soon as she saw it) and to put it in verse, hoping that would draw her on to read the more, choosing the elegiac as fittest for mourning. But never pen did more quakingly perform his office; never was paper more double moistened with ink and tears; never words more slowly married together, and never the Muses more tired than now, with changes and re-changes of his devices: fearing how to end, before he had resolved how to begin, mistrusting each word, condemning each sentence. This word was not significant; that word was too plain; this would not be conceived; the other would be ill conceived; here sorrow was not enough expressed, there he seemed too much for his own sake to be sorry; this sentence rather showed art than passion, that sentence rather foolishly passionate than forcibly moving. At last, marring with mending, and putting out better than he left, he made an end of it; being ended, was divers times ready to tear it, till his reason assuring him, the more he studied the worse it grew, he folded it up, devoutly invoking good acceptation unto it; and watching his time, when they were all gone one day to dinner, saving Mopsa to the other lodge, stole up into Pamela's chamber, and in her standish (which first he kissed, and craved of it a safe and friendly keeping) left it there to be seen at her next using her ink (himself returning again to be true prisoner to desperate sorrow) leaving her standish upon

her beds-head, to give her the more occasion to mark it: which also fell out.

It is in such a context, with just a shade of the comic about it, that *Astrophil and Stella* was written and is to be read.

But there can be nothing comic about it, except, perhaps, to an unconcerned modern observer, if the lady is the Queen. The cruel mistress to whose moods the lover is completely subject, who has power of life and death over him, may in other instances be an emotional reality or a courtly fiction; in the case of the Queen and her favorites it was the plain fact. "First of all, you must consider with whom you have to deal," Sir Edward Dyer wrote to Sir Christopher Hatton on a crisis in his relationship with Elizabeth, "and what we be towards her; who, though she do descend very much in her sex as a woman, yet we may not forget her place, and the nature of it as our Sovereign." And so the offending lover did not despair in the solitariness of the woods but in the solitariness of the Tower. There, probably in 1592, Ralegh wrote the incomplete draft of the poems of the eleventh book of *The Ocean to Cynthia*.

THE REVOLUTION IN STYLE

There is towards the end of this period a consciousness of achievement, especially in literature. This first appears in the 1590's, and indeed would not have been warranted before that decade. It was the decade of the *Faerie Queene*, of the first half of Shakespeare's work, of the first edition of Bacon's *Essays*, of Donne's most memorable poetry, and of Jonson's first great plays. There was a suddenness about the achievement that seems to call for an explanation.

But history is not a predictive science. It thinks up reasons for what has already happened, or is thought to have happened. It is what we can make of what remains of the past. And what we can make of it will depend on the nature of the remains and on our own concerns. If the remains are primarily literary, and our concerns are literary, we will look for a literary answer, though it may be only a partial answer.

Let us say, then, that the achievement of the 1590's, and of the subsequent decades, is partly a consequence of a revolution in style. For only then was there at hand an adequate instrument in poetry and in the drama. The importance of this is often overlooked. Literature, however, is not written with ideas, experiences, emotions, but with a pen, with language. And not with any language, but with a particular system of inclusions and exclusions; one writes with a style, and in poetry with a meter also, which is an aspect of style. And so a new style, a new meter, is a new attitude, a new form, new subject matter, so far unexpressed detail. Styles are innovated, and imitated, and imitation establishes a tradition.

The new styles that permitted the achievements of Elizabethan literature were innovated in the 1580's and perfected in the 1590's. This is clearest in the drama. The earlier dramas had been written, with the exception of one in blank verse (1562) in which Thomas Sackville had a hand, in mediums that would have precluded *Richard III* and all that followed. One of John Heywood's plays, for instance, printed in 1533, begins with this speech:

> God speed you, masters, every one,
> Wot ye not whither my wife is gone?
> I pray God the devil take her,
> For all that I do I can not make her
> But she will go a-gadding, very much
> Like Antony pig with an old witch
> Which leadeth her about hither and thither,
> But, by our lady, I wot not whither.

This is, of course, verse in the old Germanic tradition, a four-beat accentual meter held together by rhyme instead of alliteration. It can express simple truth and simple vulgarities, but there are many things that cannot be said in this style. Another medium is illustrated by the opening of *Cambises, King of Persia* (1570):

> My Council, grave and sapient, with lords of legal train,
> Attentive ears towards me bend, and mark what shall be sain.

This is the grave fourteener of the mid-sixteenth century, rhymed in couplets. It yielded a few impressive short poems, but nothing in drama. With such instruments not even Shakespeare could have been Shakespeare. He could at best have written in the octosyllabic tradition the verses inscribed on his tomb:

> Good friend, for Jesus sake forbear
> To dig the dust enclosed here!

Sometime in the late 1580's a new voice is heard on the London stage. The innovation was blank verse. It was not wholly new, of course; it had been used in some translations from the Latin, by Gascoigne in *The Steel Glass* (1576), in a play acted at the Third University of England, the Inns of Court. But it suddenly took on. We do not know who established the fashion, or how he hit on the new instrument. Some say Kyd, some Marlowe, and it may have been someone else. But it made the difference between Heywood and Shakespeare. This is the voice:

> When the eternal substance of my soul
> Did live imprisoned in my wanton flesh,
> Each in their function serving other's need,
> I was a courtier in the Spanish court.
> My name was Don Andrea.

From this, the opening of Kyd's *Spanish Tragedy*, to *Hamlet* is simply a matter of time and genius. The means are available.

And the innovation derives from the attempt to realize in English some of the qualities of the poetry of Classical Antiquity. For the most simple and obvious difference between that poetry and the poetry of this time is that the one was

unrhymed and the other rhymed. This is not just a difference
in effect; it is a difference in what can be said. A word to be
rhymed immediately suggests its rhymes, and at the same time
rules out all expressions that are not potentially rhymable. It is
a notable instance of a system of inclusions and exclusions.
Furthermore, unrhymed verse involves not merely a freedom
from limitations. It will have its own limitations, and one of
these is that, in a tradition in which rhymed verse is common,
the avoidance of rhyme is a positive principle of selection.

The heroic line of blank verse was developed originally in
nondramatic poetry, and with rhyme. It is, ultimately, Chaucer's
line. But something had happened to Chaucer's line in the centuries after his death, partly, no doubt, because the language
had changed. At all events, it is clear that at the court of Henry
VIII there was no commonly agreed-on metrical tradition, particularly for the heroic line. It was a situation similar to our
own, except that the possibilities of metrical confusion have
multiplied since that time. And it is a serious situation for the
history of poetry, more serious than the reader may think. For,
as prose is written in syntax, in phrases, clauses, sentences, so
poetry has a second principle of organization concurrent with
that of grammar: it is written in lines. The meter of a poem
determines the line. And as an uncertainty in grammar would
make it difficult to write good prose, so an uncertainty in meter
makes it difficult to write good poetry.

It would be a patient and delicate task to explore the whole
problem in the early sixteenth century, but a brief analysis
will show the nature of the problem. Wyatt more often than
not writes the traditional heroic line as Chaucer had established it:

> But as for me, alas, I may no more.

But he also writes a line simply of ten syllables, sometimes
counting the final unaccented syllable:

> In this also see you be not idle:

or of nine syllables, unless "laughter" is trisyllabic:

> It is but love; turn it to laughter.

or a ten-syllable line organized by the four-beat tune of the Germanic tradition:

> From under the stall, without lands or fees.

This last was the principal problem, for the Germanic and the Chaucerian traditions cannot live together; the heavy four-beat chant which we learned in our childhood ("Jóhnny is a stinker") drives out the grace and subtlety of the traditional meter. To write with both tunes in mind is to produce the baffling rhythms of Heywood's epigrams. To slip from one to the other, as Sir Thomas Elyot does, is metrical chaos:

> The poet fashioneth by some pleasant mean
> The speech of children, tender and unsure,
> Pulling their earës from wordës unclean,
> Giving to them precepts that are pure,
> Rebuking envy and wrath if it dure.
> Things well done he can by example commend;
> The needy and sick he doth also his cure
> To recomfort, if aught he can amend.

So it was that the poets of the next several generations under-took to discipline the syntax of poetry to the firm iambic line, the "drumming decasyllabon." They simplified the rules: they imposed special limitations. The ten-syllable line would be phrased in units of four and six syllables, in a limited number of syntactical patterns, and often enough the accented syllables in each phrase would be bound together and pointed by some rhetorical device, usually by alliteration and syntactical repetition:

> The life is long that loathesomely doth last;
> The doleful days draw slowly to their date.

It is a style that can handle obvious subjects, uncomplicated feelings, eternal truths, and simple sin. It is the style in which one writes from the Tower on the eve of execution. It is, furthermore, at its best an impressive style, as in Tichbourne's *Elegy*, and one that even Donne recurred to when he had an obvious subject and direct feelings about it. His *Hymn: To God the Father* is clearly in this style: let us call it the moral style. The poem is phrased for the most part in units of four and six syllables in normal iambic pattern, and the phrasing is underlined by rhetorical repetition:

> Wilt thou forgive that sin where I begun,
> Which was my sin though it were done before?
> Wilt thou forgive . . .

It is an impressive but not a sufficient style; it excludes too much. It cannot handle ordinary life. It cannot rise and fall. And so there developed in the 1580's, out of a good deal of experimenting in prose and verse, several new styles: the ornate style of Spenser, and the new plain style, modeled on the plain style of Latin Antiquity. In this the innovator was Sidney. It is not his consistent style; he is often ornate; he writes sometimes in the moral style. But there are many passages in *Astrophil and Stella* in a fully accomplished plain style:

> Dear, therefore be not jealous over me
> If you hear that they seem my heart to move;
> Not them, O no, but you in them I love.

It was there. It needed only to be recognized and imitated. It was recognized and imitated by Campian and Donne, and perfected by Jonson.

Campian (?1591):

> Whither thus hastes my little book so fast?
> *To Paul's Churchyard*. What? in those cells to stand
> With one leaf like a rider's cloak put up
> To catch a termer?

Donne (1597) on a calm at sea:

> No use of lanthorns, and in one place lay
> Feathers and dust, today and yesterday.

or:

> What are we then? How little more, alas,
> Is man now than before he was. He was
> Nothing. For us, we are for nothing fit;
> Chance or ourselves still disproportion it.

Jonson (1616):

> Think,
> All beauty doth not last until the autumn.
> You grow old while I tell you this.

It became the central style of English poetry.

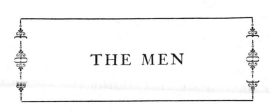

THE MEN

A Humanist Education [1529]

John Palsgrave (d. 1554), tutor to Mary, Queen of France, a sister of Henry VIII, and to the Duke of Richmond (1519–1536), natural son of Henry VIII by Elizabeth Blount. From a letter to Sir Thomas More.

I understand by Sir William Parr that the King's Grace demanded of you and Doctor Stevens whether you thought it convenient that the Duke of Richmond should learn Greek and Latin both at once, and that both you and the said Doctor duly approve mine opinion in that behalf. Wherefore I do most humbly thank you, assuring you that for my discharge in that behalf I have not only demanded the opinions of Horman, Gonnell, Rightwise, and all such as I thought could anything instruct me how I should best acquit me in the charge committed unto me, but I have also diligently read Quintilian, Maphaeus Vegius, Otho Moguntinus, Baptista Guarinus, and especially Erasmus, which all, as you know, agree in that thing.

But I remember that you showed me once how a little Latin should serve, so the said Duke might have French; and, to be plain with you, me thinketh that our shaven folk would in no wise he should be learned. Which I assure you were a great pity, for on my faith I knew never a more singular wit, neither rich nor poor, than he hath; and albeit that he hath already and every day shall have more and more sundry callers upon him to bring his mind from learning, some to hear a cry at a hare, some to kill a buck with his bow, sometime with greyhounds and sometime with buckhounds, and that it is not leefull to depart till he have taken the same, some to see a flight with a hawk, some to ride a horse, which yet he is not greatly cumbered with because of his youth, besides many other devices found within the house when he cannot go abroad, yet I trust, so you be especial good master to me, to bring him to that learning that you shall be contented worthily to approve. But I beseech you, if any that is learned shall fortune to come hither, by whom you may sufficiently be instructed whether my report of him be true or not, that you will then after your best manner confirm the King's Grace in the good opinion that he hath already to have him learned.

And to make the child love learning, I never put him in fear of any manner correction, nor never suffer him to continue at any time till he should be wearied, but devise all the ways I can possible to make learning pleasant to him, insomuch that many times his officers wot not whether I learn him or play with him; and yet have I already brought him to have a right good understanding of the principles of the grammars both of Greek and Latin, and I have read him an Eclogue (the first) of Virgil and two of the first scenes of *Adelphorum* (which he can pronounce right prettily). But I find Quintilian and Erasmus true, for the barbarous tongue of him that taught him his matins is and hath been a great hindrance to me.

Ecclesiastical Discipline [1529]

A suit in Chancery (1532) against the clerics named. The plaintiff (orator) *is shown by other evidence to have shot at marks for wagers, deserted his wife, kept a mistress. The suit was dismissed, the plaintiff censured and condemned to pay all costs.*

In most piteous-wise complaining, showeth unto your honorable Lordship your daily orator, William Waring (of the town of Pembroke in the county of Hereford, cordwainer), of and upon the wrongful vexations and troubles to him committed and done by one Sir William Higgins (parish priest of Pembroke) and by one Mr. Humphrey Ogle (clerk, Commissary of the diocese aforesaid) and his deputies.

That where your orator, which had always delighted to use and occupy his bow and to encourage other men to do so, on Tuesday in Easter Week in the twentieth year of the reign of our now sovereign lord, King Henry the Eighth, with other his neighbors and honest company, for avoiding of dice and card-tables and all other unlawful games which were then by commandment prohibited, and shooting to be used and occupied, took their bows and therewith passed their time till Matins, and then come to the church and heard there divine service: that is to say, Matins and Mass from the beginning to the ending as may be sufficiently proved. That notwithstanding, Sir William Higgins therefore cited your orator and other two of his neighbors to appear before the said Commissary at Lemster on Tuesday then next ensuing, as they then did, and the said Commissary, upon the examination of them, could find no cause of punishment and so dismissed them and discharged them thereof.

[5]

Albeit the said Sir William Higgins (still continuing his malice and intending to put your orator to hurt or vexation, slander, and cost undeserved) left the meddling with your orator's neighbors and called him three times in the church in one day. And so likewise on another day, in these words: "Come up, William Waring, and do the penance"—where he had no such penance to him injoined. Nevertheless, the said Sir William, yet of his further malice, on the day of St. Edward then next ensuing, suspended your orator, who then required a copy of the suspension and could not have it.

And whereas on the day of the holy apostles Philip and Jacob your orator come to the church to hear the divine service as belongs to every Christian man to do, the said Sir William, without any lawful authority or cause reasonable, violently put your orator out of the church (as before had done); and he desired him, if he had any suspension against him, to let him have a copy thereof. And then sued for his remedy to one John Blackston, clerk deputy to the Commissary. Albeit, by the sinister inveigling of the said Sir William, would not hear your orator till he had him first sworn to be obedient to the Church and the laws thereof, and then enjoined him (without any fault proved against him) that he should go about the church bare-foot and bare-leg in his shirt three Sundays before the Cross in procession: the first day at the cathedral church of Hereford, and the other two days in the parish church of Pembridge. And then your orator, perceiving the cruel sentence of the said Blackston, made labor by his friends and offered to give him a noble to release him of his penance, which he would in nowise do unless your orator should give him twenty shillings—which was not well in his power to do. And whereas he then offered to give him forty pence if he would respite the matter till the coming of the Commissary, which he would not but that your orator must do penance or else he would sue him for perjury.

And your orator, then seeing no remedy, brought a token from him to Sir William Higgins that he was assoiled. And on the morrow after (being Ascension Day) delivered the said token and was suffered to tary in the church all Matins, and at High Mass (to put him to rebuke and displeasure) was commanded out of the church before all his neighbors which offered to be bounden in 100 marks to save him harmless.

And the next Sunday, minding his oath, he took his journey to Hereford (being ten miles from Pembridge) in a great storm of wind, rain and cold, there to do his penance, and coming to Hereford about the hour of nine o'clock, wet through all his clothes to the skin, as the priests were ready to go procession. And then and there he was compelled to do off all his clothes to his shirt, which was wet.

And so, in his shirt, bare-foot, bare-leg and bare-head, went about before the procession with a candle in his hand.

And when the procession was come into the church, your orator was compelled to kneel upon the cold stones, and on his bare knees, while the priests sang an anthem, with the suffrages before the Rood, and likewise before Our Lady of Pity during another anthem with the suffrages there sung. And in like wise frages was there sung. And so unto the choir, where he offered also before the Saint's shrine, while an anthem with the suf- his candle and kneeled a great season, and took such cold after his labor (with kneeling on the bare stones so long) that it rooted in his body and in his head.

And afterward, by the help of God and physicians, to the great cost and charges of your said orator, it ran out as well at his ears as at his mouth, and all his hair fell off his head. And so, by the space of half a year, continued in sickness with as much pain as any man might live with.

St. Thomas More in the Tower [1534]

"When Mrs. Roper (1505-1544) had received a letter from her sister, Lady Alice Alington, she at her next repair to her father showed him the letter. And what communication was thereupon between her father and her, ye shall perceive by an answer here following, as written to the Lady Alington."

"Verily, daughter, I never intend (God being my good lord) to pin my soul at another man's back, not even the best man that I know this day living; for I know not whither he may happen to carry it. There is no man living of whom, while he liveth, I may make myself sure. Some may do for favor and some may do for fear, and so might they carry my soul a wrong way. And some might hap to frame himself a conscience and think that, while he did it for fear, God would forgive it. And some may peradventure think that they will repent and be shriven thereof, and that so God shall remit it them. And some may be peradventure of that mind that, if they say one thing and think the while the contrary, God more regardeth their heart than their tongue, and that therefore their oath goeth upon what they think and not upon what they say—as a woman reasoned once (I trow, daughter, you were by). But in good faith, Margaret, I can use no such ways in so great a matter: but like as, if mine own conscience served me, I would not let to do it though other men refused; so, though other refuse it not, I dare not do it, mine own conscience standing against it. If I had (as I told you) looked but lightly for the matter, I should have cause to fear. But now have I so looked for it and so long, that I purpose at the leastwise to have no less regard unto my soul than had once a poor honest man of the country that was called Company."

[8]

And with this he told me a tale. I ween I can scant tell it you again because it hangeth upon some terms and ceremonies of the law; but as far as I can call to mind, my father's tale was this: That there is a court belonging of course unto every fair to do justice in such things as happen within the same. This court hath a pretty fond name, but I cannot happen upon it, but it beginneth with a "pie" and the remnant goeth much like the name of a knight that I have known, I wis (and I trow you too, for he hath been at my father's oft ere this, at such time as you were there): a meetly tall black man, his name was Sir William Pounder. But, tut, let the name of the court go for this once, or call it if ye will "a court of pie Sir William Pounder." But this was the matter, lo: that upon a time, at such a court holden at Bartholomew Fair, there was an escheatour of London that had arrested a man that was outlawed, and had seized his goods that he had brought into the fair, tolling him out of the fair by a train. The man that was arrested and his goods seized was a northern man which by his friends made the escheatour within the fair to be arrested upon an action—I wot ne'er what—and so was he brought before the judge of the court of pie Sir William Pounder; and at the last the matter came to a certain ceremony to be tried by a quest of twelve men (a "jury" as I remember they call it, or else a "perjury").

Now had the clothman, by friendship of the officers, founden the means to have all the quest, almost, made of northern men such as had their booths there standing in the fair. Now was it come to the last day in the afternoon, and the twelve men had heard both the parties and their counsel tell their tales at the bar, and were from the bar had into a place to talk and commune and agree upon their sentence. (Nay, let me speak better in my terms yet: I trow the judge giveth the sentence and the quest's tale is called a "verdict.") They were scant come in together but the northern men were agreed, and in effect all the other too, to cast our London escheatour. They thought they needed no more to prove that he did wrong than even

the name of his bare office alone. But then was there then, as
the devil would, this honest man of another quarter, that was
called Company. And because the fellow seemed but a fool and
sat still and said nothing, they made no reckoning of him, but
said, "We be agreed now; come, let us go give our verdict."

Then, when the poor fellow saw that they made such haste
and his mind nothing gave him that way that theirs did (if their
minds gave them that way that they said), he prayed them to
tarry and talk upon the matter and tell him such reason therein
that he might think as they did; and when he so should do, he
would be glad to say with them, or else he said they must
pardon him. For sith he had a soul of his own to keep as they
had, he must say as he thought for his, as they must for theirs.
When they heard this, they were half angry with him.

"What, good fellow," quod one of the northern men, "where
wons thou? Be not we eleven here and you but one alone, and
all we agreed? Whereto shouldest you stick? What is thy name,
good fellow?"

"Masters," quod he, "my name is called Company."

"Company," quod they, "now by thy troth, good fellow, play
then the good companion; come thereon forth with us and pass
even for good company."

"Would God, good masters," quod the man again, "that there
lay no more weight thereby. But now when we shall hence and
come before God, and that he shall send you to heaven for doing according to your conscience and me to the devil for doing
against mine in passing at your request here for good company
now, by God, Mr. Dickenson"—that was one of the northern
men's name—"if I shall then say to all you again, 'Masters, I
went once for good company with you, which is the cause that
I go now to hell. Play you the good fellows now again with
me: as I went then for good company with you, so some of you
go now for good company with me,' would ye go, Mr.
Dickenson? Nay, nay, by our Lady, nor never one of you all.
And therefore must ye pardon me from passing as you pass,

but if I thought in the matter as you do. I dare not in such a matter pass for good company, for the passage of my poor soul passeth all good company."

And when my father had told me this tale, then said he further thus: "I pray thee now, good Margaret, tell me this: wouldest you wish your poor father, being at the leastwise somewhat learned, less to regard the peril of his soul than did there the honest unlearned man? I meddle not (you wot well) with the conscience of any man that hath sworn, nor I take not upon me to be their judge. But now, if they do well and that their conscience grudge them not, if I with my conscience to the contrary should for good company pass on with them and swear as they do, when all our souls hereafter shall pass out of this world and stand in judgement at the bar before the high Judge, if he judge them to heaven and me to the devil because I did as they did, not thinking as they thought, if I should then say (as the goodman Company said), 'Mine old good lords and friends,'—naming such a lord and such, yea, and some bishops peradventure of such as I love best—'I swore because you swore, and went that way that you went; do likewise for me now. Let me not go alone. If there be any good fellowship with you, some of you come with me.' By my troth, Margaret, I may say to thee in secret counsel here between us twain (but let it go no further, I beseech thee heartily): I find the friendship of this wretched world so fickle that, for anything that I could treat or pray that would for good fellowship go to the devil with me, among them all I ween I should not find one. And then by God, Margaret, if you think so too, best it is, I suppose, that, for any respect of them all, were they twice as many more as they be, I have myself a respect to mine own soul."

The Dissolution of the Monasteries [1538]

Dr. John London (d. 1543), D.C.L., Warden of
New College, Oxford, reporting to Thomas Crom-
well (d. 1540), Lord Privy Seal, Vicar-General.

In my most humble manner I have me commended unto your
good lordship, ascertaining the same that I have pulled down
the image of Our Lady at Caversham, whereunto was great
pilgrimage. The image is plated over with silver, and I have put
it in a chest fast locked and nailed up, and by the next barge
that cometh from Reading to London it shall be brought to
your lordship. I have also pulled down the place such stood
in, with all other ceremonies (as lights, shrouds, crosses, and
images of wax) hanging about the chapel, and have defaced the
same thoroughly in eschewing of any farther resort thither.
This chapel did belong to Notley Abbey, and there always was
a canon of that monastery which was called the warden of
Caversham, and he sung in this chapel and had the offerings for
his living. He was accustomed to show many pretty relics,
among the which were (as he made report) the holy dagger
that killed King Henry and the holy knife that killed Saint
Edward. All these, with many other, with the coats of this
image, her cap and hair, my servant shall bring unto your lordship this week, with the surrender of the friars under the con-
vent seal, and their seal also. I have sent the canon home again
to Notley, and have made fast the doors of the chapel, which
is thoroughly well covered with lead; and if it be your lordship's pleasure, I shall see it made sure to the King's Grace's use.
And, if it be not so ordered, the chapel standeth so wildly that

the lead will be stolen by night as I was served at the friars; for as soon as I had taken the friars' surrender, the multitude of the poverty of the town resorted thither, and all things that might be had they stole away, insomuch that they had conveyed the very clappers of the bells.

At Caversham is a proper lodging where the canon lay, with a fair garden and an orchard, meet to be bestowed upon some friend of your lordship in these parts, for the canon had nothing to do there but to keep the chapel and receive the offerings.

I beseech your good lordship to admit me a poor suitor for these honest men of Reading. They have a fair town and many good occupiers in it, but they lack that house necessary, of the which for the ministration of justice, they have most need of. Their town hall is a very small house, and standeth upon the river, where is the common washing place of the most part of the town; and in the session days and other court days there is such a beating with battledores as one man cannot hear another nor the quest hear the charge giving. The body of the church of the Grey Friars, which is solid with lath and lime, would be a very commodious room for them. And now I have rid all the fashion of that church in parcloses, images, and altars, it would make a goodly town hall. The mayor of the town, Mr. Richard Turner, is a very honest gentle person, with many other honest men hath expressed unto me their grief in this behalf, and have desired me to be an humble suitor unto your lordship for the same, if it should be sold. The walls beside the coin stones be but chalk and flint, and the covering but tile. And if it please the King's Grace to bestow that house upon any of his servants, he may spare the body of the church (which standeth next the street) very well and yet have room sufficient for a great man.

The Examination of Lady Jane Grey [1554]

> —✦ *Great-granddaughter (1537–1554) of Henry VII, named heir to the throne in the will of Edward VI, proclaimed Queen by her father-in-law, Northumberland, and executed seven months later, aged sixteen.*

The 12th day of February was beheaded the Lady Jane, to whom was sent Mr. Fecknam, alias Howman, from the Queen, two days before her death, to commune with her and to reduce her from the doctrine of Christ to Queen Mary's religion: the effect of which communication here follows:

FECKNAM: Madam, I lament your heavy case; and yet I doubt not but that you bear out this sorrow of yours with a constant and patient mind.

JANE: You are welcome unto me, sir, if your coming be to give Christian exhortation. And as for my heavy case, I thank God I do so little lament it that rather I account the same for a more manifest declaration of God's favor toward me than ever he showed me any time before. And therefore there is no cause why either you or others which bear me goodwill should lament or be grieved with this my case, being a thing so profitable for my soul's health.

FECKNAM: I am here come to you at this present, sent from the Queen and her Council, to instruct you in the true doctrine of the right faith, although I have so great confidence in you that I shall have, I trust, little need to travail with you much therein.

JANE: Forsooth, I heartily thank the Queen's Highness, which is not unmindful of her humble subject; and I hope, likewise, that you no less will do your duty therein both truly and faithfully according to that you were sent for.

FECKNAM: What is then required of a Christian?

JANE: That he should believe in God the Father, the Son, and the Holy Ghost, three persons and one God.

FECKNAM: What? Is there nothing else to be required or looked for in a Christian but to believe in God?

JANE: Yes, we must believe in Him, we must love Him with all our heart, with all our soul, and with all our mind, and our neighbor as ourself.

FECKNAM: Why, then faith justifies not, nor saves not?

JANE: Yes, verily: faith, as St. Paul says, only justifies.

FECKNAM: Why, St. Paul says, "If I have all faith without love, it is nothing."

JANE: True it is; for how can I love him whom I trust not, or how can I trust him whom I love not? Faith and love go both together, and yet love is comprehended in faith.

FECKNAM: How shall we love our neighbor?

JANE: To love our neighbor is to feed the hungry, to clothe the naked, and give drink to the thirsty, and to do to him as we would do to ourselves.

FECKNAM: Why, then it is necessary unto salvation to do good works also, and it is not sufficient only to believe.

JANE: I deny that, and I affirm that faith only saves; but it is meet for a Christian, in token that he doth follow his master Christ, to do good works. Yet may we not say that they profit to salvation; for when we have done all, yet we be unprofitable servants, and faith only in Christ's blood saves.

FECKNAM: How many sacraments are there?

JANE: Two: the one the sacrament of baptism, and the other the sacrament of the Lord's Supper.

FECKNAM: No, there are seven.

JANE: By what scripture find you that?

FECKNAM: Well, we will talk of that hereafter. But what is signified by your two sacraments?

JANE: By the sacrament of baptism I am washed with water and regenerated by the Spirit, and that washing is a token to me that I am the child of God. The sacrament of the Lord's Supper, offered unto me, is a sure seal and testimony that I am, by the blood of Christ which He shed for me on the Cross, made partaker of the everlasting kingdom.

FECKNAM: Why, what do you receive in the sacrament? Do you not receive the very body and blood of Christ?

JANE: No, surely; I do not so believe. I think that at the Supper I neither receive flesh nor blood, but only bread and wine: which bread when it is broken, and the wine when it is drunk, put me in remembrance how that for my sins the body of Christ was broken, and His blood shed on the Cross; and with that bread and wine, I receive the benefits that come by the breaking of His body and shedding of His blood for our sins on the Cross.

FECKNAM: Why, does not Christ speak these words, "Take, eat, this is my body"? Require we any plainer words? Does He not say it is His body?

JANE: I grant He says so, and so He says, "I am the vine, I am the door;" but He is never the more for that the door nor the vine. Does not St. Paul say that He calls things that are not as though they were? God forbid that I should say that I eat the very natural body and blood of Christ; for then either I should pluck away my redemption, either else there were two bodies, or two Christs, or else twelve bodies. One body was tormented on the Cross; and then if they did eat another body, then either He had two bodies; either else if His body were eaten, then it was not broken upon the Cross; or else if it were broken upon the Cross, it was not eaten of His disciples.

FECKNAM: Why, is it not possible that Christ by His power could make His body both to be eaten and broken, as to be born of a woman without seed of man, and as to walk upon the sea, having a body, and other such like miracles as He wrought by His power only?

JANE: Yes, verily: if God would have done at His Supper any miracle, He might have done so; but I say that then He minded no work nor miracle, but only to break His body and shed His blood on the Cross for our sins. But I pray you answer me to this one question: Where was Christ when He said, "Take, eat, this is my body"? Was He not at the table when He said so? He was at that time alive, and suffered not till the next day. Well, what took He but bread? What broke He but bread? And what gave He but bread? Look, what He took, He broke; and look, what He broke, He gave; and look, what He gave, they did eat; and yet all this while He Himself was alive and at supper before His disciples, or else they were deceived.

FECKNAM: You ground your faith upon such authors as say and unsay both with a breath, and not upon the Church to whom you ought to give credit.

JANE: No, I ground my faith upon God's word, and not upon the Church. For if the Church be a good Church, the faith of the Church must be tried by God's word, and not God's word by the Church, neither yet my faith. Shall I believe the Church because of antiquity, or shall I give credit to the Church that takes away from me the half part of the Lord's Supper, and will not let any lay man receive it in both kinds but themselves? Which thing, if they deny to us, then deny they to us part of our salvation. And I say that it is an evil Church, and not the spouse of Christ, but the spouse of the Devil, that alters the Lord's Supper, and both takes from it and adds to it. To that Church, say I, God will add plagues; and from that Church will He take their part out of the Book of Life. Do they learn that of St. Paul, when he ministered to the Corinthians in both kinds? Shall I believe this Church? God forbid!

FECKNAM: That was done for a good intent of the Church, to avoid a heresy that sprang on it.

JANE: Why, shall the Church alter God's will and ordinance for a good intent? How did King Saul? God the Lord defend!

With these and such like persuasions, he would have had her leaned to the church, but it would not be. There were many more things whereof they reasoned, but these were the chieftest. These words following were spoken openly.

After this, Fecknam took his leave, saying that he was sorry for her: "For I am sure," quoth he, "that we two shall never meet."

"True it is," said she, "that we shall never meet, except God turn your heart; for I am assured, unless you repent and turn to God, you are in an evil case. And I pray God, in the bowels of His mercy, to send you His Holy Spirit; for He has given you His great gift of utterance, if it pleased Him to open the eyes of your heart."

A Suit for Divorce [1564–1570]

--- *Sir Walter Hungerford (1532–1596), "the Knight of Farley," married Lady Anne in 1558, his second wife. She died at Louvain in 1603. "Her Grace" is Jane Dormer, the well-known Duchess of Feria, a kinswoman and a cousin of Sir Philip Sidney.*

Hugh Richard's Testimony

He saith that a month before midsummer was twelvemonth, one Miller, a servant of Mr. Darrell, came to Everope to speak with my lady; and after he had been there two hours, he returned back with a letter from my lady to Mr. Darrell; and within two days after, Darrell came himself to Everope and tarried there three days.

He saith that the morning that the said Darrell departed, he (this deponent) came up with wood in his arms to make a fire in my lady's chamber; and as soon as he came into the chamber, immediately followed Mr. Darrell and bade my lady good morrow. . . . My lady, bidding him good morrow, rose up in her bed, turning herself towards him, pulling up the bed-stuffs that were on that side, and willed him to sit down on the bedside, and then commanded the said Hugh to go forth the chamber.

Within half an hour after, Mrs. Essex willed the said Hugh to go to Mrs. Ralegh and will her to send the said lady a couple of the best chickens, which chickens were afterwards roasted in my lady's chamber; and my lady, the said Darrell, and Mrs. Essex brake their fast together in my lady's chamber. Afterward, my lady brought Mr. Darrell to horse and willed this deponent to bring him on the way.

The said Hugh brought him to Aytesbury Causey, where Mr. Darrell lighted and wrote a letter under a bush to my lady,

[19]

which, after he had sealed, he delivered to this deponent; and then the said Darrell took from about his neck a tablet of gold . . . and put it within a piece of paper; and as he rode back again, he opened the tablet, within the which was a heart in a red stone.

Lady Hungerford to William Darrell
My dear Darrell,

With my faithful commendations, this bearer maketh such haste that I have no time to write as I would—but, for the passion of God, think what you have to do and let me not be undone, for this bearer telleth me that my counsel is marvelously astonied, for that they cannot go forward according to their first instructions, so that now they know not what to say or what to lay in for answer. They have sent me to know what I could say concerning your being to me at Easter term was three year, which (to give my remembrance) you were not at that time there—but of certain I cannot tell—I rather think you were there at Trinity term, but full well I do and ever shall remember you were there at Easter. Thus putting my only trust in you, I commit you to the Almighty, who send you as well in thing as yourself would wish.

In haste at midnight,

A.H.

(read and burn)

Mister Darrell,

I, by the oath that I have sworn upon the holy Angels, do acknowledge that if Sir Walter Hungerford, my husband now living, do depart out of this life, that I, here, by the oath that I have sworn, and witness of this my hand, that I will take you to my husband. Witness thereof this, my hand, sufficeth.

Anna Hungerford

[Endorsed by William Darrell:] To his well-beloved wife, the Lady Hungerford, at the Castle of Frogges, be this delivered.

Lady Anna Hungerford to Dorothy Essex

My dear Essex,

I have received diverse letters from you and also from Her Grace. . . . I have been in that necessity that I have sold all my wearing-clothes and my table-cloth and such linens as you know I had—and all to help me to maintain my suit in law, in clearing me of mine innocence. And now I have sentence of my side, but Mr. Hungerford will not pay my charges nor yet give me living (which the law gives me), but rather will he in the Fleet, rather than to part with any penny of living with me. O, my dear Doll, what endless miseries do I live in! O what friends had I, that this most wretchedly hath utterly cast me and all mine away. I am not able to write you one quarter of my troubles which I have endured. Sir Walter Hungerford (and his brother) hath touched me in three things, but I would in no case have the duchess to know them, for giving her grief. The first was (since you went) adultery; the second, with murder; the third, that I would have poisoned him six years ago. But all this has fallen out to his shame. But I shall never recover it whilst I live; the griefs hath been and is such to me, and mine necessities so, that I fear I shall never be as I have been. . . . I have nobody to travail for me, for Gardener is gone from my father; and I have not to give him anything to serve me, so that I know not what to do. And my horses are both dead, so that I have nothing to help myself withal. . . . I am forced to put all my folks away at midsummer, for that I have not to keep them; and nothing troubles me so much as that I have not to do for Godsoll, for he has lost much by his serving of me. My children I have not heard of these eleven months and more. They are lost for want of good placing. Susan is, as I hear, clean spoiled; she has forgotten to read, and her complexion clean gone with an itch, and she hath scant to shift her withal. Jane is with a seamster in Marlborough, very evil to do. Surely I were happy if God would take them out of this life.

The Savoy, March 25, 1570

The Queen's Majesty's Answer [1566]

Queen Elizabeth I (1533–1603) "to the Commons House touching her marriage and the limitation of the succession."

If that order had been observed in the beginning of the matter and such considerations had in the prosecuting of the same as the gravity of the cause had required, the success thereof might have been taken otherwise than now it is; but those unbridled persons whose mouth was never snaffled by the rider did rashly ride into it in the Commons House of public place, where Mr. Bell with his accomplices alleged they were natural Englishmen and were bound to their country which they saw must needs perish and come to confusion unless some order were taken for limitation of succession of the Crown; and further to help the matter must needs proffer their speech to the Upper House to have you, my Lords, consent with them, whereby you were seduced and of simplicity did assent unto it, which you would not have done if you had foreseen before considerately the importance of the matter. So that there was no malice in you and so I do ascribe it, for we think and know you have cause to love us, considering our mercifulness showed to our subjects since our reign. But therein Sir Domine Doctors with their long orations sought to persuade you also with solemn matters as though you, my Lords, had not known that when my breath did fail me I had been dead unto you, and then dying without issue, what a danger were that to the whole state, which you had not known before they told you. So that it was easy to be seen *quo oratio tendit,* for they that should be stops and stays

[22]

of this great good and avoiding so many dangers and perils, how evil willing might they seem so to agree the cause against me. Was I not born in this realm? Were my parents born in any foreign country? Is not my kingdom here? Whom have I oppressed? Whom have I enriched to others' harm? What turmoil have I made to this commonwealth that I should be suspected to have no regard of the same? How have I governed since my reign? I will be tried by Envy itself. I need not to use many words, for my deeds do try me.

Well, the matter whereof (as I am informed) they would have made their petition consisteth in two points: in my marriage and the limitation of the Crown, wherein my marriage was first placed for manners' sake. I sent them answer by my council I would marry, although of my own disposition I was not inclined thereto. But that was not accepted nor credited, although spoken by their prince. And yet I used so many words that I could say no more and, were it not now I spake these words, I would never speak them again. I will never break the word of a prince spoke in public place for my honor's sake, and therefore I say again I will marry as soon as I can conveniently, if God take not him away with whom I mean to marry or myself, or else some other great let happen. I can say no more except the party were present and I hope to have children. Otherwise I would never marry.

A strange order of petitions that will make a request and cannot otherwise be ascertained but by their prince's word, and yet will not believe it when it is spoken. But they, I think, that move the same will be as ready to mislike with whom I shall marry as they are now to move it; and then it will appear that they never meant it. I thought they would have been rather ready to give me thanks than to have made a new request for the same. There have been some that, ere this, have said to me they never required more than that they once might hear me say I would marry. Well, there was never so great a treason but might be covered under as fair a pretense.

The second point was the limitation of successions of the Crown, wherein was nothing said for my safety, but only for themselves. A strange thing the foot should direct the head in so weighty a cause, which cause been so diligently weighed by us for that it toucheth us more than them. I am sure there was none of them that was ever a second person as I have been, and have tasted of the practices against my sister, who I would to God were alive again. I had great occasions to hearken to their motions, of whom some of them are in the Commons House; but when friends fall out, the truth doth appear according to the old proverb, and were it not for my honor their knavery should be known. There were occasion in me that time I stood in danger of my life, my sister was so incensed against me: I did differ from her in religion, and I was sought for divers ways. So shall never my successor be. I have conferred before this time with them that are well learned, and have asked their opinions, touching the limitation of succession, who hath been silent; not that by their silence after law-like manner they have seemed to assent unto it, but that indeed they could not tell what to say, considering the peril to the realm and most danger to myself. But now the matter must needs go very trimly and pleasantly when the bowl runneth all on the one side and, alas, not one amongst them all would answer for us, but all the speeches were for the surety of their country. They would have thirteen or fourteen limited in succession, and the more the better, and those shall be of such uprightness and so divine as they shall be divinity itself. Kings were wont to honor philosophers; but if I had such, I would honor them as angels that should have such purity in them that they would not seek when they are second to be the first, and when they are third to be the second, and so forth. It is said that I am no divine. Indeed, I studied nothing else but divinity until I came to the Crown, and then I gave myself to the study of government, as was meet for me, and I am not ignorant of histories wherein hath appeareth what hath fallen out for ambition of kingdoms as in Spain, Naples, Portugal, and at home, and what cocking hath been between the father and the son for the same.

You would have a limitation of succession. Truly, if reason did not subdue will in me, I would cause you to deal in it, so pleasant a thing it should be unto me. But I say it for your benefit; for if you should have liberty to treat of it, there be so many competitors—some kinsfolk, some servants, some tenants; some would speak for their master, some for their mistress, and every man for his friend—that it would be an occasion of a greater charge than a subsidy. And if my will did not yield to my reason, it should be the thing I would gladly desire to see you deal in. There hath been error (I will not say errors, for there were too many in the proceeding in this matter), but we will not judge that these attempts were done of any hatred to our person, but ever for lack of good foresight. I do not marvel though with you, my Lords, two of the bishops did misuse themselves therein, sithence my sister and I was bastards. Well, I wish not the death of any man; but only this I desire: that they which have been the practicers therein may before their deaths repent the same and show some open confession of their fault, whereby the scabbed ship may be known from the whole. As for mine own part, I care not for death; for all men are mortal, and though I be a woman, I have as good a courage answerable to my place as ever my father had. I am your anointed Queen. I will never be by violence constrained to do anything. I thank God I am endued with such qualities that if I were turned out of the realm in my petticoat, I were able to live in any place in Christendom.

Your petition is to deal in the limitation of succession. At this present it is not convenient, nor never shall be without some peril unto you and certain danger unto me. But were it not for your peril at this time, I would give place notwithstanding my danger. Your perils are sundry ways, for some may be touched who rest now in such terms with us as yet is not meet to be disclosed either in the Commons House or in the Upper House.

But as soon as they may be in convenient time, and that may be
done with less peril unto you (although never without great
danger unto me), I will deal therein for your safety, and offer
it unto you as your prince and head without request; for it is
monstrous that the feet should direct the head.

And therefore this is my mind and answer, which I would
have showed in the two Houses. And for the doing thereof, you,
my Lord Chief Justices, are meetest to do it in the Upper House.
And you, Cecil, in the Nether House.

And therewith speaking of the speaker, that the Lower House
would have had their Speaker there, wherein they did not consider that he was not there to speak, she said she was a speaker
indeed, and there ended.

Thomas Harman and the Doxy [1566]

Thomas Harman, Esquire, of Crayford, Kent, "a poor gentleman, have kept house these twenty years, whereunto poverty daily hath and doth repair, not without some relief."

I chanced, not long since, familiarly to commune with a doxy that came to my gate: and surely a pleasant harlot, and not so pleasant as witty, and not so witty as void of all grace and goodness. I found by her talk that she had passed her time lewdly eighteen years in walking about. I thought this a necessary instrument to attain some knowledge by; and before I would grope her mind, I made her both to eat and drink well. That done, I made her a faithful promise to give her some money if she would open and discover to me such questions as I would demand of her, and never to betray her, neither to disclose her name.

"And you should," sayeth she, "I were undone."

"Fear not that," quoth I. "But I pray thee," quoth I, "say nothing but truth."

"I will not," sayeth she.

"Then first tell me," quoth I, "how many upright men and rogues dost thou know, or hast thou known and been conversant with, and what their names be."

She paused a while and said, "Why do you ask me, or wherefore?"

"For nothing else, as I said, but that I would know them when they came to my gate."

"Now, by my troth," quoth she, "then are ye never the near, for all mine acquaintance for the most part are dead."

"Dead," quoth I, "how died they? For want of cherishing, or of painful diseases?"

Then she sighed and said they were hanged.

"What, all?" quoth I. "And so many walk abroad, as I daily see?"

"By my troth," quoth she, "I know not past six or seven by their names," and named the same to me.

"When were they hanged?" quoth I.

"Some seven years agone, some three years, and some within this fortnight." And declared the place where they were executed, which I knew well to be true by the report of others.

"Why," quoth I, "did not this sorrowful and fearful sight much grieve thee, and for thy time long and evil spent?"

"I was sorry," quoth she, "by the Mass; for some of them were good, loving men. For I lacked not when they had it, and they wanted not when I had it, and divers of them I never did forsake until the gallows parted us."

"Oh, merciful God," quoth I, and began to bless me.

"Why bless ye?" quoth she. "Alas, good gentleman, everyone must have a living."

A Day at Kenilworth [1575]

"My Lord" is the Earl of Leicester (d. 1588), and "my Lord President" is Sir Henry Sidney (1529–1586), his brother-in-law, Lord President of Wales, and father of Sir Philip Sidney.

A-mornings I rise ordinarily at seven o'clock. Then ready, I go into the chapel. Soon after eight, I get me commonly into my Lord's chamber or into my Lord's Presidents. There, at the cupboard, after I have eaten the manchet, served overnight for livery (for I dare be as bold, I promise you, as any of my friends the servants there; and indeed could I have fresh if I would tarry, but I am of wont jolly and dry a-mornings), I drink me up a good bowl of ale. When in a sweet pot it is defecated by all night's standing, drink is the better (take that of me); and a morsel in a morning with a sound draught is very wholesome and good for the eyesight. Then I am as fresh, all the forenoon after as had I eaten a whole piece of beef.

Now, sir, if the Council sit, I am at hand: wait at an inch, I warrant you. If any make babbling, "Peace!" say I, "wot ye where ye are?" If I take a listener or a pryer in at the chinks or at the lock-hole, I am by and by in the bones of him; but now they keep good order: they know me well enough. If he be a friend or such a one as I like, I make him sit down by me on a form or a chest. Let the rest walk, a' God's name!

And here doth my languages now and then stand me in good stead (my French, my Spanish, my Dutch and my Latin): sometime among ambassadors' men if their master be within the Council, sometime with the ambassador himself, if he bid call his lackey or ask me what's o'clock. And I warrant ye I answer him roundly, that they marvel to see such a fellow there. Then laugh I and say nothing.

Dinner and supper I have twenty places to go to, and heartily prayed to. And sometime get I to Mr. Pinner: by my faith, a worshipful gentleman, and as careful for his charge as any Her Highness hath. There find I alway good store of very good viands; we eat and be merry, thank God and the Queen! Himself, in feeding, very temperate and moderate as ye shall see any; and yet, by your leave, of a dish (as a cold pigeon or so, that had come to him at meat, more than he looked for) I have seen him e'en so by and by surfeit as he hath plucked off his napkin, wiped his knife, and eat not a morsel more: like enough to stick in his stomach a two days after. (Some hard message from the higher officers, perceive ye me?) Upon search, his faithful dealings and diligence hath found him faultless.

In afternoons and a-nights, sometime am I with the right worshipful Sir George Howard, as good a gentleman as any lives; and sometime at my good Lady Sidney's chamber, a noblewoman that I am as much bound unto as any poor man may be unto so gracious a lady; and sometime in some other place, but always among the gentlewomen by my good will (oh, ye know that come always of a gentle spirit). And when I see company according, then can I be as lively too. Sometime I foot it with dancing: now with my gittern, and else with my cittern, then at the virginals (ye know nothing comes amiss to me); then carol I up a song withal, that by and by they come flocking about me like bees to honey, and ever they cry, "Another, good Laneham, another!"

Shall I tell you?—when I see Mrs. _____ (ah! see a mad knave! I had almost told all!), that she gives once but an eye or an ear, why then, man, am I blessed! My grace, my courage, my cunning is doubled. She says sometime she likes it, and then I like it much the better: it doth me good to hear how well I can do. And, to say truth, what with mine eyes, as I can amorously gloat it, with my Spanish suspires, my French highs, my Italian dulcets, my Dutch wheeze, my double release, my high reaches, my fine feigning, my deep diapason, my wanton warbles, my running, my timing, my tuning and my twinkling, I can gracify the matters as well as the proudest of them—and was yet never stained, I thank God. By my troth, countryman, it is sometime by midnight ere I can get from them.

And thus have I told ye most of my trade all the livelong day. What will ye more? God save the Queen and my lord! I am well, I thank you.

Robert Lancham

Spectral Murder [1582]

—◦◦{ *From "a true and just record of the information, examination, and confession of all the witches taken at St. Osyth."*

Richard Harrison, clerk, parson of Beamond, sayeth that he and his late wife did dwell in Little Oakley in a house of his said wife and that he, the said Richard Harrison, had also the parsonage of Oakley in farm. And about summer was twelvemonth, he being at London, his wife had a duck sitting on certain eggs under a cherry tree in a hedge. And when the said duck had hatched, his said wife did suspect one Annis Herd, a light woman and a harlot, to have stolen her ducklings. And that his said wife went unto the said Annis Herd and rated her and all to-chid her, but she could get no knowledge of her ducklings, and so came home and was very angry against the said Annis. And within a short time after, the said Richard Harrison went into a chamber and there did read on his books for the space of two or three hours, bidding his said wife to go to bed with the children and that he would come to her; and she so did. And being awhile laid down in her bed, his wife did cry out, "Oh Lord, Lord, help me and keep me!" And he, running to her, asked her what she ailed. And she said, "Oh Lord, I am sore afraid, and have been diverse times, but that I would not tell you:" and said, "I am in doubt, husband, that yonder wicked harlot, Annis Herd, doth bewitch me." And the said Richard Harrison said to his wife, "I pray you be content and think not so, but trust in God and put your trust in Him only, and He will defend you from her and from the Devil himself also:" and said, moreover, "What will the people say, that I, being a preacher, should have my wife so weak in faith?"

This examinate sayeth that, within two months after, his said wife said unto him, "I pray you, as ever there was love between us (as I hope there hath been, for I have five pretty children by you, I thank God), seek some remedy for me against yonder wicked beast" (meaning the said Annis Herd). "And if you will not, I will complain to my father and I think he will see some remedy for me. For," said she, "if I have no remedy she will utterly consume me." Whereupon this examinate did exhort his wife as he had before, and desired her to pray to God, and that he would hang her, the said Annis Herd, if he could prove any such matter. And, after, he went to the parsonage and there, he sayeth, he gathered plums. And the said Annis Herd then came to the hedge-side (and Anwick's wife with her) and said unto him, "I pray you give me some plums, sir." And this examinate said unto her, "I am glad you are here, you vile strumpet," saying, "I do think you have bewitched my wife and, as truly as God doth live, if I can perceive that she be troubled any more as she hath been, I will not leave a whole bone about thee; and besides I will seek to have thee hanged." And sayeth he said unto her that his wife would make her father privy unto it and that "then, I warrant thee, he will have you hanged; for he will make good friends and is a stout man of himself." And sayeth that then he did rehearse divers things to her that were thought she had bewitched, as geese and hogs. And as he was coming down of the tree, the said Annis did suddenly depart from him without having any plums.

This examinate sayeth, after which speeches so by him used unto her, and before Christmas, his said wife was taken sore sick; and was at many times afraid both sleeping and waking; and did call this examinate, her husband, unto her not above two days before her death and said unto him, "Husband, God bless you and your children, and God send you good friends, for I must depart from you; for I am now utterly consumed

with yonder wicked creature" (naming the said Annis Herd).
Which words, he sayeth, were spoken by her in the presence of
John Pollin and Mother Pope. And within two days after, his
said wife departed out of this world in a perfect faith, repeating
these words: "Oh Annis Herd, Annis Herd: she hath consumed
me."

A Disputation at Supper [1593]

Scripture, Aristotle ("the soul is the first grade of actuality of a natural body having life potentially in it"), and Euclid ("the whole is greater than the part"), concluded with the saying of Grace.

The relation of the disputation had at Sir George Trenchard's table between Sir Walter Raleigh, Mr. Carew Raleigh and Mr. Ironside hereafter followeth, written by himself and delivered to the commissioners upon his oath:

Wednesday, seven-night before the Assizes summer last, I came to Sir George Trenchard's in the afternoon, accompanied with a fellow minister and friend of mine, Mr. Whittle, Vicar of Forthington. There were then with the knight Sir Walter Raleigh, Sir Ralph Horsey, Mr. Carew Raleigh, Mr. John Fitzjames, etc.

Towards the end of supper, some loose speeches of Mr. Carew Raleigh's being gently reproved by Sir Ralph Horsey in these words, *"Colloquia prava corrumpunt bones mores,"* Mr. Raleigh demands of me what danger he might incur by such speeches. Whereunto I answered, "The wages of sin is death." And he, making light of death as being common to all, sinner and righteous, I inferred further that as that life which is the gift of God through Jesus Christ is life eternal, so that death which is properly the wages of sin is death eternal, both of the body and of the soul also.

"Soul?" quoth Mr. Carew Raleigh. "What is that?"

"Better it were," said I, "that we would be careful how the

[35]

souls might be saved than to be curious in finding out their essence."

And so keeping silence, Sir Walter requests me that for their instruction I would answer to the question that before by his brother was proposed unto me.

"I have been," saith he, "a scholar some time in Oxford. I have answered under a Bachelor of Art, and had talk with diverse. Yet hitherunto, in this point (to wit, what the reasonable soul of man is) have I not by any been resolved. They tell us it is *primus motor*, the first mover in a man, etc."

Unto this, after, I had replied that howsoever the soul were *fons et principium*—the fountain, beginning and cause of motion in us—yet the first mover was the brain or heart.

I was again urged to show my opinion, and hearing Sir Walter Raleigh tell of his dispute and scholarship sometime in Oxford, I cited the general definition of *anima* out of Aristotle (*de Anima*, 2.1) and thence *a subiecto proprio* deduced the special definition of the soul reasonable: that it was *actus primus corporis organici animantis humani vitam habentis in potentia*.

It was misliked of Sir Walter as obscure and intricate. And I withal yielded that though it could not unto him, as being learned, yet it must seem obscure to the most present, and therefore had rather say with divines, plainly, that the reasonable soul is a spiritual and immortal substance breathed into man by God, whereby he lives and moves and understandeth, and so is distinguished from other creatures.

"Yea, but what is that spiritual and immortal substance breathed into man, etc.?" saith Sir Walter.

"The soul," quoth I.

"Nay then," saith he, "you answer not like a scholar."

Hereupon I endeavored to prove that it was scholar-like—nay, in such disputes as these, usual and necessary—to run *in circulum*: partly because *definicio rei* was *primum et imediatum principium*, and seeing *primo non est prius*, a man must of necessity come backward, and partly because *definicio et definitum* be *nature reciproce*, the one convertibly answering unto the question made upon the other. As, for example, if one ask, "What is a man?" you will say he is a creature reasonable and mortal; but if you ask again, "What is a creature reasonable and mortal?" you must, of force, come backward and answer, "It is a man." *Et sic de ceteris.*

"But we have principles in our mathematics," saith Sir Walter, "as *totum est maius quamlibet sua parte.* And ask me of it, and I can show it in the table, in the window, in a man—the whole being bigger than the parts of it."

I replied first, that he showed *quod est,* not *quid est* (that it was, but not what it was); secondly, that such demonstration as that was against the nature of man's soul being a spirit; for as his things, being sensible, were subject to the sense, so man's soul, being insensible, was to be discerned by the spirit. Nothing more certain in the world than that there is a God; yet, being a spirit, to subject Him to the sense (otherwise than perfected) it is impossible.

"Marry!" quoth Sir Raleigh. "These two be like, for neither could I learn hitherto what God is like."

Mr. Fitzjames answering that Aristotle should say he was *ens encium,* I answered that whether Aristotle, dying in a fever, should cry *"ens encium, miserere mei!"* or, drowning himself in Euripum, should say *"Quia ego te non capio tu me capies,"* it was uncertain; but that God was *ens entium*—a thing of things, having being of himself and giving being to all creatures —it was most certain, and confirmed by God Himself unto Moses.

"Yea, but what is this *ens entium?*" saith Sir Walter.

I answered, "It is God."

And being disliked, as before, Sir Walter wished that grace might be said. "For that," quoth he, "is better than this disputation."

Thus, supper ended and grace said, I departed to Dorchester with my fellow minister. And this, to my remembrance, is the substance of that speech which Sir Walter Raleigh and I had at Wolveton.

Ralph Ironside

James I and the King of Denmark [1606]

From a letter by Sir John Harington (d. 1612), the epigrammatist, and godson of Queen Elizabeth.

I came here a day or two before the Danish king came, and from the day he did come until this hour, I have been well nigh overwhelmed with carousal and sports of all kinds. The sports began each day in such manner and such sort as well nigh persuaded me of Mohammed's paradise. We had women, and indeed wine too, of such plenty as would have astonished each sober beholder. Our feasts were magnificent and the two royal guests did most lovingly embrace each other at table. I think the Dane hath strangely wrought on our good English nobles, for those whom I never could get to taste good liquor now follow the fashion and wallow in beastly delights. The ladies abandon their sobriety and are seen to roll about in intoxication. In good sooth, the Parliament did kindly provide his Majesty so seasonably with money, for there hath been no lack of good living: shows, sights, and banquetings, from morn to eve.

One day a great feast was held and, after dinner, the representation of Solomon's Temple and the coming of the Queen of Sheba was made, or (as I may better say) was meant to have been made, before their Majesties by device of the Earl of Salisbury and others. But, alas! as all earthly things do fail to poor mortals in enjoyment, so did prove our presentment hereof. The lady who did play the queen's part did carry most precious gifts to both their Majesties but, forgetting the steps arising to the canopy, overset her caskets into his Danish Majesty's lap and fell at his feet (though I rather think it was in his face). Much was the hurry and confusion; cloth and napkins were at hand to make all clean. His Majesty then got up and would dance with the Queen of Sheba, but he fell down and humbled himself before her and was carried to an inner chamber and laid on a bed of state which was not a little defiled with the presents of the Queen which had just been bestowed on his garments: such as wine, cream, jelly, beverage, cakes, spices, and other good matters.

The entertainment and show went forward, and most of the presenters went backward, or fell down, wine did so occupy their upper chambers. Now did appear, in rich dress, Hope, Faith, and Charity. Hope did assay to speak, but wine rendered her endeavors so feeble that she withdrew and hoped the King would excuse her brevity. Faith was then all alone, for I am certain she was not joined with good works, and left the Court in a staggering condition. Charity came to the King's feet and seemed to cover the multitude of sins her sisters had committed: in some sort, she made obeisance and brought gifts, but said she would return home again, as there was no gift which Heaven had not already given his Majesty. She then returned to Hope and Faith, who were both sick and spewing in the lower hall. Next came Victory, in bright armor, and presented a rich sword to the King (who did not accept it, but put it by with his hand) and, by a strange medley of versification, did endeavor to make suit to the King. But Victory did not triumph long, for after much lamentable utterance, she was led away like a silly captive and laid to sleep in the outer steps of the ante-chamber. Now did Peace make entry and strive to get foremost to the King; but I grieve to tell how great wrath she did dis-cover unto those of her attendants and, much contrary to her own semblance, most rudely made war with her olive branch, and laid on the pates of those who did oppose her coming.

I have much marvelled at these strange pageantries, and they do bring to my remembrance what passed of this sort in our Queen's days, of which I was sometime an humble presenter and assistant; but I ne'er did see such lack of good order, discretion, and sobriety as I have now done. I have passed much time in seeing the royal sports of hunting and hawking, where the manners were such as made me devise the beasts were pursuing the sober creation, and not man in quest of exercise or food. I will now, in good sooth, declare to you, who will not blab, that the Gunpowder fright is got out of all our heads, and we are going on, hereabouts, as if the Devil was contriving every man should blow up himself by wild riot, excess, and devastation of time and temperance. The great ladies do go wellmasked, and indeed it be the only show of their modesty, to conceal their countenance; but, alack, they meet with such countenance to uphold their strange doings, that I marvel not at ought that happens.

Marriage [1618]

*⇥ John Hoskyns (1566–1638), Serjeant-at-law,
wrote on November 13, 1601, to his bride of three and
a half months: "For I swear, might I dissemble my
habit, I had rather be in your scullion boy's place
than where I am; so should I be a creature whereas
now I am a shadow divided from mine own life
and essence."*

6th Feb., 1617 [i.e. 1618]

This is now the eighth day I have kept my bed. Yesterday I
took a purge by Dr. Gifford's advice. He would had me this
day let blood; I would stay till this frost thaws, he would not
have me stay. And I am willing to do as please him, for he doth
all things discreetly and safely.

There are but three ways. Either this sudden obstruction
will bring death, which is most welcome of all, and to speak
the truth I most earnestly desire it: first, to enjoy my Saviour;
secondly, I have seen enough and known enough and too much
of this world; thirdly, God hath led me by His hand past the
difficulties of malice, misery, and debt—there is but one enemy
to conquer, death, whom my Saviour hath conquered for me,
and I long to step over his back. And when I am gone an old
objection will be ended: whether I wanted others or others
wanted me. I shall sin no more, I shall be reprehended no more.

The second way is, if this be a cold it cannot be long; my
strength or physic will break it. The third is, if it grow to be
a consumption I shall have the longer time to repent, but that
will be the most miserable of all. I shall have them saucy with
me that ought not to be so. I shall be upbraided to be a waster
of a poor estate. It grieves me of what is lost already; to save
the rest and obtain peace it were best die now, and best die
here where nobody dares interrupt my thoughts.

To be a true judge of myself, I think the greatest part of this is melancholy, yet God grant never worse melancholy possess my mind. Be you merry, for I feel no pain but a deep long cough, sometimes labor for breath without any pain, and some danger to be choked when I sleep. This ten days I have eaten once a day toward night, well enough but without any great desire, my stomach is so full of phlegm. Yet sometimes I am thirsty, as I drink seldom but physic drink, and that not twice a day.

The loss of my practise makes me sad. I know you could be contented to endure me longer with money. If I scape this and come home, be not froward, be not cross, withdraw not your heart nor counsel from me, practise not upon me, reprehend me no more. For then my next sickness I will certainly die if I can, and would now if I could. The reason may be guessed. Do you think I see not what I do amiss? Do you think I speak not more bitterly to my own heart for every offence than you can? Do you think it can be pleasing to me to see you suffer such things under your eyes and authority as you do in others, and reserve your gall for me?

This hath made me ask. I have been sometimes stung a fortnight to break out in a rage. But God and your soul knows who begins. Self and sudden will and presumption above your sex in you, riot and misdiet in me must be amended. I by the laws of God am your governor; you are not mine. If you desire a sole supremacy, marry no more when I am dead; there be enough that can speak you fair and undo you, and you shall find none to deal with mine as I have dealt with yours. Change that wicked axiom which you repeat so often, that you desire to be kindly used though it be by a dissembler. For I dreamt I saw a dissembler pawning your plate, selling your leases, feasting in your house, and putting my boy to keep his hawks and dogs, and you making much of him.

I will leave you all, and therefore give me leave to leave you this, and I pray you make better use of it than to grieve. For

God knows I desire your health and contentment rather than my own life. When I am gone never do what you suddenly desire or determine, follow no counsel of them that flatter you, give them good words, or rather money, than the government of yourself. Be not tied to the service of any one too much, for you will so endure anything rather than to lose such a one that you and your children will become servants ere you be aware, and therefore hearken for exchange in time and use them all well. Stuff not your house with too many people. Let my boy be continually kept at his book. Choose an honest man for Bess; for little Dick neither you nor I but God must provide an husband.

It grieves me that the living which I shall leave you is so little, and that he must have a pension out of it in whom there never was courage, and now I descry sneaking lewd vices and unthriftiness. I have bitterly reproved him. I hope he will amend; therefore speak not of it. Will Harbin stays here to bring me home if it be God's will. If I come, give me no ill words; if I come not, you are rid of one that offended you much. I pray you forgive him for God's sake, and he with all his soul prays for your health and contentment in this world, and to see you in the kingdom of heaven long hence.

J. Hoskyns

God bless the poor children.

Ben Jonson on Himself [1619]

"Informations" by Ben Jonson to William Drummond, Laird of Hawthornden, "when he came to Scotland on foot."

His grandfather came from Carlisle, and he thought from Annandale to it; he served King Henry VIII and was a gentleman. His father lost all his estate under Queen Mary; having been cast in prison and forfeited, at last turned minister. So he was a minister's son. He himself was posthumous, born a month after his father's decease, brought up poorly, put to school by a friend (his master, Camden), after taken from it and put to another craft (I think was to be a wright or bricklayer) which he could not endure. Then went he to the Low Countries; but returning soon, he betook himself to his wonted studies. In his service in the Low Countries he had, in the face of both the camps, killed an enemy and taken *opima spolia* from him. And since his coming to England, being appealed to the fields, he had killed his adversary, which had hurt him in the arm and whose sword was ten inches longer than his, for the which he was imprisoned and almost at the gallows. Then took he his religion by trust of a priest who visited him in prison. Thereafter he was twelve years a Papist.

He was Master of Arts in both the universities—by their favor, not his study.

He married a wife who was a shrew, yet honest. Five years he had not bedded with her, but remained with my Lord Albany.

In the time of his close imprisonment under Queen Elizabeth, his judges could get nothing of him to all their demands but Aye and No. They placed two damned villains, to catch advantage of him, with him, but he was advertised by his keeper. Of the spies he hath an epigram.

When the King came in England, at that time the pest was in London. He being in the country at Sir Robert Cotton's house with old Camden, he saw in a vision his eldest son (then a child, and at London) appear to him with the mark of a bloody cross on his forehead, as if it had been cutted with a sword. At which amazed, he prayed unto God; and in the morning he came to Mr. Camden's chamber to tell him, who persuaded him it was but an apprehension of his fantasy at which he should not be disjected. In the meantime comes there letters from his wife of the death of that boy in the plague. He appeared to him, he said, of a manly shape, and of that growth that he thinks he shall be at the resurrection.

He was delated by Sir James Murray to the King for writing something against the Scots in a play, *Eastward Ho,* and voluntarily imprisoned himself with Chapman and Marston, who had written it among them. The report was that they should then had their ears cut, and noses. After their delivery, he banqueted all his friends: there was Camden, Selden, and others. At the midst of the feast, his old mother drank to him and shew him a paper which she had (if the sentence had taken execution) to have mixed in the prison among his drink, which was full of lusty strong poison. And that she was no churl, she told she minded first to have drunk of it herself.

He had many quarrels with Marston, beat him and took his pistol from him, wrote his *Poetaster* on him. The beginning of them were that Marston represented him in the stage.

In his youth given to venery. He thought the use of a maid nothing in comparison to the wantonness of a wife, and would never have another mistress. He said two accidents strange befell him. One, that a man made his own wife to court him, whom he enjoyed two years ere he knew of it, and one day finding them by chance, was passingly delighted with it. One other, lay diverse times with a woman who shew him all that he wished except the last act, which she would never agree unto.

Sir Walter Ralegh sent him governor with his son, *anno* 1613, to France. This youth being knavishly inclined, among other pastimes (as the setting of the favor of damosels on a cod-piece) caused him to be drunken and dead drunk, so that he knew not where he was; thereafter laid him on a car which he made to be drawn by pioneers through the streets, at every corner showing his governor stretched out and telling them that was a more lively image of the crucifix than any they had. At which sport young Ralegh's mother delighted much (saying his father, young, was so inclined), though the father abhorred it.

He can set horoscopes, but trusts not in them. He, with the consent of a friend, cozened a lady with whom he had made an appointment to meet an old astrologer in the suburbs, which she kept; and it was himself, disguised in a long gown and a white beard, at the light of a dim burning candle up in a little cabinet reached unto by a ladder.

Every first day of the new year, he had twenty pounds sent him from the Earl of Pembroke to buy books.

After he was reconciled with the Church and left off to be a recusant, at his first communion, in token of true reconciliation, he drank out all the full cup of wine.

Being at the end of my Lord Salisbury's table with Inigo Jones, and demanded by my Lord why he was not glad, "My Lord," said he, "you promised I should dine with you, but I do not." For he had none of his meat; he esteemed only it his meat which was of his own dish.

He hath consumed a whole night in lying looking to his great toe, about which he hath seen Tartars and Turks, Romans and Carthaginians fight in his imagination.

Northampton was his mortal enemy for brawling on a St.

George's Day one of his attenders. He was called before the Council for his *Sejanus,* and accused both of popery and treason by him.

Sundry times he hath devoured his books, i.e. sold them all for necessity.

He hath a mind to be a churchman; and so he might have favor to make one sermon to the King, he careth not what thereafter should befall him, for he would not flatter though he saw death.

THE KNOWLEDGE

A Universal Method [1524]

From The Art or Craft of Rhetoric *by*
Leonard Cox, a schoolmaster.

Here must be noted that logic is a plain and a sure way to
instruct a man of the truth of everything. And that in it the
natures, causes, parts, and effects of things are by certain rules
discussed and searched out. So that nothing can be perfectly
and properly known but by rules of logic, which is nothing
but an observation or a diligent marking of nature, whereby in
everything man's reason doth consider what is first, what last,
what proper, what improper.

Order and the Public Weal [1531]

From The Governor *by Sir Thomas Elyot (d. 1546), who speaks of himself as "being continually trained in some daily affairs of the public weal . . . almost from my childhood."*

A public weal is a body living, compact or made of sundry estates and degrees of men, which is disposed by the order of equity and governed by the rule and moderation of reason. In the Latin tongue it is called *respublica*, of which the word *res* hath diverse significations and doth not only betoken that that is called a thing, which is distinct from a person, but also signifieth estate, condition, substance, and profit. In our old vulgar, profit is called *weal*. And it is called a wealthy country wherein is all thing that is profitable. And he is a wealthy man that is rich in money and substance. *Public* (as Varro saith) is derived of *people*, which in Latin is called *populus*, wherefore it seemeth that men have been long abused in calling *rempublicam* a common weal. And they which do suppose it so to be called for that, that every thing should be to all men in common without discrepancy of any estate or condition, be thereto moved more by sensuality than by any good reason or inclination to humanity. And that shall soon appear unto them that will be satisfied either with authority or with natural order and example.

First, the proper and true signification of the words *public* and *common*, which be borrowed of the Latin tongue for the insufficiency of our own language, shall sufficiently declare the blindness of them which have hitherto holden and maintained the said opinions. As I have said, *public* took his beginning of *people*, which in Latin is *populus*, in which word is contained all the inhabitants of a realm or city, of what estate or condition so ever they be.

Plebs in English is called the *commonalty*, which signifieth only the multitude, wherein be contained the base and vulgar inhabitants not advanced to any honor or dignity, which is also used in our daily communication; for in the city of London and other cities, they that be none aldermen or sheriffs be called commoners; and in the country, at a sessions or other assembly, if no gentlemen be thereat, the saying is that there was none but the commonalty; which proveth, in mine opinion, that *plebs* in Latin is in English *commonalty*, and *plebeii* be *commoners*. And consequently, there may appear like diversity to be in English between a public weal and a common weal as should be in Latin between *res publica* and *res plebeia*. And after that signification, if there should be a common weal, either the commoners only must be wealthy and the gentle and noble men needy and miserable, or else, excluding gentility, all men must be of one degree and sort, and a new name provided. For as much as *plebs* in Latin and *commoners* in English be words only made for the discrepancy of degrees, whereof proceedeth order: which in things as well natural as supernatural hath ever had such a pre-eminence, that thereby the incomprehensible majesty of God, as it were by a bright leam of a torch or candle, is declared to the blind inhabitants of this world. Moreover, take away order from all things, what should then remain? Certes nothing finally, except some man would imagine eftsoons *chaos*, which of some is expound a confuse mixture. Also, where there is any lack of order, needs must be perpetual conflict; and in things subject to Nature, nothing of himself only may be nourished, but when he hath destroyed that wherewith he doth participate by the order of his creation, he himself of necessity must then perish, whereof ensueth universal dissolution.

A Worcester Grammar School [1544]

Prayers to be Said in School in the Morning
At six o'clock in the morning the usher shall go into school, and with all the scholars of the school in turns say the Psalm, The king shall rejoice in thy strength, O Lord; Lord have mercy upon us, Christ have mercy upon us; The Lord's Prayer, and lead us not into temptation, etc.; O Lord, show thy mercy upon us, etc.; O Lord, save the King, etc.; Be a strong tower, O Lord, etc.; Let the enemy have no advantage, etc.; Lord, hear our prayer, etc.

Prayers to be Said in School in the Evening
At five o'clock, when about to leave school, they shall say in turns the Psalm, Behold, now praise the Lord, etc.; Lord have mercy upon us, Christ; Our Father, etc.; Rise, Lord, and help us, etc.; Lord of all power and might, etc., with the prayer, Lighten our darkness, we beseech thee, O Lord, etc.

Of the School and Classes, and the Order
to be Observed in it
The usual qualities which are found in an architect and other overseers of works in pressing on their work, namely, industry and diligence, ought also to be found in pedagogues and teachers of the tender youth, that they may, as it were, enter into a friendly conspiracy and contention between themselves to im-

bue thoroughly the scholars committed to their trust with piety and good letters, and not to study their own advantage or indulge their own love of ease, so much as to look to their proficiency and the public benefit, so that they may be seen to do their duty fairly in everything. And this they will be able to do much more successfully if they endeavor sedulously to follow the order we have prescribed.

The whole number of the scholars shall be divided into five or six ranks or classes. The Under Master shall teach the three lower, and the Head Master the three upper classes.

No one shall be admitted into the school who cannot read readily, or does not know by heart in the vernacular the Lord's Prayer, the Angelic Salutation, the Apostle's Creed, and the Ten Commandments. Those who are wholly ignorant of grammar shall learn the accidence of nouns and verbs, as it were out of class. When they have learned these they shall be taken into the First Class.

In the First Class they shall learn thoroughly by heart the rudiments in English. They shall learn to put together the parts of speech, and to turn a short phrase of English into Latin, and gradually to approach other easy constructions.

In the Second Class they shall learn a little higher. They shall know the genders of nouns and the inflection of verbs written in Latin. They shall run through Cato's verses, Aesop's *Fables*, and some *Familiar Colloquies*.

In the Third Class they shall endeavor to make correct varyings on the nouns and anomalous verbs, so that no noun or verb can be found anywhere which they do not know how to inflect in every detail. In this form, too, they shall make Terence's *Comedies*, Mantuanus' *Eclogues*, and other things of that sort thoroughly familiar to them.

These classes the Under Master shall have the care of, gradually instilling and inculcating the lesser rudiments into his pupils so as to make them fit and prepared to receive higher instruction.

The Usher shall come into school at six A.M. and, immediately after saying the prayers to God which we have prescribed, shall make his scholars say by heart daily one of the eight parts of speech until they are ready in each. Nor shall he omit on any other day to dictate to his pupils an English sentence, which he shall teach them to turn exactly into Latin, and to write it carefully in their parchment notebooks.

In anything to be done in the school the Under Master shall be subject to and shall obey the Head Master, and shall consult him on the method and plan of teaching so that they may both agree in their zeal for the profit of the scholars. Both, too, shall endeavor to teach their pupils to speak openly, finely, and distinctly, keeping due decorum both with their body and their mouth.

In the Fourth Form the boys shall be taught to know the Latin syntax readily, and shall be practised in the stories of poets, and familiar letters of learned men, and the like.

In the Fifth Form they shall commit to memory the figures of Latin oratory and the rules for making verses, and at the same time shall be practised in making verses and polishing themes. Then they shall be versed in translating the chastest poets and the best historians.

Lastly, in the Sixth Form they shall be instructed in the formulas of *The Copiousness of Words and Things* written by Erasmus, and learn to master varyings of speech in every mode so that they may acquire the faculty of speaking Latin, as far as is possible for boys. Meanwhile, they shall taste Horace, Cicero, and other authors of that class. Meanwhile, they shall compete with one another in declamations so that they may leave well learned in the school of argument.

These classes principally the Head Master shall try to polish in Latin.

He shall come into school by seven o'clock to perform his duty of teaching thoroughly. He shall, too, every other day make some English sentence into Latin, and teach the flock committed to him to change it into many forms.

Moreover, let him understand that he has charge of the whole school. So every week he ought to visit the whole flock, once, twice, or three times, and diligently test the abilities of the scholars, and ascertain their progress in learning. If he shall prove any of them, after testing them in every way, to be slow and wholly strangers to the Muses, he shall warn their friends not to let them, being wholly unfit for letters, waste their time in vain and fill the places of others. But those he shall find to be fit and industrious he shall, at least three times a year, call up to the higher forms: namely, from the first to the second, from the second to the third, and so on as each shall be thought fit. This shall be done in the presence of and after consultation with the Under Master in the case of those entrusted to his care.

Moreover, at six P.M. the scholars shall return to school, and until seven P.M. shall do their repetition, and render to their fellow pupils who have become ripe in learning, several masters also being present, whatever they have learned through the day.

When leave to play is given they shall play and sport together, not wandering about here and there, lest they incur loss of character, and their minds become set on other things and estranged from learning. And they shall not practise any games which are not of a gentlemanly appearance and free of all lowness.

Lastly, whatever they are doing, in earnest or in play, they shall never use any language but Latin or Greek.

The Elements and the Spheres [1556]

From The Castle of Knowledge *by Robert Recorde* (d. 1558), *a minor official.*

MASTER: I have already said that of all the parts of the world, the earth is the least; whereby you may conceive that within it is nothing, for so should that (whatsoever it were) be lesser than the earth. But without the earth, doth the water lie, which covereth a great part of the same; about them both doth the air run, and occupieth (as we may easily consider) much more room than both the sea and the land; above the air and round about it (after the agreement of most wise men) doth the fire occupy his place. And these four, that is, earth, water, air and fire, are named the four elements: that is to say, the first simple and original matters whereof all mixed and compound bodies be made and into which all shall turn again.

SCHOLAR: Oftentimes have I heard it that both man and beasts are made of earth and into earth shall return again; but I thought not that they had been made of water, and much less of air or fire.

MASTER: Of earth only, nothing is made but earth; for an herb or tree cannot grow (as all men confess) except it be helped and nourished with air convenient, and due watering, and also have the heat of the sun. And generally, since all thing is maintained by his like and is destroyed by his contrary, then if man cannot be maintained without fire, air, and water, it must needs appear that he is made of them as well as of earth, and so likewise as other things that be compound.

SCHOLAR: This talk delighteth me marvelously, so that I cannot be weary of it as long as it shall please you to continue it.

MASTER: This talk is not for this place: partly for that it is more physical than astronomical, and partly because I determined, in this first part, to omit the causes and reasons of all things, and briefly to declare the parts of the world; whereof these four elements, being uncompound of themselves (that is, simple and unmixed), are accounted as one part of the world, which therefore is called the elementary part. And because those elements do daily increase and decrease in some parts of them (though not in all parts at once) and are subject to continual corruption, they are distinct from the rest of the world, which hath no such alteration nor corruption. Which part is above all the four elements and compasseth them about, and is called the sky, or welkin, and also the heavens. This part hath in it diverse lesser or special parts, named commonly spheres: as the sphere of the moon, which is lowest and next unto the elements; then above it, the sphere of Mercury; and next to it the sphere of Venus; then followeth the sun with his sphere; and then Mars in his order; above him is Jupiter; and above him is Saturn. These seven are named the seven planets, every one having his sphere by himself severally, and his motion also several and unlike in time to any other. But above these seven planets is there another heaven or sky, which commonly is named the firmament, and hath in it an infinite number of stars, whereof it is called the starry sky. And because it is eighth in order of the heavens or spheres, it is named also the eighth sphere. This heaven is manifest enough to all men's eyes, so that no man needeth to doubt of it; for it is that sky wherein are all those stars that we see, except the five lesser planets which I did name before: that is, Saturn, Jupiter, Mars, Venus, and Mercury.

The Making of a Delectable Poem [1575]

--◆{ *From* Certain Notes of Instruction Concerning
the Making of Verse or Rhyme in English, *by*
George Gascoigne (1542–1577). Aliquid salis, *"some*
salt"; vix, *"scarcely";* tamquam in oratione perpetua,
"as in run-on talk"; trita et obvia, *"trite and obvious";*
per allegoriam, *"by allegory."*

The first and most necessary point that ever I found meet to be
considered in making of a delectable poem is this, to ground it
upon some fine invention. For it is not enough to roll in pleasant
words, nor yet to thunder in *rym, ram, ruff* by letter (quoth
my master Chaucer), nor yet to abound in apt vocables or
epithets unless the invention have in it also *aliquid salis*. By this
aliquid salis I mean some good and fine device showing the quick
capacity of a writer. And where I say some good and fine invention I mean that I would have it both fine and good, for
many inventions are so superfine that they are *vix* good, and,
again, many inventions are good and yet not finely handled. And
for a general forewarning, what theme soever you do take in
hand, if you do handle it but *tamquam in oratione perpetua* and
never study for some depth of device in the invention and some
figures also in the handling thereof, it will appear to the skilful
reader but a tale of a tub. To deliver unto you general examples
it were almost unpossible, sithence the occasions of inventions
are, as it were, infinite; nevertheless, take in worth mine opinion
and perceive my further meaning in these few points. If I should
undertake to write in praise of a gentlewoman I would neither
praise her chrystal eye nor her cherry lip, etc., for these things
are *trita et obvia*. But I would either find some supernatural
cause whereby my pen might walk in the superlative degree, or

else I would undertake to answer for any imperfection that she hath and thereupon raise the praise of her commendation. Likewise, if I should disclose my pretense in love, I would either make a strange discourse of some intolerable passion, or find occasion to plead by the example of some history, or discover my disquiet in shadows *per allegoriam,* or use the covertest mean that I could to avoid the uncomely customs of common writers. Thus much I adventure to deliver unto you, my friend, upon the rule of invention, which of all other rules is most to be marked and hardest to be prescribed in certain and infallible rules. Nevertheless, to conclude therein, I would have you stand most upon the excellency of your invention and not stick to study deeply for some fine device. For that being found, pleasant words will follow well enough and fast enough.

Law [1580]

—⧫ *The judgment of the King of Macedon, towards
the end of Sidney's* Arcadia, *on the disguised
Daiphantus, his son, and the disguised Palladius,
Prince of Thessalia, his nephew, for their complicity
in the supposed murder of the King of Arcadia
and their elopement with his daughters and heirs.
Everything comes out all right a few pages later.*

This weighty matter, whereof presently we are to determine,
doth at the first consideration yield two important doubts: the
first, whether these men be to be judged; the second, how they
are to be judged. The first doubt ariseth because they give themselves out for princes absolute, a sacred name, and to which any
violence seems to be an impiety. For how can any laws, which
are the bonds of all human society, be observed if the law-givers
and law-rulers be not held in an untouched admiration? But
hereto, although already they have been sufficiently answered,
yet thus much again will I repeat unto you. That whatsoever
they be or be not, here they be no princes, since betwixt prince
and subject there is as necessary a relation as between father and
son; and as there is no man a father but to his child, so is not a
prince a prince but to his own subjects. Therefore is not this the
place to acknowledge in them any principality without it should
at the same time, by a secret consent, confess subjugation.

Yet hereto may be objected that the universal civility, the
law of nations (all mankind being as it were co-inhabitors or
world-citizens together), hath ever required public persons
should be of all parties especially regarded, since not only in
peace but in war, not only princes but heralds and trumpets
are with great reason exempted from injuries. This point is true,
but yet so true as they that will receive the benefit of a custom

must not be the first to break it; for then can they not complain
if they be not helped by that which they themselves hurt. If a
prince do acts of hostility without denouncing war, if he breaks
his oath of amity, or innumerable such other things contrary to
the law of arms, he must take heed how he fall into their hands
whom he so wrongeth; for then is courtesy the best custom he
can claim. Much more these men, who have not only left to do
like princes, but to be like princes; not only entered into Arcadia, and so into the Arcadian orders, but into domestical services, and so, by making themselves private, deprived themselves
of respect due to their public calling. For no proportion it were
of justice that a man might make himself no prince when he
would do evil, and might anew create himself a prince when he
would not suffer evil. Thus, therefore, by all laws of nature and
nations, and especially by their own putting themselves out of
the sanctuary of them, these young men cannot in justice avoid
the judgement, but, like private men, must have their doings
either cleared, excused, or condemned.

There resteth, then, the second point: how to judge well. And
that must undoubtedly be done not by a free discourse of reason and skill of philosophy, but must be tied to the laws of
Greece and municipal statutes of this kingdom. For although
out of them these came, and to them must indeed refer their
offspring, yet because philosophical discourses stand in the general consideration of things, they leave to every man a scope of
his own interpretation; where the laws, applying themselves to
the necessary use, fold us within assured bounds: which, once
broken, man's nature infinitely rangeth. Judged therefore they
must be, and by your laws judged.

Now the action offereth itself to due balance betwixt the ac-
cuser's twofold accusation and their answer accordingly applied. The questions being, the one of a fact simply, the other
of the quality of a fact. To the first they use direct denial, to
the second qualification and excuse. They deny the murder of

the King and, against mighty presumptions, bring forth some probable answers which they do principally fortify with the Queen's acknowledging herself only culpable. Certainly, as in equality of conjectures, we are not to take hold of the worse, but rather to be glad we may find any hope that mankind is not grown monstrous (being undoubtedly less evil a guilty man should escape than a guiltless perish); so if in the rest they be spotless, then is no farther to be remembered. But if they have aggravated these suspicions with new evils, then are those suspicions so far to show themselves as to cause the other points to be thoroughly examined, and with less favor weighted, since this no man can deny: they have been accidental, if not principal, causes of the King's death.

Now then we are to determine of the other matters which are laid to them, wherein they do not deny the fact, but deny or at least diminish the fault. But first I may remember, though it were not first alleged by them, the services they had before done, truly honorable and worthy of great reward, but not worthy to countervail a following wickedness. Reward is proper to well-doing, punishment to evil-doing, which must not be confounded no more than good and evil are to be mingled. Therefore hath it been determined in all wisdoms that no man, because he hath done well before, should have his present evils spared, but rather so much the more punished as having showed he knew how to be good, yet would against his knowledge be naught.

The fact is then nakedly, without passion or partiality, to be viewed: wherein without all question they are equally culpable. For though he that terms himself Daiphantus were sooner disappointed of his purpose of conveying away the Lady Philoclea than he that persuaded the Princess Pamela to fly her country, and accompanied her in it; yet seeing, in causes of this nature, the will by the rules of justice standeth for the deed, they are both alike to be found guilty, and guilty of heinous ravishment.

For though they ravished them not from themselves, yet they ravished them from him that owned them, which was their father: an act punished by all the Grecian laws by the loss of the head, as a most execrable theft. For if they must die who steal from us our goods, how much more they who steal from us that for which we gather our goods? And if our laws have it so in private persons, much more forcibly are they to be in princes' children, where one steals as it were the whole state and well-being of that people, being tied by the secret of long use to be governed by none but the next of blood. Neither let any man marvel our ancestors have been so severe in these cases, since the example of the Phoenician Europa, but especially of Grecian Helen, hath taught them what destroying fires have grown of such sparkles. And although Helen was a wife and this but a child, that booteth not, since the principal cause of marrying wives is that we may have children of our own.

But now let us see how these young men, truly for their persons worthy of pity, if they had rightly pitied themselves, do go about to mitigate the vehemency of their errors. Some of their excuses are common to both, some peculiar only to him that was the shepherd. Both remember the force of love and, as it were, the mending up of the matter by their marriage. If that unbridled desire which is entitled love might purge such a sickness as this, surely we should have many loving excuses of hateful mischief. Nay, rather no mischief should be committed that should not be veiled under the name of love. For as well he that steals might allege the love of money; he that murders, the love of revenge; he that rebels, the love of greatness, as the adulterer the love of a woman; since they do in all speeches affirm they love that which an ill-governed passion maketh them to follow. But love may have no such privilege. That sweet and heavenly uniting of the minds which properly is called love hath no other knot but virtue; and therefore if it be a right love, it can never slide into any action that is not virtuous.

The other and indeed more effectual reason is that they may be married unto them, and so honorably redress the dishonor of them whom this matter seemeth most to touch. Surely if the question were what were convenient for the parties, and not what is just in the never-changing justice, there might be much said in it. But herein we must consider that the laws look how to prevent by due examples that such things be not done, and not how to salve such things when they are done. For if the governors of justice shall take such a scope as to measure the foot of the law by the show of conveniency, and measure that conveniency not by the public society but by that which is fittest for them which offend, young men, strong men, and rich men shall ever find private conveniences how to palliate such committed disorders as to the public shall not only be inconvenient but pestilent. The marriage perchance might be fit for them, but very unfit were it to the state to allow a pattern of such procurations of marriage.

And thus much do they both allege. Further goes he that went with the Princess Pamela, and requireth the benefit of a counsellor, who hath place of free persuasion, and the reasonable excuse of a servant that did but wait of his mistress. Without all question, as counsellors have great cause to take heed how they advise anything directly opposite to the form of that present government, especially when they do it singly without public allowance, yet so is the case much more apparent, since neither she was an effectual princess (her father being then alive, and though he had been dead, she not come to the years of authority) nor he her servant in such manner to obey her, but by his own preferment first belonging to Dametas and then to the King, and therefore (if not by Arcadian laws, yet by household orders) bound to have done nothing without his agreement.

Thus therefore, since the deeds accomplished by these two are both abominable and inexcusable, I do, in the behalf of justice and by the force of Arcadian laws, pronounce that Daiphantus should be thrown out of a high tower to receive his

death by his fall, Palladius shall be beheaded: the time, before
the sunset; the place, in Mantinea; the executioner, Dametas,
which office he shall execute all the days of his life for his beastly
forgetting the careful duty he owed to his charge.

Bugbears [1584]

᪥ *Reginald Scot* (*d. 1599*), *M.P.*, *in* The Discovery of Witchcraft. *"Witchcraft is incomprehensible to the wise, learned, or faithful; a probable matter to children, fools, melancholic persons, and papists."*

In our childhood our mother's maids have so terrified us with an ugly devil having horns on his head, fire in his mouth, and a tail in his breech, eyes like a basin, fangs like a dog, claws like a bear, a skin like a nigger, and a voice roaring like a lion, whereby we start and are afraid when we hear one cry "boo." And they have so fraid us with bull-beggars, spirits, witches, urchins, elves, hags, fairies, satyrs, pans, fauns, silenes, Kit with the canstick, tritons, centaurs, dwarfs, giants, imps, calcars, conjurors, nymphs, changelings, incubus, Robin Goodfellow, the spoorn, the mare, the man in the oak, the hellwain, the firedrake, the puckle, Tom Thumb, hobgoblin, Tom Tumbler, boneless, and other such bugs that we are afraid of our own shadows: in so much as some never fear the devil but in a dark night. And then a polled sheep is a terrible beast, and many times is taken for our father's soul, specially in a churchyard, where a right hardy man heretofore scant durst pass by night but his hair would stand upright.

Mr. Bacon in Praise of Knowledge [?1592]

This is probably a speech delivered before the Queen at some formal entertainment, some "conference of pleasure."

Silence were the best celebration of that which I mean to commend; for who would not use silence, where silence is not made, and what crier can make silence in such a noise and tumult of vain and popular opinions?

My praise shall be dedicated to the mind itself. The mind is the man and the knowledge of the mind. A man is but what he knoweth. The mind itself is but an accident to knowledge; for knowledge is a double of that which is; the truth of being and the truth of knowing is all one.

Are not the pleasures of the affections greater than the pleasures of the senses? And are not the pleasures of the intellect greater than the pleasures of the affections? Is not knowledge a true and only natural pleasure, whereof there is no satiety? Is it not knowledge that doth alone clear the mind of all perturbation? How many things are there which we imagine not! How many things do we esteem and value otherwise than they are! This ill proportioned estimation, these vain imaginations, these be the clouds of error that turn into the storms of perturbation. Is there any such happiness as for a man's mind to be raised above the confusion of things, where he may have the prospect of the order of nature and the error of men?

But is this a vein only of delight, and not of discovery? of contentment, and not of benefit? Shall he not as well discern the riches of nature's warehouse, as the benefit of her shop? Is truth ever barren? Shall he not be able thereby to produce worthy effects, and to endow the life of man with infinite commodities?

But shall I make this garland to be put upon a wrong head? Would anybody believe me, if I should verify this upon the knowledge that is now in use? Are we the richer by one poor invention, by reason of all the learning that hath been these many hundred years? The industry of artificers maketh some small improvement of things invented; and chance sometimes in experimenting maketh us to stumble upon somewhat which is new; but all the disputation of the learned never brought to light one effect of nature before unknown. When things are known and found out, then they can descant upon them, they can knit them into certain causes, they can reduce them to their principles. If any instance of experience stand against them, they can range it in order by some distinctions. But all this is but a web of the wit, it can work nothing. I do not doubt but that common notions, which we call reason, and the knitting of them together, which we call logic, are the art of reason and studies. But they rather cast obscurity than gain light to the contemplation of nature. All the philosophy of nature which is now received, is either the philosophy of the Grecians, or that other of the Alchemists. That of the Grecians hath the foundations in words, in ostentation, in confutation, in sects, in schools, in disputations. The Grecians were (as one of themselves saith), *you Grecians, ever children.* They knew little antiquity; they knew (except fables) not much above five hundred years before themselves; they knew but a small portion of the world. That of the alchemists hath the foundation in imposture, in auricular traditions and obscurity; it was catching hold of religion, but the principle of it is, *Populus vult decipi.* So that I know no great difference between these great philosophies, but that the one is a loud crying folly, and the other is a whispering folly. The one is gathered out of a few vulgar observations, and the other out of a few experiments of a furnace. The one never faileth to multiply words, and the other ever faileth to multiply gold. Who would not smile at Aristotle, when he admireth the eternity and invariableness of the heavens, as there were not the like in the bowels of the earth? Those be the confines and borders of these two kingdoms, where the continual alteration and incursion are. The superficies and upper parts of the earth are full of varieties. The superficies and lower parts of the heavens (which we call the middle region of the air) is full of variety. There is much spirit in the one part that cannot be brought into mass. There is much massy body in the other place that cannot be refined to spirit. The common air is as the waste ground between the borders. Who would not smile at the astronomers, I mean not these new carmen which drive the earth about, but the ancient astronomers, which feign the moon to be the swiftest of the planets in motion, and the rest in order, the higher the slower; and so are compelled to imagine a double motion; whereas how evident is it, that that which they call a contrary motion is but an abatement of motion. The fixed stars overgo Saturn, and so in them and the rest all is but one motion, and the nearer the earth the slower; a motion also whereof air and water do participate, though much interrupted.

But why do I in a conference of pleasure enter into these great matters, in sort that pretending to know much, I should forget what is seasonable? Pardon me, it was because all other things may be endowed and adorned with speeches, but knowledge itself is more beautiful than any apparel of words that can be put upon it.

And let not me seem arrogant, without respect to these great reputed authors. Let me so give every man his due, as I give Time his due, which is to discover truth. Many of these men had greater wits, far above mine own, and so are many in the universities of Europe at this day. But alas, they learn nothing there but to believe: first to believe that others know that which they know not; and after that themselves know that which they know not. But indeed facility to believe, impatience to doubt, temerity to answer, glory to know, doubt to contradict, end to gain, sloth to search, seeking things in words, resting in part of nature; these, and the like, have been the things which have forbidden the happy match between the mind of man and the nature of things, and in place thereof have married it to vain notions and blind experiments. And what the posterity and issue of so honourable a match may be, it is not hard to consider. Printing, a gross invention; artillery, a thing that lay not far out of the way; the needle, a thing partly known before; what a change have these three made in the world in these times; the one in state of learning, the other in state of the war, the third in the state of treasure, commodities, and navigation. And those, I say, were but stumbled upon and lighted upon by chance. Therefore, no doubt the sovereignty of man lieth hid in knowledge; wherein many things are reserved, which kings with their treasure cannot buy, nor with their force command; their spials and intelligencers can give no news of them, their seamen and discoverers cannot sail where they grow. Now we govern nature in opinions, but we are thrall unto her in necessity; but if we would be led by her in invention, we should command her in action.

Reason and Will [1593]

Richard Hooker (1554–1600), Rector of Bishopsbourne, Of the Laws of Ecclesiastical Polity. "There be certain words, as Nature, Reason, Will, and such like, which wheresoever you find named you suspect them presently as bugs-words, because what they mean you do not indeed as you ought apprehend."

By reason man attaineth unto the knowledge of things that are and are not sensible. It resteth therefore that we search how man attaineth unto the knowledge of such things unsensible as are to be known that they may be done. Seeing then that nothing can move unless there be some end the desire whereof provoketh unto motion, how should that divine power of the soul, that "spirit of our mind," as the Apostle termeth it, ever stir itself unto action unless it have also the like spur? The end for which we are moved to work is sometimes the goodness which we conceive of the very working itself, without any further respect at all, and the cause that procureth action is the mere desire of action, no other good besides being thereby intended. Of certain turbulent wits it is said, *Illis quieta movere magna merces videbatur:* "They thought the very disturbance of things established an hire sufficient to set them on work." Sometimes that which we do is referred to a further end, without the desire whereof we would leave the same undone, as in their actions that gave alms to purchase thereby the praise of men.

Man, in perfection of nature being made according to the likeness of his Maker, resembleth him also in the manner of working; so that whatsoever we work as men, the same we do wittingly work and freely. Neither are we, according to the manner of natural agents, any way so tied but that it is in our power to leave the things we do undone. The good which either is gotten by doing, or which consisteth in the very doing itself, causeth not action unless, apprehending it as good, we so like and desire it; that we do unto any such end, the same we choose and prefer before the leaving of it undone. Choice there is not, unless the thing which we take be so in our power that we might have refused and left it. If fire consume the stubble, it chooseth not so to do, because the nature thereof is such that it can do no other. To choose is to will one thing before another, and to will is to bend our souls to the having or doing of that which they see to be good. Goodness is seen with the eye of the understanding. And the light of that eye is reason. So that two principal fountains there are of human action: Knowledge and Will. Which Will, in things tending towards any end, is termed Choice. Concerning Knowledge, "Behold," saith Moses, "I have set before you this day good and evil, life and death." Concerning Will, he addeth immediately, "Choose life"; that is to say, the things that tend unto life, them choose.

But of one thing we must have special care, as being a thing of no small moment. And that is how the Will, properly and strictly taken, as it is of things which are referred unto the end that man desireth, differeth greatly from that inferior natural desire which we call Appetite. The object of Appetite is whatsoever sensible good may be wished for; the object of Will is that good which Reason doth lead us to seek. Affections, as joy and grief and fear and anger, with such like, being as it were the sundry fashions and forms of Appetite, can neither rise at the conceit of a thing indifferent nor yet choose but rise at the sight of some things. Wherefore it is not altogether in our power whether we will be stirred with affections or no, whereas actions which issue from the disposition of the Will are in the power thereof to be performed or stayed. Finally, Appetite is the Will's solicitor, and the Will is Appetite's controller. What we covet according to the one, by the other we often reject.

Neither is any other desire termed properly Will, but that where Reason and Understanding, or the show of Reason, prescribeth the thing desired.

It may be therefore a question whether those operations of men are to be counted voluntary wherein that good which is sensible provoketh Appetite, and Appetite causeth action, Reason being never called to counsel: as when we eat or drink, and betake ourselves unto rest, and such like. The truth is that such actions, in men having attained to the use of Reason, are voluntary. For as the authority of higher powers hath force even in those things which are done without their privity, and are of so mean reckoning that to acquaint them therewith it needeth not; in like sort, voluntarily we are said to do that also which the Will, if it listed, might hinder from being done, although about the doing thereof we do not expressly use our reason or understanding and so immediately apply our wills thereunto. In cases therefore of such facility, the Will doth yield her assent as it were with a kind of silence, by not dissenting; in which respect her force is not so apparent as in express mandates or prohibitions, especially upon advice and consultation going before.

Where understanding therefore needeth, in those things Reason is the director of man's Will by discovering in action what is good. For the laws of well-doing are the dictates of right Reason. Children, which are not as yet come unto those years whereat they may have; again, innocents, which are excluded by natural defect from ever having; thirdly, madmen, which for the present cannot possibly have the use of right Reason to guide themselves, have for their guide the Reason that guideth other men, which are tutors over them to seek and to procure their good for them. In the rest there is that light of Reason whereby good may be known from evil and which, discovering the same rightly, is termed right.

The Will, not withstanding, doth not incline to have or do that which Reason teacheth to be good unless the same do also teach it to be possible. For albeit the Appetite, being more general, may wish anything which seemeth good, be it never so impossible, yet for such things the reasonable Will of man doth never seek. Let Reason teach impossibility in anything, and the Will of man doth let it go; a thing impossible it doth not affect, the impossibility thereof being manifest.

There is in the Will of man naturally that freedom whereby it is apt to take or refuse any particular object whatever being presented to it. Whereupon it followeth that there is no particular object so good but it may have the show of some difficult or unpleasant quality annexed to it, in respect whereof the Will may shrink and decline it; contrariwise (for so things are blended), there is no particular evil which hath not some appearance of goodness whereby to insinuate itself. For evil as evil cannot be desired. If that be desired which is evil, the cause is the goodness which is or seemeth to be joined with it. Goodness doth not move by being, but by being apparent; and therefore many things are neglected which are most precious, only because the value of them lieth hid. Sensible goodness is most apparent, near, and present, which causeth the Appetite to be therewith strongly provoked. Now pursuit and refusal in the Will do follow, the one the affirmation and the other the negation of goodness which the understanding apprehendeth, grounding itself upon sense unless some higher reason do chance to teach the contrary. And if Reason have taught it rightly to be good, yet not so apparently that the mind receiveth it with utter impossibility of being otherwise, still there is place left for the Will to take or leave. Whereas therefore amongst so many things as are to be done, there are so few the goodness whereof Reason in such sort doth or easily can discover, we are not to marvel at the choice of evil even then when the contrary is probably known. Hereby it cometh to pass that custom, inuring the mind by long practice, and so leaving there a sensible impression, prevaileth more than reasonable persuasion what way

soever. Reason therefore may rightly discern the thing which
is good, and yet the Will of man not incline itself thereunto,
as oft as the prejudice of sensible experience doth oversway.

Nor let any man think that this doth make anything for the
just excuse of iniquity. For there was never sin committed
wherein a less good was not preferred before a greater, and that
willfully; which cannot be done without the singular disgrace
of Nature and the utter disturbance of that divine order,
whereby the pre-eminence of chiefest acceptation is by the best
things worthily challenged. There is not that good which con-
cerneth us, but it hath evidence enough for itself if Reason
were diligent to search it out. Through neglect thereof, abused
we are with the show of that which is not; sometimes the
subtlety of Satan inveigling us as it did Eve; sometimes the
hastiness of our Wills preventing the more considerate advice
of sound Reason, as in the Apostles, when they no sooner saw
what they liked not, but they forthwith were desirous of fire
from heaven; sometimes the very custom of evil making the
heart obdurate against whatever instructions to the contrary,
as in them over whom our Savior spake weeping, "O Jerusalem,
how often, and thou wouldst not!" Still, therefore, that therewith we stand blameable and can no way excuse it is, in doing
evil, we prefer a less good before a greater, the greatness whereof
is by reason investigable and may be known. The search of
knowledge is a thing painful; and the painfulness of knowledge
is that which maketh the Will so hardly inclinable thereunto.
The root hereof, divine malediction, whereby the instruments
being weakened wherewithal the soul (especially in reasoning)
doth work, it preferreth rest in ignorance before wearisome labor
to know. For a spur of diligence, therefore, we have a natural
thirst after knowledge ingrafted in us. But by reason of that
original weakness in the instruments without which the understanding part is not able in this world by discourse to work,
the very conceit of painfulness is as a bridle to stay us. For

which cause the Apostle, who knew right well that the weariness of the flesh is an heavy clog to the Will, striketh mightily upon this key, "Awake thou that sleepest; cast off all which presseth down; watch, labor, strive to go forward and to grow in knowledge."

The Trinity and the Incarnation [1597]

Hooker: "And forasmuch as there is no union of God with man without that mean between both which is both, it seemeth requisite that we first consider how God is in Christ, then how Christ is in us."

"The Lord our God is but one God." In which indivisible unity notwithstanding, we adore the Father as being altogether of himself, we glorify that consubstantial Word which is the Son, we bless and magnify that co-essential Spirit eternally proceeding from both which is the Holy Ghost. Seeing therefore the Father is of none, the Son is of the Father, and the Spirit is of both, they are by these their several properties really distinguishable each from other. For the substance of God with this property *to be of none* doth make the Person of the Father; the very selfsame substance in number with this property *to be of the Father* maketh the Person of the Son; the same substance having added unto it the property of *proceeding from the other two* maketh the person of the Holy Ghost. So that in every person there is implied both the substance of God which is one, and also that property which causeth the same person really and truly to differ from the other two. Every person hath his own subsistence which no other besides hath, although there be others besides that are of the same substance. As no man but Peter can be the person which Peter is, yet Paul hath the selfsame nature which Peter hath. Again, angels have every of them the nature of pure and invisible spirits, but every angel is not that angel which appeared in a dream to Joseph.

[79]

Now when God became man, lest we should err in applying this to the Person of the Father or of the Spirit, St. Peter's confession unto Christ was, "Thou art *the Son* of the living God," and St. John's exposition thereof was plain, that it is *the Word* which was made Flesh. "The Father and the Holy Ghost," saith Damascene, "have no communion with the incarnation of the Word otherwise than only by approbation and assent."

Notwithstanding, forasmuch as the Word and Deity are one subject, we must beware we exclude not the nature of God from incarnation, and so make the Son of God incarnate not to be very God. For undoubtedly even the nature of God itself in the only person of the Son is incarnate, and hath taken to itself flesh. Wherefore incarnation may neither be granted to any person but only one, nor yet denied to that nature which is common to all three.

Concerning the cause of which incomprehensible mystery, forasmuch as it seemeth a thing unconstant that the world should honor any other as the Savior but Him whom it honoreth as the Creator of the world, and in the wisdom of God it hath not been thought convenient to admit any way of saving man but by man himself: though nothing should be spoken of the love and mercy of God towards man, which this way are become such a spectacle as neither men nor angels can behold without a kind of heavenly astonishment, we may hereby perceive there is cause sufficient why divine nature should assume human, that so God might be in Christ reconciling to Himself the world. And if some cause be likewise required why rather to this end and purpose the Son than either the Father or the Holy Ghost should be made man, could we which are born the children of wrath be adopted the sons of God through grace any other than the natural Son of God being mediator between God and us? It became therefore Him by whom all things are to be the way of salvation to all, that the institution and restitution of the world might be both wrought by one hand. The world's salvation was, without the incarnation of the Son of

God, a thing impossible: not simply impossible, but impossible it being presupposed that the will of God was no otherwise to have it saved than by the death of his own Son. Wherefore taking to himself our flesh, and by his incarnation making it his own flesh, he had now of his own (although from us) what to offer unto God for us.

And as Christ took manhood that by it he might be capable of death whereunto he humbled himself, so because manhood is the proper subject of compassion and feeling pity (which maketh the scepter of Christ's regency even in the kingdom of heaven amiable), he which without our nature could not on earth suffer for the sins of the world, doth now also by means thereof both make intercession to God for sinners and exercise dominion over all men with a true, a natural, and a sensible touch of mercy.

It is not in man's ability either to express perfectly or conceive the manner how this was brought to pass. But the strength of our faith is tried by those things wherein our wits and capacities are not strong.

On Speech and Style [1599]

From Directions for Speech and Style *by John Hoskyns (1566–1638), "containing all the figures of rhetoric and the art of the best English, exemplified either all out of* Arcadia, *which it censureth, or by instances, the matter whereof may benefit conversation."*

The conceits of the mind are pictures of things and the tongue is interpreter of those pictures. The order of God's creatures in themselves is not only admirable and glorious but eloquent; then he that could apprehend the consequences of things in their truth and utter his apprehensions as truly were a right orator. Therefore Cicero said much when he said, *dicere recte nemo potest nisi qui prudenter intellegit* [no man can speak rightly who is not morally intelligent].

The shame of speaking unskilfully were small if the tongue were only disgraced by it. But as the image of the king in a seal of wax, ill represented, is not so much a blemish to the wax or the signet that sealeth it as to the king whom it resembleth, so disordered speech is not so much injury to the lips which give it forth or the thoughts which put it forth as to the right proportion and coherence of things in themselves, so wrongfully expressed. Yet cannot his mind be thought in tune whose words do jar, nor his reason in frame whose sentences are preposterous, nor his fancy clear and perfect whose utterance breaks itself into fragments and uncertainties. Were it an honor to a prince to have the majesty of his embassage spoiled by a careless ambassador? And is it not as great an indignity that an excellent conceit and capacity by the indiligence of an idle tongue should be defaced? Careless speech doth not only discredit the personage of the speaker but it doth discredit the opinion of his reason and judgement; it discrediteth the truth, force, and uniformity of the matter and substance. If it be so, then, in words which fly and escape censure, and where one good phrase begs pardon for many incongruities and faults, how shall he be thought wise whose penning is thin and shallow? How shall you look for wit from him whose leisure and whose head, assisted with the examination of his eyes, could yield you no life and sharpness in his writing?

The rule of a metaphor is that it be not too bold or too farfetched. And though all metaphors go beyond the signification of things, yet are they requisite to match the compassing sweetness of men's minds, that are not content to fix themselves upon one thing but they must wander into the confines, like the eye that cannot choose but view the whole knot when it beholds but one flower in a garden of purpose, or like an archer that, knowing his bow will overcast or carry too short, takes an aim on this side or beyond the mark. Besides, a metaphor is pleasant because it enricheth our knowledge with two things at once, with the truth and with similitude: as this, "heads disinherited of their natural seigniories," whereby we understand both beheading and the government of the head over the body, as the heir hath over the lordship which he inheriteth.

The ears of men are not only delighted with store and exchange of divers words but feel great delight in repetition of the same; which, because it beginneth in the middle, and in the end, and in sundry correspondencies of each of their places, one to another, it happeneth, therefore, it hath purchased several names of figures, as a repetition of the same word or sound immediately or without interposition of any other is called epizeuxis. "O let not, let not from you be poured upon me destruction!" "Tormented? Tormented? torment of my soul, Philoclea, tormented?" This figure is not to be used but in passion.

Not only Lyly, whose posy at the beginning of his book was stamped with cognizance (*Commend it or Amend it*), but even with Dr. Mathew this figure [agnomination] was of great account, and he lost no estimation by it: "Our paradise is a pair of dice, our almës-deeds are turned into all misdeeds, our praying into playing, our fasting into feasting." But that kind of breaking words into another meaning is pretty to play with among gentlewomen, as, "You will have but a bare gain of this bargain." Otherwise it will best become the tuftaffeta orators to skip up and down the neighborhood of these words that differ more in sense than in sound, tending nearer to meter than to matter, in whose mouth long may that phrase prosper, a man not only fit for the gown but for the gun, for the pen but for the pike, for the book but for the blade.

See to what preferment a figure may aspire if it once get in credit in a world that hath not much true rhetoric! That was the cause Sir Philip Sidney would not have his style be much beholding to this kind of garnish. And of a truth, if the times gives itself too much to any one flourish, it makes it a toy and bars a learned man's writings from it, lest it seem to come more of the general humor than the private judgement.

To amplify and illustrate are two the chiefest ornaments of eloquence and gain of men's minds two the chiefest advantages, admiration and belief. For how can you commend a thing more acceptably to our attention than by telling us it is extraordinary and by showing us that it is evident?

Sententia if it be well used is a figure; if ill and too much, it is a style, whereof none that writes humorously or factiously nowadays can be clear. For now there are such schisms of eloquence that it is enough for any ten years that all the bravest wits do imitate some figure which a critic hath taught some great personage. So it may be within this two hundred years we shall go through the whole body of rhetoric. It is true that we study according to the predominancy of courtly inclinations. Whilst mathematics were in requests all our similitudes came from lines, circles, and angles. Whilst moral philosophy is now a while spoken of, it is rudeness not to be sententious. And for my part I'll make one. I have used and outworn six several styles since I was first Fellow of New College, and am yet able to bear the fashion of writing company. Let our age, therefore, only speak morally, and let the next age live morally.

But he that will truly set down a man in a figured story must first learn truly to set down an humor, a passion, a virtue, a vice, and therein keeping decent proportion add but names and knit together the accidents and encounters.

There is in the best writers sometimes a vein of speech wherein the vulgar conceits are exceedingly pleased, for they admire this most, that there is some excellency in it and yet they themselves suspect that it excells their admiration. In some examples I would gladly discover the reason thereof. It cannot be but if either the meaning or the words be obscure or unfamiliar unto a man's mind, that the speech so consisting should be much accepted. And yet it is impossible that there should be any extraordinary delight in ordinary words and plain meaning. How then shall we determine? It is as it is in many dishes at our tables; our eyes and taste give them commendation, not for the substance but for the dressing and service. What plainer meaning than sleep among thieves? And verily, *sleep, life, trust* are common English words. Yet it is not a common fashion of speech to say, "trust a sleeping life among thieves." In the same sense, "when they had slept a while" is ordinary, but "when they had a while hearkened to the persuasion of sleep" is extraordinary. Though all the words of it by themselves are most known and familiar, yet the bringing in and fetch of it is strange and admirable to the ignorant. We therefore call it periphrasis or circumlocution, and it is much helped by metaphors: as before, *inclined to sleep* is expressed by a metaphor taken from an orator who moves and inclines by persuasion, and to be so moved it is to *hearken*.

On Knowledge [1614]

From Sir Walter Ralegh's History of the
World, *written while he was in the Tower. This
is a more formal statement of the position taken
in the "Disputation at Supper."*

But for myself, I shall never be persuaded that God hath shut
up all light of learning within the lantern of Aristotle's brains,
or that it was ever said unto him, as unto Esdras, *Accendam in
corde tuo lucernam intellectus*, that God hath given invention
but to the heathen, and that they only have invaded Nature
and found the strength and bottom thereof, the same Nature
having consumed all her store and left nothing of price to after-
ages. That these and these be the causes of these and these
effects, time hath taught us, and not reason; and so hath experience, without art. The cheese-wife knoweth it as well as
the philosopher that sour rennet doth coagulate her milk into
a curd. But if we ask a reason of this cause, why the sourness
doth it, whereby it doth it, and the manner how, I think that
there is nothing to be found in vulgar philosophy to satisfy this
and many other like vulgar questions. But man, to cover his
ignorance in the least things, who cannot give a true reason for
the grass under his feet, why it should be green rather than red
or of any other color; that could never yet discover the way
and reason of Nature's working in those which are far less noble
creatures than himself, who is far more noble than the heavens
themselves; "man," saith Solomon, "that can hardly discern the
things that are upon the earth, and with great labor find out
the things that are before us"; that hath so short a time in the

world as he no sooner begins to learn than to die; that hath in
his memory but borrowed knowledge, in his understanding
nothing truly; that is ignorant of the essence of his own soul,
and which the wisest of the naturalists (if Aristotle be he) could
never so much as define but by the action and effect, telling us
what it works (which all men know as well as he) but not
what it is, which neither he nor any else doth know but God
that created it ("For though I were perfect, yet I know not
my soul," saith Job)—man, I say, that is but an idiot in the next
cause of his own life and in the cause of all the actions of his
life, will, notwithstanding, examine the art of God in creating
the world; of God, who, saith Job, "is so excellent as we know
him not"; and examine the beginning of the work which had
end before mankind had a beginning of being. He will disable
God's power to make a world without matter to make it of.
He will rather give the motes of the air for a cause; cast the
work on necessity or chance; bestow the honor thereof on Nature; make two powers, the one to be the author of the matter,
the other of the form; and lastly, for want of a workman, have
it eternal. Which latter opinion Aristotle, to make himself the
author of a new doctrine, brought into the world.

The Circulation of the Blood [1615]

*—◦ Robert Boyle (1627–1691), the formulator
of Boyle's Law, on Dr. William Harvey, Physician
to James I and Charles I. As Lumleian Lecturer
at the College of Physicians he presented, from
1615 on, his discovery of the circulation of the
blood; he published his work on the subject in
1628.*

And I remember that when I asked our famous Harvey in the
only discourse I had with him, which was but a while before
he died, what were the things that induced him to think of a
circulation of the blood, he answered me that when he took
notice that the valves in the veins of so many several parts of
the body were so placed that they gave free passage to the
blood towards the heart, but opposed the passage of the venal
blood the contrary way, he was invited to imagine that so
provident a cause as Nature had not so placed so many valves
without design; and no design seemed more probable than that,
since the blood could not well, because of the interposing valves,
be sent by the veins to the limbs, it should be sent through the
arteries, and return through the veins, whose valves did not
oppose its course that way.

The Element of Fire [1623]

Drummond of Hawthornden, developing the famous lines from Donne's First Anniversary *(1611): "new philosophy calls all in doubt; / The element of fire is quite put out / . . . 'Tis all in pieces, all coherence gone."*

The element of fire is quite put out; the air is but water rarified; the earth is found to move, and is no more the center of the universe, is turned into a magnet. Stars are not fixed, but swim in the etherial spaces; comets are mounted above the planets. Some affirm there is another world of men and sensitive creatures, with cities and palaces in the moon. The sun is lost, for it is but a light made of the conjunction of many shining bodies together, a cleft in the lower heavens through which the rays of the highest diffuse themselves, is observed to have spots. Thus, sciences by the diverse motions of this globe of the brain of man are become opinions, nay, errors, and leave the imagination in a thousand labyrinths.

Ignorance [1628]

From a sermon by John Donne, D.D.,
(1572–1631), Dean of St. Paul's.

The Schools have made so many divisions, and sub-divisions, and re-divisions, and post-divisions of ignorance that there goes as much learning to understand ignorance as knowledge. One much elder than all they, and elder (as some will have it) than any but some of the first secretaries of the Holy Ghost, that is, Trismegistus, hath said as much as all: *nequitia animae ignorantia.* Ignorance is not only the drowsiness, the silliness, but "the wickedness of the soul." Not only dis-estimation in this world and damnification here, but damnation in the next world proceeds from ignorance. And yet, here in this world, knowledge is but as the earth and ignorance as the sea; there is more sea than earth, more ignorance than knowledge. And as if the sea do gain in one place it loses in another, so is it with knowledge too; if new things be found out, as many and as good that were known before are forgotten and lost.

What anatomist knows the body of man thoroughly, or what casuist the soul? What politician knows the distemper of the state thoroughly, or what master the disorders of his own family? Princes glory *in arcanis,* that they have secrets which no man shall know, and, God knows, they have hearts which they know not themselves. Thoughts and purposes indigested fall upon them and surprise them. It is so in natural, in moral, in civil things; we are ignorant of more things than we know.

And it is so in divine and supernatural things, too. For, for them, the Scripture is our only light, and of the Scripture St. Augustine professes, *plura se nescire quam scire*, that there are more places in Scripture that he does not than that he does understand.

Hell is darkness, and the way to it is the cloud of ignorance. Hell itself is but condensed ignorance, multiplied ignorance.

THE LITERATURE

JOHN SKELTON

"*Skelton, Laureate*" (*d. 1529*), *Parson of Diss, tutor to Prince Henry (Henry VIII)*, "*upon a dead man's head that was sent to him from an honorable gentlewoman for a token, devised this ghostly meditation in English—convenable in sentence, commendable, lamentable, lacrimable, profitable for the soul.*"

Upon a Dead Man's Head

Your ugly token
My mind hath broken
From wordly lust.
For I have discussed
We are but dust
And die we must.
It is general
To be mortal.
I have well espied
No man may him hide
From Death hollow-eyed,
With sinews withered,
With bones shivered,
With his worm-eaten maw,
And his ghastly jaw
Gasping aside,
Naked of hide,
Neither flesh nor fell.
Then by my counsel,
Look that ye spell
Well this gospel:

[95]

For whereso we dwell,
Death will us quell
And with us mell.
For all our pampered paunches
There may be no franchise,
Nor worldly bliss
Redeem us from this.
Our days be dated
To be checkmated,
With draughts of Death
Stopping our breath—
Our eyes sinking,
Our bodies stinking,
Our gums grinning,
Our souls burning.
To whom, then, shall we sue
For to have rescue,
But to sweet Jesu
On us then to rue?
O goodly Child
Of Mary mild,
Then be our shield,
That we be not exiled
To the dun dale
Of bottomless bale,
Nor to the lake
Of fiends black.
But grant us grace
To see Thy face,
And to purchase
Thine heavenly place,
And Thy palace
Full of solace
Above the sky
That is so high,

Eternally
To behold and see
The Trinity.
Amen.

The Tunning of Elinour Rumming

*⫷ In August 1525 the Aletaster of Leatherhead,
Surrey, certified Elinour Rumming, common tippler
of ale, of the Running Horse, for selling "at
excessive price by small measures." She was fined
2d. The poem has been reduced to about a fourth
of its original length.*

Tell you I will,
If that ye will
A while be still,
Of a comely gill
That dwelt on a hill,
Droopy and drowsy,
Scurvy and lousy,
Her face all bowsy,
Comely crinkled,
Wondrously wrinkled,
Like a roast pig's ear,
Bristled with hair.
And this comely dame,
I understand her name
Is Elinour Rumming,
And as men say
She dwelt in Surrey.
But to make up my tale,
She breweth noppy ale,
And maketh thereof port-sale

To travelers, to tinkers,
To sweaters, to swinkers,
And all good ale drinkers,
That will nothing spare
But drink till they stare
And bring themself bare,
With "Now away the mare,"
And "Let us slay care,"
As wise as an hare!
Come whoso will
To Elinour on the hill,
With "Fill the cup, fill,"
And sit thereby still,
Early and late.
Thither cometh Kate,
Cisly, and Sare,
With their legs bare,
And also their feet
Hardily full unsweet,
With their naked paps
That flips and flaps,
It wigs and it wags
Like tawney saffron bags.
Such a lewd sort
To Elinour resort
From tide to tide.
Abide, abide,
And to you shall be told
How her ale is sold
To Mawt and to Mold.
Instead of coin and money
Some bring her a cony,
And some a pot with honey,
Some a salt, and some a spoon,
Some their hose, some their shoon.

Some ran a good trot
With a skillet or a pot.
Some go straight thither,
Be it sleety or slither.
They hold the highway,
They care not what men say,
Be that as be may.
Some loathe to be espied,
Some start in at the back side,
Over the hedge and pale,
And all for the good ale.
Then start in mad Kit
That had little wit.
She seemed somedeal sick,
And brought up a penny chick
To Dame Elinour
For a draught of liquor.
Then Margery Milkduck
Her kirtle she did up tuck
An inch above her knee,
Her legs that ye might see.
But they were sturdy and stubbed,
Mighty pestles and clubbed,
As fair and as white
As the foot of a kite.
She was somewhat foul,
Crook-necked like an owl.
And yet she brought her fees—
A cantle of Essex cheese
Was well a foot thick,
Full of maggots quick.
It was huge and great,
And mighty strong meat
For the Devil to eat.
Maud Ruggy thither skipped.

She was ugly hipped,
And ugly thick-lipped,
Like an onion sided,
Like tan leather hided.
She had her so guided
Between the cup and the wall
That she was therewithal
Into a palsy fall.
With that her head shaked,
And her hands quaked.
One's head would have ached
To see her naked!
"Soft!" quoth one hight Sybil,
"And let me with you bibble."
She sat down in the place
With a sorry face.
"This ale," said she, "is noppy.
Let us sip and soppy,
And not spill a droppy,
For so might I hoppy,
It cooleth well my croppy."
But, sir, among all
That sat in that hall,
There was a prick-me-dainty
Sat like a sainty,
And began to panty
As though she would fainty.
She was not half so wise
As she was peevish nice.
She said never a word,
But rose from the board
And called for our dame,
Elinour, by name.
"I have no penny nor groat
To pay," said she, "God wote,

For washing of my throat.
But my beads of amber,
Bear them to your chamber."
Then Elinour did them hide
Within her bed's side.
But some then sat right sad
That nothing had.
Such were there many
That had not a penny,
But, when they should walk,
Were faln with a chalk
To score on the balk
Or score on the tally.
God give it ill hail!
For my fingers itch.
I have written too much
Of this mumming
Of Elinour Rumming.
Thus endeth the gest
Of this worthy feast!
> *Quoth Skelton, Laureate.*

THOMAS MORE

St. Thomas More (1478–1535), Knight, of Lincoln's Inn, Speaker of the House of Commons, Lord Chancellor of England, indicted for high treason and executed 1535, canonized 1935. The Utopia relates a conversation between More, Peter Giles, and Raphael Hythloday, a traveler who had seen many new and strange countries, including the new island of Nowhere (Utopia). Our selection, Hythloday's report of a conversation at Cardinal Morton's table, shortly after the Cornish Rebellion (1497), is from the first of the two books of Utopia, in Robinson's translation of 1551. The original is in Latin.

A Dialogue [1516]

"I pray you, sir," quod I, "have you been in our country?"

"Yea, forsooth," quod he, "and there I tarried for the space of four or five months together, not long after the insurrection that the western Englishmen made against their king, which by their own miserable and pitiful slaughter was suppressed and ended. In the mean season I was much bound and beholden to the Right Reverend Father John Morton, Archbishop and Cardinal of Canterbury, and at that time also Lord Chancellor of England: a man, Mr. Peter (for Mr. More knoweth already that I will say), not more honorable for his authority than for his prudence and virtue. He was of a mean stature and, though stricken in age, yet bare he his body upright. In his face did shine such an amiable reverence as was pleasant to behold. Gentle in communication, yet earnest and sage. He had great delight many times with rough speech to his suitors to prove, but without harm, what prompt wit and what bold spirit were in every man; in the which, as in a virtue much agreeing with his nature (so that therewith were not joined impudency) he took great delectation; and the same person, as apt and meet to have an administration in the weal public, he did lovingly embrace. In his speech he was fine, eloquent and pithy; in the law he had profound knowledge; in wit he was incomparable; and in memory wonderful excellent. These qualities, which in him were by nature singular, he by learning and use had made perfect.

"The King put much trust in his counsel; the weal public also in a manner leaned unto him when I was there. For even in the chief of his youth he was taken from school into the Court, and there passed all his time in much trouble and business, and was continually troubled and tossed with diverse misfortunes and adversities. And so, by many and great dangers, he learned the experience of the world, which so being learned cannot easily be forgotten.

"It chanced on a certain day when I sat at his table, there was also a certain layman, cunning in the laws of your realm; which, I cannot tell whereof taking occasion, began diligently and busily to praise that strait and rigorous justice which at that time was there executed upon felons, who, as he said, were for the most part twenty hanged together upon one gallows. And seeing so few escaped punishment, he said he could not choose but greatly wonder and marvel how, and by what evil luck, it should so come to pass that thieves nevertheless were in every place so rife and rank.

" 'Nay, sir,' quod I (for I durst boldly speak my mind before the cardinal), 'marvel nothing hereat; for this punishment of thieves passeth of the limits of justice, and is also very hurtful to the weal public. For it is too extreme and cruel a punishment for theft, and yet not sufficient to refrain men from theft. For simple theft is not so great an offence that it ought to be punished with death; neither is there any punishment so horrible that it can keep them from stealing which have no other craft whereby to get their living. Therefore, in this point, not you only, but also the most part of the world, be like evil schoolmasters which be readier to beat than to teach their scholars. For great and horrible punishments be appointed for thieves; whereas much rather provision should have been made that there were some means whereby they might get their living so that no man should be driven to this extreme necessity, first to steal and then to die.'

" 'Yes,' quod he, 'this matter is well enough provided for already. There be handicrafts, there is husbandry, to get their living by if they would not willingly be naught.'

" 'Nay,' quod I, 'you shall not scape so. For first of all, I will speak nothing of them that come home out of war maimed and lame, as not long ago out of Blackheath Field and a little before that out of the wars in France: such, I say, as put their lives in jeopardy for the weal public's or the King's sake and by the reason of weakness and lameness be not able to occupy their old crafts and be too aged to learn new. Of them I will speak nothing, because war like the tide ebbeth and floweth. But let us consider those things that chance daily before our eyes.

" 'First, there is a great number of gentlemen which cannot be content to live idle themselves, like dors, of that which other have labored for: their tenants, I mean, whom they poll and shave to the quick by raising their rents (for this only point of frugality do they use, men else through their lavish and prodigal spending able to bring themselves to very beggary). These gentlemen, I say, do not only live in idleness themselves, but also carry about with them at their tails a great flock or train of idle and loitering servingmen which never learned any craft whereby to get their livings. These men, as soon as their master is dead or be sick themselves, be incontinent thrust out of doors. For gentlemen had rather keep idle persons than sick men; and many times the dead man's heir is not able to maintain so great a house and keep so many servingmen as his father did. Then, in the mean season, they that be thus destitute of service either starve for hunger or manfully play the thieves. For what would you have them to do? When they have wandered abroad so long until they have worn threadbare their apparel and also appaired their health, then gentlemen, because of their pale and sick faces and patched coats, will not take them into service. And husbandmen dare not set them a-work, knowing well enough that he is nothing meet to do true and faithful service to a poor man with a spade and a mattock, for small wages and hard fare, which being daintily and tenderly pampered up in idleness and pleasure was wont with a sword and buckler by his side to jet through the street with a bragging look, and to think himself too good to be any man's mate.'

" 'Nay, by Saint Mary, sir,' quod the lawyer, 'not so, for this kind of men must we make most of. For in them, as men of stouter stomachs, bolder spirits, and manlier courages than handicraftsmen and plowmen be, doth consist the whole power, strength, and puissance of our host when we must fight in battle.'

" 'Forsooth, sir, as well you might say,' quod I, 'that for war's sake you must cherish thieves. For surely you shall never lack thieves whiles you have them. No, nor thieves be not the most false and fainthearted soldiers, nor soldiers be not the cowardliest thieves: so well these two crafts agree together. But this fault, though it be much used among you, yet is it not peculiar to you only, but common also almost to all nations. Yet France, besides this, is troubled and infected with a much sorer plague. The whole realm is filled and besieged with hired soldiers in peace time (if that be peace), which be brought in under the same color and pretense that hath persuaded you to keep these idle servingmen. For these wise-fools and very archdolts thought the wealth of the whole country herein to consist, if there were ever in a readiness a strong and a sure garrison, specially of old practiced soldiers; for they put no trust at all in men unexercised. And therefore they must be fain to seek for war, to the end they may ever have practiced soldiers and cunning manslayers, lest that (as it is prettily said of Sallust) their hands and their minds, through idleness or lack of exercise, should wax dull.

" 'But how pernicious and pestilent a thing it is to maintain such beasts, the Frenchmen by their own harms have learned, and the examples of the Romans, Carthaginians, Syrians, and of many other countries, do manifestly declare. For not only the empire, but also the fields and cities of all these, by diverse occasions have been overrunned and destroyed of their own armies beforehand had in a readiness. Now how unnecessary a thing this is, hereby it may appear: that the French soldiers, which from their youth have been practiced and ured in feats of arms, do not crack nor advance themselves to have very often got the upper hand and mastery of your new-made and unpracticed soldiers. But in this point I will not use many words, lest perchance I may seem to flatter you.

" 'No, nor those same handicraftmen of yours in cities, nor yet the rude and uplandish plowmen of the country, are not supposed to be greatly afraid of your gentlemen's idle serving-men, unless it be such as be not of body or stature correspondent to their strength and courage, or else whose bold stomachs be discouraged through poverty. Thus you may see that it is not to be feared lest they should be effeminated if they were brought up in good crafts and laborsome works whereby to get their living: whose stout and sturdy bodies (for gentlemen vouch-safe to corrupt and spill none but picked and chosen men) now, either by reason of rest and idleness be brought to weakness, or else by too easy and womanly exercises be made feeble and unable to endure hardness. Truly, howsoever the case standeth, this methinketh is nothing available to the weal public, for war's sake (which you never have but when you will yourselves) to keep and maintain an unnumerable flock of that sort of men that be so troublesome and noyous in peace, whereof you ought to have a thousand times more regard than of war.

" 'But yet this is not only the necessary cause of stealing.

There is another which, as I suppose, is proper and peculiar to you Englishmen alone.'

" 'What is that?' quod the cardinal.

" 'Forsooth,' quod I, 'your sheep, that were wont to be so meek and tame and so small eaters, now, as I hear say, be become so great devourers and so wild that they eat up and swallow down the very men themselves. They consume, destroy, and devour whole fields, houses, and cities. For look in what parts of the realm doth grow the finest and therefore dearest wool; there noblemen and gentlemen, yea and certain abbots (holy men, God wot), not contenting themselves with the yearly revenues and profits that were wont to grow to their fore-fathers and predecessors of their lands, nor being content that they live in rest and pleasure, nothing profiting (yea, much noying) the weal public, leave no ground for tillage. They en-close all in pastures; they throw down houses; they pluck down towns and leave nothing standing but only the church, to make of it a sheep-house. And, as though you lost no small quantity of ground by forests, chases, lands and parks, those good holy men turn all dwelling-places and all glebe land into desolation and wilderness.

" 'Therefore, that one covetous and unsatiable cormorant and very plague of his native country may compass about and en-close many thousand acres of ground to gather within one pale or hedge, the husbandmen be thrust out of their own; or else, either by covin or fraud or by violent oppression, they be put besides it; or by wrongs and injuries they be so wearied that they be compelled to sell all. By one means therefore or by other, either by hook or crook, they must needs depart away, poor, silly, wretched souls: men, women, husbands, wives, fatherless children, widows, woeful mothers with their young babes, and their whole household small in substance and much in number, as husbandry requireth many hands. Away they trudge, I say, out of their known and accustomed houses, find-ing no places to rest in. All their household stuff, which is very little worth, though it might well abide the sale, yet, being suddenly thrust out, they be constrained to sell it for a thing of nought. And when they have wandering about soon spent that, what can they else do but steal and then justly (God wot) be hanged, or else go about a-begging? And yet then also they be cast in prison as vagabonds, because they go about and work not whom no man will set a-work, though they never so willingly offer themselves thereto. For one shepherd or herdman is enough to eat up that ground with cattle to the occupying whereof about husbandry many hands were requisite.

" 'And this is also the cause that victuals be now in many places dearer. Yea, besides this, the price of wool is so risen that poor folks, which were wont to work it and make cloth of it, be now able to buy none at all. And by this means very many be fain to forsake work and to give themselves to idleness. For after that so much ground was enclosed for pasture, an infinite multitude of sheep died of the rot: such vengeance God took of their inordinate and unsatiable covetousness, sending among the sheep that pestiferous murrain which much more justly should have fallen on the sheep-masters' own heads. And though the number of sheep increase never so fast, yet the price falleth not one mite because there be so few sellers. For they be almost all commen into a few rich men's hands, whom no need driveth to sell before they lust; and they lust not before they may sell as dear as they lust. Now the same cause bringeth in like dearth of other kinds of cattle; yea, and that so much the more because that, after farms plucked down and husbandry decayed, there is no man that passeth for the breeding of young store. For these rich men bring not up the young ones of great cattle as they do lambs; but first they buy them abroad very cheap, and afterward, when they be fatted in their pastures, they sell them again exceeding dear. And therefore, as I suppose, the whole incommodity hereof is not yet felt. For yet they make dearth only in those places where they sell; but when they shall fetch them away from thence where they be bred faster than they can be brought up, then shall there also be felt great dearth when store beginneth to fail there where the ware is bought.

" 'Thus the unreasonable covetousness of a few hath turned that thing to the utter undoing of your island, in the which thing the chief felicity of your realm did consist. For this great dearth of victuals causeth every man to keep as little houses and as small hospitality as he possibly may, and to put away their servants—whither, I pray you, but a-begging or else, which these gentle bloods and stout stomachs will sooner set their minds unto, a-stealing?

" 'Now to amend the matters, to this wretched beggary and miserable poverty is joined great wantonness, importunate super-fluity, and excessive riot. For not only gentlemen's servants, but also handicraftmen, yea, and almost the plowmen of the country, with all other sorts of people, use much strange and proud newfangleness in their apparel and too much prodigal riot and sumptuous fare at their table. Now bawds, queens, whores, harlots, strumpets, brothel-houses, stews, and yet another stews, wine-taverns, ale-houses, and tippling-houses, with so many naughty, lewd and unlawful games as dice, cards, tables-tennis, bowls, quoits: do not all these send the haunters of them straight a-stealing when their money is gone?

" 'Cast out these pernicious abominations; make a law that they which plucked down farms and towns of husbandry shall build them up again, or else yield and uprender the possession of them to such as will go to the cost of building them anew. Suffer not these rich men to buy up all, to engross and forstall and, with their monopoly, to keep the market alone as please them. Let not so many be brought up in idleness; let cloth-working be renewed, that there may be honest labors for this idle sort to pass their time in profitably: which hitherto either poverty hath caused to be thieves, or else now be either vaga-bonds or idle servingmen, and shortly will be thieves. Doubt-less, unless you find a remedy for these enormities, you shall in vain advance yourselves of executing justice upon felons.

For this justice is more beautiful than just or profitable. For by suffering your youth wantonly and viciously to be brought up, and to be infected even from their tender age by little and little with vice; then (o' God's name) to be punished when they commit the same faults, after they be commen to man's state, which from their youth they were ever like to do. In this point, I pray you, what other thing do you than make thieves and then punish them?' "

"Now as I was thus speaking, the lawyer began to make himself ready to answer, and was determined with himself to use the common fashion and trade of disputers, which be more diligent in rehearsing than answering, as thinking the memory worthy of the chief praise.

" 'Indeed, sir,' quod he, 'you have said well, being but a stranger, and one that might rather hear something of these matters than have any exact or perfect knowledge of the same, as I will incontinent by open proof make manifest and plain. For first I will rehearse in order all that you have said. Then I will declare wherein you be deceived through lack of knowledge in all our fashions, manners, and customs. And last of all, I will answer your arguments, and confute them every one. First, therefore, I will begin where I promised. Four things you seemed to me—"

" 'Hold your peace,' quod the cardinal, 'for by like you will make no short answer which make such a beginning. Wherefore at this time you shall not take the pains to make your answer, but keep it to your next meeting, which I would be right glad that it might be even tomorrow next, unless either you or Mr. Raphael have any earnest let.

" 'But now, Mr. Raphael, I would very gladly hear of you why you think theft not worthy to be punished with death, or what other punishment you can devise more expedient to the weal public. For I am sure you are not of that mind that you would have theft escape unpunished. For if now the extreme punishment of death cannot cause them to leave stealing, then if ruffians and robbers should be sure of their lives, what violence, what fear, were able to hold their hands from robbing, which would take the mitigation of the punishment as a very provocation to the mischief?'

" 'Surely, my lord,' quod I, 'I think it no right nor justice that the loss of money should cause the loss of man's life. For mine opinion is that all the goods in the world are not able to countervail man's life. But if they would thus say that the breaking of justice and the transgression of the laws is recompensed with this punishment, and not the loss of the money, then why may not this extreme and rigorous justice well be called plain injury? For so cruel governance, so strait rules and unmerciful laws be not allowable, that if a small offense be committed, by-and-by the sword should be drawn. Nor so stoical ordinances are to be borne withal, as to count all offenses of such equality that the killing of a man or the taking of his money from him were both a matter, and the one no more heinous offense than the other, between the which two, if we have any respect to equity, no similitude or equality consisteth.

" 'God commandeth us that we shall not kill. And be we then so hasty to kill a man for taking a little money? And if any man would understand killing by this commandment of God to be forbidden after no larger wise than man's constitutions define killing to be lawful, then why may it not likewise by man's constitutions be determined after what sort whoredom, fornication, and perjury may be lawful? For whereas by the permission of God no man hath power to kill neither himself nor yet any other man, then if a law made by the consent of men concerning slaughter of man ought to be of such strength, force, and virtue that they, which contrary to the commandment of God have killed those whom this constitution of man commanded to be killed, be clean quit and exempt out of the bonds and danger of God's commandment, shall it not then by this reason follow that the power of God's commandment shall extend no further than man's law doth define and permit? And so it shall come to pass that in like manner man's constitutions in all things shall determine how far the observation of all God's commandments shall extend. To be short: Moses' law, though it were ungentle and sharp, as a law that was given to bondmen (yea, and them very obstinate, stubborn, and stiff-necked), yet it punished theft by the purse and not with death. And let us not think that God, in the new law of clemency and mercy under the which he ruleth us with fatherly gentleness, as his dear children, hath given us greater scope and license to execute cruelty, one upon another.

" 'Now ye have heard the reasons whereby I am persuaded that this punishment is unlawful. Furthermore, I think there is nobody that knoweth not how unreasonable (yea, how pernicious) a thing it is to the weal public that a thief and an homicide or murderer should suffer equal and like punishment. For the thief, seeing that man that is condemned for theft in no less jeopardy nor judged to no less punishment than him that is convict of manslaughter, through this cogitation only he is strongly and forcibly provoked, and in a manner constrained, to kill him whom else he would have but robbed. For the murder once done, he is in less care and in more hope that the deed shall not be betrayed or known, seeing the party is now dead and rid out of the way which only might have uttered and disclosed it. But if he chance to be taken and described, yet he is in no more danger and jeopardy than if he had committed but a single felony. Therefore, whiles we go about with such cruelty to make thieves afeared, we provoke them to kill good men.

" 'Now as touching this question what punishment were more commodious and better, that truly in my judgement is easier to be found than what punishment were worse. For why should we doubt that to be a good and profitable way for the punishment of offenders which we know did in times past so long please the Romans, men, in the administration of a weal public, most expert, politic, and cunning? Such as among them were convict of great and heinous trespasses, them they condemned into stone quarries, and into mines to dig metal, there to be kept in chains all the days of their life.

" 'But as concerning this matter, I allow the ordinance of no nation so well as that I saw, whiles I travelled abroad about the world, used in Persia among the people that commonly be called the Polylerites, whose land is both large and ample, and also well and wittily governed, and the people in all conditions free and ruled by their own laws, save that they pay a yearly tribute to the great king of Persia. But because they be far from the sea, compassed and closed in almost round about with high mountains, and do content themselves with the fruits of their own land, which is of itself very fertile and fruitful, for this cause neither they go to other countries nor other come to them. And according to the old custom of the land they desire not to enlarge the bounds of their dominions; and those that they have by reason of the high hills be easily defended; and the tribute which they pay to the mighty king setteth them quit and free from warfare. Thus their life is commodious rather than gallant, and may better be called happy or wealthy than notable or famous. For they be not known as much as by name, I suppose, saving only to their next neighbors and borders.

" 'They that in this land be attainted and convict of felony make restitution of that they stole to the right owner, and not (as they do in other lands) to the king, whom they think to have no more right to the thief-stolen thing than the thief himself hath. But if the thing be lost or made away, then the value of it is paid of the goods of such offenders, which else remaineth all whole to their wives and children. And they themselves be condemned to be common laborers and, unless the theft be very heinous, they be neither locked in prison nor fettered in gyves, but be untied and go at large, laboring in the common works. They that refuse labor or go slowly and slackly to their work be not only tied in chains but also pricked forward with stripes. But being diligent about their work, they live without check or rebuke. Every night they be called in by name and be locked in their chambers. Beside their daily labor, their life is nothing hard or incommodious. Their fare is indifferent good, borne at the charges of the weal public because they be common servants to the commonwealth.

" 'But their charges in all places of the land is not borne alike. For in some parts, that bestowed upon them is gathered of alms. And though that way be uncertain, yet the people be so full of mercy and pity that none is found more profitable or plentiful. In some places, certain lands be appointed hereunto, of the revenues whereof they be found. And in some places, every man giveth a certain tribute for the same use and purpose. Again in some parts of the land, these servingmen (for so be these damned persons called) do no common work, but as every private man needeth laborers, so he cometh into the market-place and there hireth some of them for meat and drink and a certain limited wages by the day, somewhat cheaper than he should hire a free man. It is also lawful for them to chastise the sloth of these servingmen with stripes. By this means they never lack work, and besides the gaining of their meat and drink, every one of them bringeth daily something into the common treasury.

" 'All and every one of them be appareled in one color. Their heads be not polled or shaven, but rounded a little above the ears. And the tip of the one ear is cut off. Every one of them may take meat or drink of their friends, and also a coat of their own color; but to receive money is death, as well to the giver as to the receiver. And no less jeopardy is it for a free man to re-ceive money of a servingman for any manner of cause, and like-wise for a servingman to touch weapons. The servingmen of every several shire be distinct, and known from other by their several and distinct badges, which to cast away is death, as it is also to be seen out of the precinct of their own shire or to talk with a servingman of another shire. And it is no less danger to them for to intend to run away than to do it in deed. Yea, and to conceal such an enterprise, in a servingman it is death, in a free man servitude. Of the contrary part, to him that openeth and uttereth such counsels be decreed large gifts: to a free man a great sum of money, to a servingman freedom, and to them both forgiveness and pardon of that they were of counsel in that pretense. So that it can never be so good for them to go forward in their evil purpose as by repentance to turn back.

" 'This is the law and order in this behalf, as I have showed you. Wherein what humanity is used, how far it is from cruelty, and how commodious it is, you do plainly perceive. Forasmuch as the end of their wrath and punishment intendeth nothing else but the destruction of vices and saving of men, with so using and ordering them that they cannot choose but be good, and what harm soever they did before, in the residue of their life to make amends for the same. Moreover, it is so little feared that they should turn again to their vicious conditions, that wayfaring men will for their safeguard choose them to their guides before any other, in every shire changing and taking new. For if they would commit robbery, they have nothing about them meet for that purpose: they may touch no weapons; money found about them should betray the robbery. They should be no sooner taken with the manner, but forthwith they should be punished. Neither can they have any hope at all to 'scape away by flying. For how should a man that in no part of his apparel is like other men fly privily and unknown, unless he would run away naked? Howbeit so, also flying he should be described by the rounding of his head and his ear-mark.

" 'But it is a thing to be doubted that they will lay their heads together and conspire against the weal public. No, no, I warrant you. For the servingmen of one shire alone could never hope to bring to pass such an enterprise without soliciting, enticing, and alluring the servingmen of many other shires to take their parts. Which thing is to them so impossible that they may not as much as speak or walk togethers or salute one another. No, it is not to be thought that they would make their own countrymen, and companions, of their counsel in such a matter, which they know well should be jeopardy to the counselor thereof and great commodity and goodness to the opener of the same. Whereas on the other part, there is none of them all hopeless or in despair to recover again his freedom by humble obedience, by patient suffering, and by giving good tokens and likelihood of himself that he will ever after that live like a true and honest man. For every year divers be restored to their freedom through the commendation of their patience.'

"When I had thus spoken, saying, moreover, that I could see no cause why this order might not be had in England with much more profit than the justice which the lawyer so highly praised, 'Nay,' quod the lawyer, 'this could never be so 'stablished in England but that it must needs bring the weal public into great jeopardy and hazard.' And as he was thus saying, he shaked his head and made a wry mouth, and so held his peace. And all that were present with one assent agreed to his saying.

" 'Well,' quod the cardinal, 'yet it were hard to judge without a proof whether this order would do well here or no. But when the sentence of death is given, if then the king should command execution to be deferred and spared, and would prove this order and fashion (taking away the privileges of all sanctuaries), if then the proof would declare the thing to be good and profitable, then it were well done that it were 'stablished; else the condemned and reprieved persons may as well and justly be put to death after this proof as when they were first cast. Neither any jeopardy can in the mean space grow hereof. Yea, and me thinketh that these vagabonds may very well be ordered after the same fashion, against whom we have hitherto made so many laws and so little prevailed.'

"When the cardinal had thus said, then every man gave great praise to my sayings, which a little before they had disallowed. But most of all was esteemed that which was spoken of vagabonds, because it was the cardinal's own addition.

"I cannot tell whether it were best to rehearse the communication that followed, for it was not very sad. But yet you shall hear it, for there was no evil in it, and partly it pertained to the matter before said.

"There chanced to stand by a certain jesting parasite, or scoffer, which would seem to resemble and counterfeit the fool. But he did in such wise counterfeit that he was almost the very same indeed that he labored to represent: he so studied, with words and sayings brought forth so out of time and place, to make sport and move laughter that he himself was oftener laughed at than his jests were. Yet the foolish fellow brought out now and then such indifferent and reasonable stuff, that he made the proverb true which sayeth, 'He that shooteth oft, at the last shall hit the mark.' So that when one of the company said that through my communication a good order was found for thieves, and that the cardinal also had well provided for vagabonds, so that only remained some good provision to be made for them that through sickness and age were fallen into poverty and were become so impotent and unwieldy that they were not able to work for their living, 'Tush!' quod he, 'let me alone with them; you shall see me do well enough with them. For I had rather than any good that this kind of people were driven somewhere out of my sight: they have so sore troubled me, many times and oft, when they have with their lamentable tears begged money of me. And yet they could never, to my mind, so tune their song that thereby they ever got of me one farthing. For evermore the one of these two chanced: either that I would not, or else that I could not because I had it not. Therefore, now they be waxed wise. When they see me go by, because they would not lose their labor, they let me go and say not one word to me. So they look for nothing of me: no, in good sooth, no more than if I were a priest. But I will make a law that all these beggars shall be distributed and bestowed into houses of religion. The men shall be made lay brethren, and the women nuns.'

"Hereat the cardinal smiled, and allowed it in jest, yea, and all the residue in good earnest. But a certain friar, graduate in divinity, took such pleasure and delight in this jest of priests and monks, that he also, being else a man of grisly and stern gravity, began merrily and wantonly to jest and taunt.

" 'Nay,' quod he, 'you shall not be so rid and dispatched of beggars unless you make some provision also for us friars.'

" 'Why,' quod the jester, 'that is done already, for my lord himself set a very good order for you when he decreed that vagabonds should be kept strait and set to work; for you be the greatest and veriest vagabonds that be.'

"This jest also, when they saw the cardinal not disprove it, every man took it gladly, saving only the friar. For he (and that no marvel), when he was thus touched on the quick and hit on the gall, so fret, so fumed and chafed at it, and was in such a rage, that he could not refrain himself from chiding, scolding, railing, and reviling. He called the fellow ribald, villain, javel, back-biter, slanderer, and the son of perdition, citing therewith terrible threatenings out of holy scripture. Then the jesting scoffer began to play the scoffer indeed, and verily he was good at that, for he could play a part in that play, no man better.

" 'Patience yourself, good master friar,' quod he, 'and be not angry, for scripture sayeth: *In your patience you shall save your souls.*'

"Then the friar (for I will rehearse his very words): 'No, gallows wretch, I am not angry,' quod he, 'or at the leastwise, I do not sin, for the psalmist saith: *Be you angry and sin not.*'

"Then the cardinal spake gently to the friar, and desired him to quiet himself.

" 'No, my lord,' quod he, 'I speak not but of a good zeal, as I ought, for holy men had a good zeal. Wherefore it is said: *The zeal of thy house hath eaten me.* And it is sung in the church: *The scorners of Helizeus, whiles he went up into the house of God, felt the zeal of the bald,* as peradventure this scorning villain ribald shall feel.'

" 'You do it,' quod the cardinal, 'perchance of a good mind

and affection; but me thinketh you should do (I cannot tell whether more holily) certes more wisely, if you would not set your wit to a fool's wit, and with a fool take in hand a foolish contention.'

" 'No, forsooth, my lord,' quod he, 'I should not do more wisely. For Solomon the Wise sayeth: *Answer a fool according to his folly* (like as I do now), and so show him the pit that he shall fall into if he take not heed. For if many scorners of Helizeus, which was but one bald man, felt the zeal of the bald, how much more shall one scorner of many friars feel, among whom be many bald men? And we have also the Pope's Bulls, whereby all that mock and scorn us be excommunicate, suspended, and accursed.'

"The cardinal, seeing that none end would be made, sent away the jester by a privy beck, and turned the communication to another matter. Shortly after, when he was risen from the table, he went to hear his suitors, and so dismissed us.

A Merry Tale

From A Dialogue of Comfort against Tribulation (*1534*). *"Whereas you demand me whether in tribulation men may not sometimes refresh themself with worldly mirth and recreation, I can no more say but, he that cannot long endure to hold up his head and hear talking of heaven except he be now and then between, as though heaven were heaviness, refreshed with a merry foolish tale, there is none other remedy but you must let him have it." The speakers are two Hungarians, Anthony and his nephew Vincent.*

ANTHONY: My mother had, when I was a little boy, a good old woman that took heed to her children. They called her Mother Maud, I trow you have heard of her.

VINCENT: Yea, yea, very much.

ANTHONY: She was wont when she sat by the fire with us to tell us, that were children, many childish tales. But as Plinius saith that there is no book lightly so bad but that some good thing a man may pick out thereof, so think I there is almost no tale so foolish but that yet, in one matter or other, to some purpose it may hap to serve. For I remember me that, among other of her fond tales, she told us once that the Ass and the Wolf came to confession to the Fox. The poor Ass came to shrift in the Shrovetide, a day or two before Ash Wednesday. But the Wolf would not come to confession till he saw first Palm Sunday past, and then foded yet forth farther until Good Friday.

The Fox asked the Ass, before he began "Benedicite," wherefore he came to confession so soon, before Lent begin? The poor beast answered him again, for fear of deadly sin if he should lose his part of any of those prayers that the priest in the cleansing days pray for them that are then confessed already. Then in his shrift he had a marvellous grudge in his inward conscience, that he had one day given his master a cause of anger, in that that with his rude roaring before his master arose he had awaked him out of his sleep and bereaved him of his rest. The Fox for that fault, like a good discreet confessor, charged him to do so no more, but lie still and sleep like a good son himself till his master were up and ready to go to work, and so should he be sure that he should not wake him no more.

To tell you all the poor Ass's confession, it were a long work. For every thing that he did was deadly sin with him, the poor soul was so scrupulous. But his wise wily confessor accounted them for trifles, as they were, and swear after unto the Badger that he was so weary to sit so long and hear him that, saving for the manner sake, he had liefer have sitten all that while at breakfast with a good fat goose.

But when it came to the penance giving, the Fox found that the most weighty sin in all his shrift was gluttony, and therefore he discreetly gave him in penance that he should never for greediness of his meat do any other beast any harm or hindrance, and then eat his meat and study for no more.

Now, as good Mother Maud told us, when the Wolf came to Father Reynard (that was, she said, the Fox's name), to confession upon Good Friday, his confessor shook his great pair of beads upon him, almost as big as bowls, and asked him wherefore he came so late? "Forsooth, Father Reynard," quoth he, "I must needs tell you the truth: I come, you wot well, therefor. I durst come no sooner for fear lest you would for any gluttony have given me in penance to fast some part of this Lent." "Nay, nay," quoth the Father Fox, "I am not so unreasonable, for I fast none of it myself. For I may say to thee, son, between us twain here in confession, it is no commandment of God, this fasting, but an invention of man. The priests make folk fast, and put them to pain about the moonshine in the water, and do but make folk fools. But they shall make me no such fool, I warrant thee, son. For I ate flesh all this Lent myself, I. Howbeit indeed, because I will not be occasion of slander, I therefore ate it secretly in my chamber, out of sight of all such foolish brethren as for their weak scrupulous conscience would wax offended withal. And so would I counsel you to do."

"Forsooth, Father Fox," quoth the Wolf, "and so, I thank God, I do as near as I can. For when I go to my meat I take none other company with me but such sure brethren as are of mine own nature, whose consciences are not weak, I warrant you, but their stomachs as strong as mine."

"Well, then, no force," quoth Father Fox.

But when he heard after by his confession that he was so great a ravener that he devoured and spent sometime so much victual at one meal as the price thereof would well find some poor man with his wife and his children almost all the week, then he prudently reproved that point in him, and preached him a process of his own temperance, which never used, as he said, to pass upon himself the value of six pence at a meal, no, nor yet so much neither. "For when I bring home a goose," quoth he, "not out of the poulter's shop where folk find them out of the feathers ready plucked, and see which is the fattest, and yet for six pence buy and choose the best, but out of the housewife's house at the first hand, which may somewhat better cheap afford them, you wot well, than the poulter may. Nor yet cannot be suffered to see them plucked, and stand and choose them by day, but am fain by night to take at adventure, and when I come home am fain to do the labor to pluck her myself, too. Yet for all this, though it be lean and I ween not well worth a groat, serveth it me sometime for all that, both dinner and supper, too. And therefore, as for that you live of raven, therein can I find no fault. You have used it so long that I think you can do none other, and therefore were it folly to forbid it you, and, to say the truth, against good conscience too. For live you must, I wot well, and other craft can you none. And therefore, as reason is, must you live by that. But yet you wot well too much is too much, and measure is a merry mean, which I perceive by your shrift you have never used to keep. And therefore, surely this shall be your penance, that you shall all this year never pass upon yourself the price of six pence at a meal, as near as your conscience can guess the price."

Their shrift have I showed you as Mother Maud showed it us. But now serveth for our matter the conscience of them both in the true performing of their penance.

The poor Ass, after his shrift when he waxed enhungered, saw a sow lie with her pigs well lapped in new straw, and near he drew and thought to have eaten of the straw. But anon his scrupulous conscience began therein to grudge him. For while his penance was that for greediness of his meat he should do none other body none harm, he thought he might not eat one straw there lest for lack of that straw some of those pigs might hap to die for cold. So held he still his hunger till one brought him meat. But when he should fall thereto then fell he yet in a far farther scruple. For then it came in his mind that he should yet break his penance if he should eat any of that either, sith he was commanded by his ghostly father that he should not for his own meat hinder any other beast. For he thought that if he ate not that meat some other beast might hap to have it, and so should he by the eating of it peradventure hinder another. And thus stood he still fasting till, when he told the cause, his ghostly father came and informed him better, and then he cast off that scruple, and fell mannerly to his meat, and was a right honest ass many a fair day after.

The Wolf now coming from shrift, clean soiled from his sins, went about to do as a shrewd wife once told her husband that she would do when she came from shrift. "Be merry, man," quoth she now, "for this day, I thank God, was I well shriven. And I purpose now, therefore, to leave off all mine old shrewdness and begin even afresh."

VINCENT: Ah well, uncle, can you report her so? That word heard I her speak, but she said it in sport to make her good man laugh.

ANTHONY: Indeed it seemed she spake it half in sport. For that she said she would cast away all her old shrewdness, therein, I trow, she sported. But in that she said she would begin it all afresh, her husband found that good earnest.

VINCENT: Well, I shall show her what you say, I warrant you.

ANTHONY: Then will you make me make my word good. But whatsoever she did, at the leastwise so fared now this Wolf which had cast out in confession all his old raven, and then hunger pricked him forward that, as the shrewd wife said, he should begin all afresh. But yet the prick of conscience withdrew and held him back, because he would not for breaking of his penance take any prey for his meal tide that should pass the price of six pence.

It happed him, then, as he walked prowling for his gear about, he came where a man had in few days before cast off two old lean and lame horses, so sick that no flesh was there left upon them. And the one, when the Wolf came by, could scant stand on his legs, and the other already dead, and his skin ripped off and carried away. And as he looked upon them suddenly, he was first about to feed upon them and whet his teeth on their bones. But as he looked aside he spied a fair cow in a close, walking with her young calf by her side. And as soon as he saw them, his conscience began to grudge him against both those two horses. And then he sighed and said unto himself, "Alas, wicked wretch that I am, I had almost broken my penance ere I was ware. For yonder dead horse, because I never saw no dead horse sold in the market (and I should even die therefor by the way that my sinful soul shall, too), I cannot devise what price I should set upon him. But in my conscience I set him far above six pence, and therefore I dare not meddle with him. Now, then, is yonder quick horse of likelihood worth a great deal of money. For horse be dear in this country, specially such soft amblers. For I see by his pace he trotteth not, nor can scant shift a foot, and therefore I may not meddle with him for he very far passeth my six pence. But kine this country here hath enough, but money have they very little. And therefore, considering the plenty of the kine and the scarcity of the money, as for yonder peevish cow, seemeth unto me in my conscience, worth not past a groat, an she be worth so much. Now then, as for her calf, is not so much as she by half. And therefore, while the cow is in my conscience worth but four pence, my conscience cannot serve me for sin of my soul to praise her calf above two pence, and so pass they not six pence between them both. And therefore them twain may I well eat at this one meal, and break not my penance at all." And so thereupon he did without any scruple of conscience.

If such beasts could speak now, as Mother Maud said they could then, some of them would, I ween, tell a tale almost as wise as this, wherein, save for minishing of old Mother Maud's tale, else would a shorter process have served.

The Carpenter's Wife

ANTHONY: There was here in Buda, in King Ladislaus' days, a good poor honest man's wife. This woman was so fiendish that the devil, perceiving her nature, put her in the mind that she should anger her husband so sore that she might give him occasion to kill her, and then should he be hanged for her.

VINCENT: This was a strange temptation indeed. What the devil should she be the better then?

ANTHONY: Nothing, but that it eased her shrewd stomach before to think that her husband should be hanged after. And peradventure if you look about the world and consider it well, you shall find more such stomachs than a few. Have you never heard no furious body plainly say that, to see some such man have a mischief, he would with good will be content to lie as long in Hell as God liveth in Heaven?

VINCENT: Forsooth, and some such have I heard of.

ANTHONY: This mind of his was not much less mad than hers, but rather, haply, the more mad of the twain. For the woman, peradventure, did not cast so far peril therein. But to tell you now to what good pass her charitable purpose came. As her husband (the man was a carpenter) stood hewing with his chip axe upon a piece of timber, she began after her old guise so to revile him that the man waxed wroth at last, and bade her get her in or he would lay the helm of his axe about her back, and said also that it were little sin even with that axe head to chop off that unhappy head of hers that carried such an ungracious tongue therein. At that word the devil took his time and whetted her tongue against her teeth. And when it was well sharped she swore to him in very fierce anger, "By the mass, whoreson husband, I would thou wouldest. Here lieth mine head, lo!" and therewith down she laid her head upon the same timber log.

"If thou smite it not off, I beshrew thine whoreson's heart."

With that, like wise as the devil stood at her elbow, so stood, as I heard say, his good angel at his, and gave him ghostly courage, and bade him be bold and do it. And so the good man up with his chip axe and at a chop chopped off her head indeed. There were standing other folk by, which had a good sport to hear her chide, but little they looked for this chance till it was done ere they could let it. They said they heard her tongue babble in her head, and call, "Whoreson, whoreson," twice after that the head was from the body. At the least wise afterward unto the King thus they reported all, except only one and that was a woman, and she said that she heard it not.

VINCENT: Forsooth, this was a wonderful work. What came, uncle, of the man?

ANTHONY: The King gave him his pardon.

VINCENT: Verily, he might in conscience do no less.

ANTHONY: But then was it farther, almost, at another point, that there should have been a statute made that in such case there should never after pardon be granted but, the truth being able to be proved, none husband should need any pardon, but should have leave by the law to follow the sample of that carpenter and do the same.

VINCENT: How happed it, uncle, that that good law was left unmade?

ANTHONY: How happed it? As it happeth, cousin, that many more be left unmade as well as it, and within a little as good as it, too, both here and in other countries, and sometime some worse made in their stead. But, as they say, the let of that law was the Queen's grace (God forgive her soul). It was the greatest thing I ween, good Lady, that she had to answer for when she died. For, surely, save for that one thing she was a full blessed woman.

ANTONY ST. LEGER

~ *Sir Antony St. Leger (1496?-1559),* Lord *Deputy of Ireland.*

On Sir Thomas Wyatt

Thus liveth the dead that whilom livéd here
Among the dead that quick go on the ground.
Though he be dead yet doth he quick appear
By immortal fame that death cannot confound;
His life for aye his fame in trump shall sound.
Though he be dead yet is he thus alive:
No death can that life from Wyatt's life deprive.

THOMAS WYATT

--✦| *Sir Thomas Wyatt (1503–1542), M.A., of Allington Castle, Kent; Marshal of Calais; Ambassador to the court of Charles V. It is possible that the "touch me not" (Noli me tangere) hind is Ann Boleyn; Wyatt was sent to the Tower for several months at the time of her fall, 1536.*

"Whoso list to hunt"

Whoso list to hunt, I know where is an hind
But as for me, alas, I may no more.
The vain travail hath wearied me so sore
I am of them that farthest cometh behind.
Yet may I by no means my wearied mind
Draw from the Deer, but as she fleeth afore
Fainting I follow. I leave off therefore
Since in a net I seek to hold the wind.
Whoso list her hunt, I put him out of doubt
As well as I may spend his time in vain.
And graven with diamonds in letters plain
There is written her fair neck round about:
*Noli me tangere, for Caesar's I am
And wild for to hold though I seem tame.*

"If in the world there be more woe"

If in the world there be more woe
Than I have in my heart,
Where so it is it doth come fro,
And in my breast there doth it grow
For to increase my smart.
Alas, I am receipt of every care

And of my life each sorrow claims his part.
Who list to live in quietness
By me let him beware,
For I by high disdain
Am made without redress,
And unkindness, alas, hath slain
My poor true heart, all comfortless.

"Who hath heard of such cruelty before?"

Who hath heard of such cruelty before?
That when my plaint remembered her my woe
That caused it, she, cruel more and more,
Wished each stitch, as she did sit and sew,
Had pricked mine heart for to increase my sore.
And, as I think, she thought it had been so.
For, as she thought, "This is his heart indeed,"
She pricked hard and made her self to bleed.

"They flee from me"

They flee from me that sometime did me seek
With naked foot stalking in my chamber.
I have seen them gentle, tame, and meek
That now are wild and do not remember
That sometime they put themselves in danger
To take bread at my hand. And now they range,
Busily seeking with a continual change.

Thankèd be fortune, it hath been otherwise
Twenty times better, but once in special:
In thin array, after a pleasant guise,
When her loose gown from her shoulders did fall
And she me caught in her arms long and small,
Therewithal sweetly did me kiss
And softly said, "Dear heart, how like you this?"

It was no dream, I lay broad waking.
But all is turned thorough my gentleness
Into a strange fashion of forsaking.
And I have leave to go of her goodness,
And she also to use newfangleness.
But since that I so kindly am served,
I would fain know what she hath deserved.

"It was my choice, it was no chance"

It was my choice, it was no chance,
That brought my heart in other's hold,
Whereby it hath had sufferance
Longer, perdie, than reason would.
Since I it bound where it was free,
Methinks, iwis, of right it should
   Accepted be.

Accepted be without refuse,
Unless that fortune have the power
All right of love for to abuse;
For, as they say, one happy hour
May more prevail than right or might.
If fortune, then, list for to lower,
   What 'vaileth right?

What 'vaileth right if this be true?
Then trust to chance, and go by guess.
Then whoso loveth may well go sue
Uncertain hope for his redress.
Yet some would say assuredly
Thou mayest appeal for thy release
   To fantasy.

To fantasy pertains to choose.
All this I know, for fantasy

First unto love did me induce.
But yet I know as steadfastly
That, if love have no faster knot,
So nice a choice slips suddenly;
    It lasteth not.

It lasteth not that stands by change.
Fancy doth change, fortune is frail.
Both these to please, the way is strange.
Therefore, methinks, best to prevail
There is no way that is so just
As truth to lead, though tother fail,
    And thereto trust.

Satire

*Addressed to Sir Francis Bryan (d. 1550),
Privy Councillor and favorite of Henry VIII. "Some
men being never so old and spent by years will still
be full of youthful conditions, as was Sir F. Bryan,
and evermore would have been."*

A spending hand that alway poureth out
Had need to have a bringer in as fast.
And on the stone that still doth turn about

There groweth no moss. These proverbs yet do last.
Reason hath set them in so sure a place
That length of years their force can never waste.

When I remember this and eke the case
Wherein thou stands, I thought forthwith to write,
Bryan, to thee, who knows how great a grace

In writing is, to counsel man the right—
To thee, therefore, that trots still up and down
And never rests, but running day and night

From realm to realm, from city, street, and town.
Why dost thou wear thy body to the bones
And mightst at home sleep in thy bed of down

And drink good ale, so nappy for the nonce,
Feed thyself fat and heap up pound by pound?
Likest thou not this? *No.* Why? *For swine so groans*

In sty, and chew the turds moulded on the ground,
And drivel in pearls, the head still in the manger,
Then of the harp, the ass, to hear the sound;

So sacks of dirt be filled up in the cloister
That serves for less than do these fatted swine.
Though I seem lean and dry, without moisture,

Yet will I serve my prince, my lord and thine,
And let them live to feed the paunch that list
So I may live to feed both me and mine.

By God, well said. But what and if thou wist
How to bring in as fast as thou dost spend?
That would I learn. And it shall not be missed

To tell thee how. Now hark what I intend.
Thou knowest well, first, who so can seek to please
Shall purchase friends where truth shall but offend;

Flee, therefore, truth. It is both wealth and ease.
For though that truth of every man hath praise
Full near that wind goeth truth in great misease.

Use Virtue as it goeth nowadays:
In word alone to make thy language sweet
And of the deed yet do not as thou says.

Else be thou sure thou shalt be far unmeet
To get thy bread, each thing is now so scant.
Seek still thy profit upon thy bare feet.

Lend in nowise for fear that thou do want,
Unless it be as to a dog a cheese,
By which return be sure to win a cant

Of half at least; it is not good to lese.
Learn at Kitson that in a long white coat
From under the stall, without lands or fees,

Hath lept into the shop, who knoweth by rote
This rule that I have told thee here before.
Sometime, also, rich age beginneth to dote:

See thou, when there thy gain may be the more,
Stay him by the arm where so he walk or go,
Be near alway, and if he cough too sore,

When he hath spit tread out and please him so.
A diligent knave that picks his master's purse
May please him so that he, withouten mo,

Executor is, and what is he the worse?
But if so chance you get nought of the man
The widow may for all thy charge deburse.

A riveled skin, a stinking breath, what then?
A toothless mouth shall do thy lips no harm.
The gold is good, and though she curse or ban

Yet where thee list thou mayst lie good and warm.
Let the old mule bite upon the bridle
Whilst there do lie a sweeter in thine arm.

In this also see you be not idle:
Thy niece, thy cousin, thy sister or thy daughter,
If she be fair, if handsome be her middle,

If thy better hath her love besought her,
Advance his cause and he shall help thy need.
It is but love; turn it to laughter.

But ware, I say, so gold thee help and speed!
That in this case thou be not so unwise
As Pandar was in such a like deed,

For he, the fool, of conscience was so nice
That he no gain would have for all his pain.
Be next thyself, for friendship bears no price.

Laughst thou at me? Why? Do I speak in vain?
No, not at thee, but at thy thrifty jest.
Wouldst thou I should for any loss or gain

Change that for gold that I have ta'en for best:
Next godly things, to have an honest name?
Should I leave that, then take me for a beast!

Nay, then, farewell! And if thou care for shame
Content thee then with honest poverty,
With free tongue what thee mislikes to blame,

And for thy truth sometime adversity.
And therewithal this thing I shall thee give:
In this world now little prosperity,
And coin to keep as water in a sieve.

—⋅◄{ *Heywood (d. in exile, about 1580) married a
niece of Thomas More, and was the grandfather of
John Donne. Works, 1562.*

A Prisoner

In prison a prisoner, condemned to die
And for execution waiting daily,
In his hands for worms looking on a day,
Smiling to himself these words did say:
"Since my four quarters in four quarters shall stand,
Why harm I these silly worms eating my hand?
Nought else in this deed do I but myself show
Enemy to the worm and friend to the crow."

An Old Wife's Boon

In old world when old wives bitterly prayed
One devoutly as by way of a boon
Asked vengeance on her husband, and to him said,
"Thou wouldst wed a young wife ere this week were done
Were I dead, but thou shalt wed the Devil as soon."
"I cannot wed the Devil," quoth he. "Why?" quoth she.
"For I have wedded his dam before," quoth he.

THOMAS SACKVILLE

Earl of Dorset (1536–1608), Lord High Treasurer of England. He was co-author of the first English tragedy in blank verse, Gorboduc *(1562). The following work, reduced to about one-fourth of its original length, is the* Induction to the Mirror for Magistrates *(1563), a series of narrative poems on the fall of princes.*

A Vision of Hell

The wrathful winter, 'proaching on apace,
With blustering blasts had all ybared the treen,
And old Saturnus, with his frosty face,
With chilling cold had pierced the tender green:
The mantles rent wherein enwrapped been
The gladsome groves that now lay overthrown,
The tapets torn, and every bloom down blown.

And sorrowing I to see the summer flowers,
The lively green, the lusty leas forlorn,
The sturdy trees so shattered with the showers,
The fields so fade that flourished so beforn—
It taught me well all earthly things be born
To die the death, for naught long time may last:
The summer's beauty yields to winter's blast.

Then looking upward to the heaven's gleams,
With night's stars thick-powdered everywhere,
Which erst so glistened with the golden streams
That cheerful Phoebus spread down from his sphere—
Beholding dark oppressing day so near,

The sudden sight reduced to my mind
The sundry changes that in earth we find.

That musing on this worldly wealth in thought,
Which comes and goes more faster than we see
The flickering flame that with the fire is wrought,
My busy mind presented unto me
Such fall of peers as in this realm had be,
That oft I wished some would their woes describe,
To warn the rest whom Fortune left alive.

And straight forth stalking with redoubled pace
For that I saw the night draw on so fast,
In black all-clad there fell before my face
A piteous wight whom woe had all forwaste;
Forth from her eyes the crystal tears outburst,
And sighing sore, her hands she wrung and fold,
Tear all her hair, that ruth was to behold.

Her body small, forwithered and forspent
As is the stalk that summer's drought oppressed;
Her welked face with woeful tears besprent,
Her color pale and, as it seemed her best,
In woe and plaint reposed was her rest;
And as the stone that drops of water wears,
So dinted were her cheeks with fall of tears.

"Alas! I, wretch, whom thus thou seest distrained
With wasting woes that never shall aslake,
Sorrow I am: in endless torments pained
Among the furies in the infernal lake
Where Pluto, god of Hell, so grisly black,
Doth hold his throne, and Letheus' deadly taste
Doth reave remembrance of each thing forepast.

"Whence come I am, the dreary destiny
And luckless lot for to bemoan of those
Whom Fortune in this maze of misery,
Of wretched chance, most woeful mirrors chose;
That when thou seest how lightly they did lose
Their pomp, their power, and that they thought most sure,
Thou mayest soon deem no earthly joy may dure.

"I shall thee guide first to the grisly lake
And thence unto the blissful place of rest
Where thou shalt see and hear the plaint they make
That whilom here bore swinge among the best.
This shalt thou see, but great is the unrest
That thou must bide before thou canst attain
Unto the dreadful place where these remain."

And with these words, as I upraised stood,
And gan to follow her that straight forth paced,
Ere I was ware, into a desert wood
We now were come, where, hand in hand embraced,
She led the way and through the thick so traced
As, but I had been guided by her might,
It was no way for any mortal wight.

And first, within the porch and jaws of Hell,
Sat deep Remorse of Conscience, all besprent
With tears; and to herself oft would she tell
Her wretchedness, and cursing never stent
To sob and sigh, but ever thus lament
With thoughtful care as she that, all in vain,
Would wear and waste continually in pain.

And next, within the entry of this lake,
Sat fell Revenge, gnashing her teeth for ire,
Devising means how she may vengeance take;

Never in rest till she have her desire,
But frets within so far forth with the fire
Of wreaking flames, that now determines she
To die by death, or venged by death to be.

And next in order sad Old Age we found,
His beard all hoar, his eyes hollow and blind,
With drooping cheer still poring on the ground
As on the place where nature him assigned
To rest when that the Sisters had untwined
His vital thread and ended with their knife
The fleeting course of fast-declining life.

Crookbacked he was, tooth-shaken, and blear-eyed,
Went on three feet, and sometime crept on four,
With old lame bones that rattled by his side,
His scalp all pilled and he with eld forlore,
His withered fist still knocking at Death's door,
Fumbling and driveling as he draws his breath—
For brief, the shape and messenger of Death.

Lastly, stood War, in glittering arms yclad,
With visage grim, stern looks, and blackly hued;
In his right hand a naked sword he had
That to the hilts was all with blood embrewed;
And in his left, that kings and kingdoms rued,
Famine and fire he held, and therewithal
He razed towns and threw down towers and all.

Herefrom when scarce I could mine eyes withdraw,
That filled with tears as doth the springing well,
We passed on so far forth till we saw
Rude Acheron, a loathesome lake to tell,
That boils and bubs up swelth as black as hell,
Where grisly Charon, at their fixed tide,
Still ferries ghosts unto the farther side.

Thence came we to the horror and the hell,
The great large kingdoms and the dreadful reign
Of Pluto in his throne where he did dwell,
The wide waste places and the hugy plain,
The wailings, shrieks, and sundry sorts of pain,
The sighs, the sobs, the deep and deadly groan,
Earth, air, and all, resounding plaint and moan.

"Lo, here," quoth Sorrow, "princes of renown,
That whilom sat on top of Fortune's wheel,
Now laid full low like wretches whirled down
Even with one frown, that stayed but with a smile.
And now behold the thing that thou, erewhile,
Saw only in thought, and what thou now shalt hear,
Recount the same to caesar, king, and peer."

Then first came Henry, Duke of Buckingham,
His coat of black all pilled and quite forworn,
Wringing his hands, and Fortune oft doth blame
Which of a duke hath made him now her scorn;
With ghastly looks, as one in manner lorn,
Oft spread his arms; stretched hands he joins as fast,
With rueful cheer and vapored eyes upcast.

Thrice he began to tell his doleful tale,
And thrice the sighs did swallow up his voice,
At each of which he shrieked so withal
As though the heavens rived with the noise;
Till at the last, recovering his voice,
Supping the tears that all his breast berained,
On cruel Fortune, weeping, thus he plained.

GEORGE GASCOIGNE

"Written to the Lord Grey of Wilton (1536–1593) upon this occasion: the said Lord Grey, delighting (amongst many other good qualities) in choosing of his winter deer and killing the same with his bow, did furnish Mr. Gascoigne (1542–1577) with a crossbow cum pertinenciis *and vouchsafed to use his company in the said exercise, calling him one of his woodmen. Now the author, shooting very often, could never hit any deer; yea, and oftentimes he let the herd pass by as though he had not seen them. Whereat when this noble lord took some pastime, and had often put him in remembrance of his good skill in choosing and readiness in killing of a winter deer, he thought good thus to excuse it in verse."*

Gascoigne's Woodmanship [1573]

My worthy lord, I pray you wonder not
To see your woodman shoot so oft awry,
Nor that he stands amazed like a sot,
And lets the harmless deer (unhurt) go by.
Or if he strike a doe which is but carrion,
Laugh not, good lord, but favor such a fault.
Take will in worth, he would fain hit the barren;
But though his heart be good, his hap is naught.
     And therefore now I crave your Lordship's leave
To tell you plain what is the cause of this.
First, if it please your honor to perceive
What makes your woodman shoot so oft amiss,
Believe me, lord, the case is nothing strange:
He shoots awry almost at every mark.

His eyes have been so used for to range,
That now, God knows, they be both dim and dark.
    For proof, he bears the note of folly now,
Who shot sometimes to hit philosophy.
And ask you why? Forsooth, I make avow,
Because his wanton wits went all awry.
    Next that, he shot to be a man of law,
And spent some time with learned Littleton;
Yet in the end he proved but a daw,
For law was dark and he had quickly done.
Then could he with Fitzherbert such a brain
As Tully had, to write the law by art,
So that with pleasure or with little pain
He might, perhaps, have caught a truant's part.
But all too late; he most misliked the thing
Which most might help to guide his arrow straight:
He winked wrong, and so let slip the string,
Which cast him wide for all his quaint conceit.
    From thence he shot to catch a courtly grace,
And thought even there to wield the world at will;
But out, alas, he much mistook the place,
And shot awry at every rover still.
The blazing baits which draw the gazing eye
Unfeathered there his first affection.
No wonder then although he shot awry,
Wanting the feathers of discretion.
Yet more than them, the marks of dignity
He much mistook and shot the wronger way,
Thinking the purse of prodigality
Had been best mean to purchase such a prey.
He thought the flattering face which fleereth still
Had been full fraught with all fidelity,
And that such words as courtiers use at will
Could not have varied from the verity.
But when his bonnet buttoned with gold,

His comely cape beguarded all with gay,
His bombast hose with linings manifold,
His knit silk stocks and all his quaint array
Had picked his purse of all the Peter pence
Which might have paid for his promotion,
Then (all too late) he found that light expense
Had quite quenched out the court's devotion,
So that since then the taste of misery
Hath been always full bitter in his bit.
And why? Forsooth, because he shot awry,
Mistaking still the marks which others hit.

   But now behold what mark the man doth find:
He shoots to be a soldier in his age.
Mistrusting all the virtues of the mind,
He trusts the power of his personage,
As though long limbs led by a lusty heart
Might yet suffice to make him rich again.
But Flushing frays have taught him such a part,
That now he thinks the wars yield no such gain.

   And sure I fear, unless your lordship deign
To train him yet into some better trade,
It will be long before he hit the vein
Whereby he may a richer man be made.
He cannot climb as other catchers can
To lead a charge before himself be led.
He cannot spoil the simple sakeless man
Which is content to feed him with his bread.
He cannot pinch the painful soldier's pay,
And shear him out his share in ragged sheets.
He cannot stoop to take a greedy prey
Upon his fellows groveling in the streets.
He cannot pull the spoil from such as pill
And seem full angry at such foul offence,
Although the gain content his greedy will
Under the cloak of contrary pretence.

And nowadays the man that shoots not so
May shoot amiss even as your woodman doth.
But then you marvel why I let them go,
And never shoot, but say farewell forsooth.

   Alas, my lord, while I do muse hereon
And call to mind my youthful years misspent,
They give me such a bone to gnaw upon
That all my senses are in silence pent.
My mind is rapt in contemplation
Wherein my dazzled eyes only behold
The black hour of my constellation
Which framed me so luckless on the mold.
Yet therewithal I can not but confess
That vain presumption makes my heart to swell;
For thus I think not all the world (I guess)
Shoots bet than I. Nay, some shoots not so well.
In Aristotle somewhat did I learn
To guide my manners all by comeliness,
And Tully taught me somewhat to discern
Between sweet speech and barbarous rudeness.
Old Perkins, Rastall, and Dan Bracton's books
Did lend me somewhat of the lawless law.
The crafty courtiers with their guileful looks
Must needs put some experience in my maw.
Yet can not these, with many mysteries mo,
Make me shoot straight at any gainful prick,
Where some that never handled such a bow
Can hit the white or touch it near the quick.
Who can nor speak nor write in pleasant wise,
Nor lead their life by Aristotle's rule,
Nor argue well on questions that arise,
Nor plead a case more than my Lord Mayor's mule;
Yet can they hit the marks that I do miss
And win the mean which may the man maintain.
Now when my mind doth mumble upon this,

No wonder then although I pine for pain;
And whiles mine eyes behold this mirror thus,
The herd goeth by, and farewell gentle does,
So that your Lordship quickly may discuss
What blinds my eyes so oft (as I suppose).

But since my Muse can to my lord rehearse
What makes me miss, and why I do not shoot,
Let me imagine in this worthless verse
If right before me at my standing's foot
There stood a doe and I should strike her dead,
And then she prove a carrion carcass too,
What figure might I find within my head
To 'scuse the rage which ruled me so to do?

Some might interpret by plain paraphrase
That lack of skill or fortune led the chance,
But I must otherwise expound the case:
I say Jehovah did this doe advance
And made her bold to stand before me so
Till I had thrust mine arrow to her heart,
That by the sudden of her overthrow
I might endeavor to amend my part
And turn mine eyes that they no more behold
Such guileful marks as seem more than they be,
And though they glister outwardly like gold
Are inwardly but brass as men may see.
And when I see the milk hang in her teat,
Methinks it saith: old babe, now learn to suck,
Who in thy youth couldst never learn the feat
To hit the whites which live with all good luck.
Thus have I told, my lord, (God grant in season)
A tedious tale in rhyme, but little reason.

EDMUND SPENSER

-----◄◄ "A spousal verse ... in honor of the double
marriage of the two honorable and virtuous ladies, the
Lady Elizabeth and the Lady Katherine Somerset,
daughters to the right honorable the Earl of
Worcester, and espoused to the two worthy
gentlemen, Mr. Henry Guilford and Mr. William
Petre, Esquires." The party goes upstream with the
tide in swan boats, from the Court at Greenwich past
the Temple to Essex House, where they are
welcomed by Essex, just returned from the successful
expedition to Cadiz.

Prothalamium [1596]

Calm was the day, and through the trembling air
Sweet breathing Zephyrus did softly play,
A gentle spirit that lightly did delay
Hot Titan's beams which then did glister fair;
When I (whom sullen care,
Through discontent of my long fruitless stay
In princes' court, and expectation vain
Of idle hopes which still do fly away,
Like empty shadows, did afflict my brain)
Walked forth to ease my pain
Along the shore of silver-streaming Thames;
Whose rutty bank, the which his river hems,
Was painted all with variable flowers,
And all the meads adorned with dainty gems
Fit to deck maidens' bowers,
And crown their paramours
Against the bridal day, which is not long:
   Sweet Thames! run softly till I end my song.

There in a meadow by the river's side
A flock of nymphs I chancéd to espy,
All lovely daughters of the flood thereby,
With goodly greenish locks, all loose untied,
As each had been a bride.
And each one had a little wicker basket
Made of fine twigs entrailéd curiously
In which they gathered flowers to fill their flasket,
And with fine fingers cropt full feateously
The tender stalks on high.
Of every sort which in that meadow grew
They gathered some: the violet, pallid blue,
The little daisy that at evening closes,
The virgin lily, and the primrose true,
With store of vermeil roses,
To deck their bridegroom's posies
Against the bridal day, which was not long:
  Sweet Thames! run softly till I end my song.

With that I saw two swans of goodly hue
Come softly swimming down along the Lea;
Two fairer birds I yet did never see.
The snow which doth the top of Pindus strew
Did never whiter shew,
Nor Jove himself when he a swan would be
For love of Leda whiter did appear;
Yet Leda was, they say, as white as he,
Yet not so white as these, nor nothing near;
So purely white they were
That even the gentle stream the which them bare
Seemed foul to them, and bade his billows spare
To wet their silken feathers lest they might
Soil their fair plumes with water not so fair,
And mar their beauties bright
That shone as heaven's light

Against their bridal day, which was not long:
  Sweet Thames! run softly till I end my song.

Eftsoons the nymphs, which now had flowers their fill,
Ran all in haste to see that silver brood
As they came floating on the crystal flood;
Whom when they saw, they stood amazéd still,
Their wondering eyes to fill;
Them seemed they never saw a sight so fair
Of fowls so lovely, that they sure did deem
Them heavenly born or to be that same pair
Which through the sky draw Venus' silver team;
For sure they did not seem
To be begot of any earthly seed,
But rather angels or of angels' breed;
Yet were they bred of summer's heat, they say,
In sweetest season when each flower and weed
The earth did fresh array;
So fresh they seemed as day,
Even as their bridal day, which was not long:
  Sweet Thames! run softly till I end my song.

Then forth they all out of their baskets drew
Great store of flowers, the honor of the field,
That to the sense did fragrant odors yield,
All which upon those goodly birds they threw
And all the waves did strew
That like old Peneus' waters they did seem
When down along by pleasant Tempe's shore,
Scattered with flowers, through Thessaly they stream,
That they appear, through lilies' plenteous store,
Like a bride's chamber floor.
Two of those nymphs meanwhile two garlands bound
Of freshest flowers which in that mead they found,
The which presenting all in trim array

Their snowy foreheads there withal they crowned,
Whilst one did sing this lay,
Prepared against that day,
Against their bridal day, which was not long:
 Sweet Thames! run softly till I end my song.

"Ye gentle birds! the world's fair ornament,
And heaven's glory, whom this happy hour
Doth lead unto your lover's blissful bower,
Joy may you have and gentle heart's content
Of your love's couplement;
And let fair Venus that is queen of love
With her heart-quelling son upon you smile,
Whose smile, they say, hath virtue to remove
All love's dislike, and friendship's faulty guile
Forever to assoil;
Let endless peace your steadfast hearts accord
And blessed plenty wait upon your board;
And let your bed with pleasures chaste abound
That fruitful issue may to you afford
Which may your foes confound,
And make your joys redound
Upon your bridal day, which is not long:"
 Sweet Thames! run softly till I end my song.

So ended she, and all the rest around
To her redoubled that her undersong,
Which said their bridal day should not be long.
And gentle Echo from the neighbor ground
Their accents did resound.
So forth those joyous birds did pass along,
Adown the Lea that to them murmured low
As he would speak but that he lacked a tongue,
Yet did by signs his glad affection show,
Making his stream run slow.

And all the fowl which in his flood did dwell
'Gan flock about these twain that did excel
The rest so far as Cynthia doth shend
The lesser stars. So they, enrangéd well,
Did on those two attend
And their best service lend
Against their wedding day, which was not long:
   Sweet Thames! run softly till I end my song.

At length they all to merry London came,
To merry London, my most kindly nurse,
That to me gave this life's first native source,
Though from another place I take my name,
An house of ancient fame.
There when they came whereas those bricky towers
The which on Thames' broad, aged back do ride,
Where now the studious lawyers have their bowers,
There whilom wont the Templar Knights to bide
Till they decayed through pride
(Next whereunto there stands a stately place
Where oft I gainéd gifts and goodly grace
Of that great Lord, which therein wont to dwell,
Whose want too well now feels my friendless case)—
But ah! here fits not well
Old woes, but joys, to tell
Against the bridal day, which is not long:
   Sweet Thames! run softly till I end my song.

Yet therein now doth lodge a noble peer,
Great England's glory and the world's wide wonder,
Whose dreadful name late through all Spain did thunder,
And Hercules' two pillars standing near
Did make to quake and fear:
Fair branch of honor, flower of chivalry!
That fillest England with thy triumph's fame,

Joy have thou of thy noble victory
And endless happiness of thine own name
That promiseth the same;
That through thy prowess and victorious arms
Thy country may be freed from foreign harms,
And great Elisa's glorious name may ring
Through all the world, filled with thy wide alarms,
Which some brave muse may sing
To ages following
Upon the bridal day, which is not long:
   Sweet Thames! run softly till I end my song.

From those high towers this noble lord issuing,
Like radiant Hesper when his golden hair
In th' ocean billows he hath bathéd fair,
Descended to the river's open viewing,
With a great train ensuing.
Above the rest were goodly to be seen
Two gentle knights of lovely face and feature
Beseeming well the bower of any queen,
With gifts of wit and ornaments of nature
Fit for so goodly stature
That like the twins of Jove they seemed in sight,
Which deck the baldrick of the heavens bright;
They two, forth pacing to the river's side,
Received those two fair brides, their love's delight;
Which at th' appointed tide
Each one did make his bride
Against their bridal day, which is not long:
   Sweet Thames! run softly till I end my song.

PHILIP SIDNEY

*——⋖ "This is that Sidney" (1554–1586) "who, as
Providence seems to have sent him into the world to
give the present age a specimen of the ancients, so
did it on a sudden recall him and snatch him from us
as more worthy of heaven than earth. Thus where
virtue comes to perfection, it is gone in a trice, and
the best things are never lasting." The first part of
the following episode from the* Arcadia *is related
by Kalendar's Steward to one of the heroes; the
second is directly narrated.*

Argalus and Parthenia

Part One

"My Lord," said he, "when our good King Basilius, with better
success than expectation, took to wife (even in his more than
decaying years) the fair young princess Gynecia, there came
with her a fair young lord, cousin-german to herself, named
Argalus, led hither partly with the love and honor of his noble
kinswoman, partly with the humor of youth, which ever thinks
that good whose goodness he sees not. And in this court he received so good increase of knowledge that, after some years
spent, he so manifested a most virtuous mind in all his actions
that Arcadia gloried such a plant was transported unto them,
being a gentleman indeed most rarely accomplished, excellently
learned but without all vainglory; friendly without factious-
ness; valiant so as, for my part, I think the earth hath no man
that hath done more heroical acts than he (howsoever now of
late the fame flies of the two princes of Thessalia and Macedon, and hath long done of our noble Prince Amphialus who,
indeed, in our parts is only accounted likely to match him);
but I say, for my part I think no man for valor of mind and

ability of body to be preferred, if equalled, to Argalus; and yet
so valiant as he never durst do anybody injury. In behavior,
some will say ever sad, surely sober and somewhat given to
musing, but never uncourteous; his word ever led by his thought
and followed by his deed; rather liberal than magnificent, though
the one wanted not and the other had ever good choice of the
receiver: in sum (for I perceive I shall easily take a great draught
of his praises, whom both I and the country love so well), such
a man was (and I hope is) Argalus, as hardly the nicest eye
can find a spot in, if the over-vehement constancy of yet spotless affection may not, in hard-wrested constructions, be counted
a spot, which in this manner began that work in him which
hath made both him, and itself in him, over all this country
famous.

"My master's son, Clitophon (whose loss gives the cause to
this discourse, and yet gives me cause to begin with Argalus,
since his loss proceeds from Argalus), being a young gentleman
as of great birth (being our king's sister's son) so truly of good
nature, and one that can see good and love it, haunted more
the company of this worthy Argalus than of any other; so as
if there were not a friendship (which is so rare as it is to be
doubted whether it be a thing indeed, or only a word), at least
there was such a liking and friendliness as hath brought forth
the effects which you shall hear.

"About two years since, it so fell out that he brought him
to a great lady's house, sister to my master, who had with her
her only daughter, the fair Parthenia: fair indeed (fame, I
think, itself daring not to call any fairer, if it be not Helena
Queen of Corinth, and the two incomparable sisters of Arcadia), and that which made her fairness much the fairer was
that it was but a fair ambassador of a most fair mind, full of
wit, and a wit which delighted more to judge itself than to
show itself; her speech being as rare as precious, her silence
without sullenness, her modesty without affectation, her shamefastness without ignorance: in sum, one that to praise well, one

must first set down with himself what it is to be excellent, for so she is.

"I think you think that these perfections, meeting, could not choose but find one another and delight in that they found, for likeness of manners is likely in reason to draw liking with affection. Men's actions do not always cross with reason; to be short, it did so indeed. They loved, although for a while the fire thereof (hope's wings being cut off) were blown by the bellows of despair, upon this occasion.

"There had been a good while before, and so continued, a suitor to this same lady, a great nobleman (though of Laconia, yet near neighbor to Parthenia's mother) named Demagoras: a man mighty in riches and power, and proud thereof, loving nobody but himself and, for his own delights, Parthenia. And pursuing vehemently his desire, his riches had so gilded over all his other imperfections that the old Lady (though contrary to my Lord her brother's mind) had given her consent and, using a mother's authority upon her fair daughter, had made her yield thereunto: not because she liked her choice but because her obedient mind had not yet taken upon it to make choice. And the day of their assurance drew near when my young Lord Clitophon brought this noble Argalus, perchance principally to see so rare a sight as Parthenia by all well-judging eyes was judged.

"But although few days were before the time of assurance appointed, yet Love (that saw he had a great journey to make in short time) hasted so himself that before her word could tie her to Demagoras, her heart had vowed her to Argalus, with so grateful a receipt in mutual affection that, if she desired above all things to have Argalus, Argalus feared nothing but to miss Parthenia. And now Parthenia had learned both liking and misliking, loving and loathing, and out of passion began to take the authority of judgement. Insomuch that, when the time came that Demagoras (full of proud joy) thought to receive the gift of her self, she with words of resolute refusal (though with tears showing she was sorry she must refuse) assured her mother she would first be bedded in her grave than wedded to Demagoras.

"The change was no more strange than unpleasant to the mother who, being determinately (lest I should say of a great lady, willfully) bent to marry her to Demagoras, tried all ways which a witty and hard-hearted mother could use upon so humble a daughter in whom the only resisting power was love. But the more she assaulted, the more she taught Parthenia to defend; and the more Parthenia defended, the more she made her mother obstinate in assault; who, at length finding that Argalus' standing between them was it that most eclipsed her affection from shining upon Demagoras, she sought all means how to remove him, so much the more as he manifested himself as unremoveable suitor to her daughter. First, by employing him in as many dangerous enterprises as ever the evil stepmother Juno recommended to the famous Hercules; but the more his virtue was tried, the more pure it grew, while all the things she did to overthrow him did set him up upon the height of honor: enough to have moved her heart, especially to a man every way so worthy as Argalus. But she, struggling against all reason because she would have her will and show her authority in matching her with Demagoras, the more virtuous Argalus was, the more she hated him, thinking herself conquered in his conquests and therefore still employing him in more and more dangerous attempts. Meanwhile she used all extremities possible upon her fair daughter to make her give over herself to her direction. But it was hard to judge whether he in doing, or she in suffering, showed greater constancy of affection; for as to Argalus, the world sooner wanted occasions than he valor to go through them, so to Parthenia, malice sooner ceased than her unchanged patience. Lastly, by treasons Demagoras and she would have made away Argalus; but he with providence and courage so passed over all that the mother took such a spiteful grief at it that her heart brake withal and she died.

"But then, Demagoras assuring himself that now Parthenia was her own she would never be his, and receiving as much by her own determinate answer, not more desiring his own happiness than envying Argalus, whom he saw with narrow eyes even ready to enjoy the perfection of his desires, strengthening his conceit with all the mischievous counsels which disdained love and envious pride could give unto him, the wicked wretch (taking a time that Argalus was gone to his country to fetch some of his principal friends to honor the marriage which Parthenia had most joyfully consented unto), the wicked Demagoras I say, desiring to speak with her, with unmerciful force (her weak arms in vain resisting) rubbed all over her face a most horrible poison, the effect whereof was such that never leper looked more ugly than she did; which done, having his men and horses ready, departed away in spite of her servants, as ready to revenge as they could be in such an unexpected mischief.

"But the abominableness of this fact being come to my lord Kalander, he made such means, both by our king's intercession and his own, that by the king and senate of Lacedemon, Demagoras was upon pain of death banished the country: who, hating the punishment where he should have hated the fault, joined himself with all the powers he could make unto the Helots, lately in rebellion against that state; and they (glad to have a man of such authority among them) made him their general, and under him have committed divers the most outrageous villainies that a base multitude full of desperate revenge can imagine.

"But within a while after this pitiful fact committed upon Parthenia, Argalus returned (poor gentleman), having her fair image in his heart and already promising his eyes the uttermost of his felicity, when they (nobody else daring to tell it him) were the first messengers to themselves of their own misfortune. I mean not to move passions with telling you the grief of both when he knew her, for at first he did not, nor at first knowledge could possibly have Virtue's aid so ready as not even weakly to lament the loss of such a jewel, so much the more as that skillful men in that art assured it was unrecoverable. But within a while, truth of love (which still held the first face in his memory), a virtuous constancy and even a delight to be constant, faith given, and inward worthiness shining through the foulest mists took so full hold of the noble Argalus that not only in such comfort which witty arguments may bestow upon adversity, but even with the most abundant kindness that an eye-ravished lover can express, he labored both to drive the extremity of sorrow from her and to hasten the celebration of their marriage; whereunto he unfeignedly showed himself no less cheerfully earnest than if she had never been disinherited of that goodly portion which nature had so liberally bequeathed unto her; and for that cause deferred his intended revenge upon Demagoras, because he might continually be in her presence, showing more humble serviceableness and joy to content her than ever before.

"But as he gave this rare example, not to be hoped for of any other but of another Argalus, so, of the other side, she took as strange a course in affection. For where she desired to enjoy him more than to live, yet did she overthrow both her own desire and his, and in no sort would yield to marry him: with a strange encounter of love's affects and effects, that he, by an affection sprung from excessive beauty, should delight in horrible foulness, and she, of a vehement desire to have him, should kindly build a resolution never to have him. For truth is that so in heart she loved him as she could not find in her heart that he should be tied to what was unworthy of his presence.

"Truly, sir, a very good orator might have a fair field to use eloquence in if he did but only repeat the lamentable and truly affectionated speeches while he conjured her, by remembrance of her affection and true oaths of his own affection, not to make him so unhappy as to think he had not only lost her face, but her heart; that her face, when it was fairest, had been but a marshall to lodge the love of her in his mind, which now was so well placed as it needed no further help of any outward harbinger; beseeching her, even with tears, to know that his love was not so superficial as to go no further than the skin, which yet now to him was most fair since it was hers; how could he be so ungrateful as to love her the less for that which she had only received for his sake; that he never beheld it but therein he saw the loveliness of her love toward him; protesting unto her that he would never take joy of his life if he might not enjoy her for whom principally he was glad he had life.

"But (as I heard by one that overheard them) she, wringing him by the hand, made no other answer but this: "My Lord," said she, "God knows I love you. If I were Princess of the whole world and had withal all the blessings that ever the world brought forth, I should not make delay to lay my self and them under your feet. Or if I had continued but as I was, though I must confess far unworthy of you, yet would I, with too great a joy for my heart to think of, have accepted your vouchsafing me to be yours, and with faith and obedience would have supplied all other defects. But first let me be much more miserable than I am ere I match Argalus to such a Parthenia. Live happy, dear Argalus; I give you full liberty and I beseech you to take it. And I assure you I shall rejoice, whatsoever become of me, to see you so coupled as may be fit both for your honor and satisfaction." With that she burst out in crying and weeping, not able longer to contain herself from blaming her fortune and wishing her own death.

"But Argalus with a most heavy heart still pursuing his desire, she fixed of mind to avoid further entreaty and to fly all company, which (even of him) grew unpleasant unto her. One night she stole away, but whither as yet is unknown, or indeed what is become of her."

Part Two

As they had newly dined, there came in to Kalander a messenger that brought him word a young noble lady, near kinswoman to the fair Helen, Queen of Corinth, was come thither and desired to be lodged in his house. Kalander, most glad of such an occasion, went out and all his other worthy guests with him, saving only Argalus who remained in his chamber, desirous that this company were once broken up, that he might go in his solitary quest after Parthenia.

But when they met this lady, Kalander straight thought he saw his niece Parthenia, and was about in such familiar sort to have spoken to her; but she in grave and honorable manner giving him to understand that he was mistaken, he, half-ashamed, excused himself with the exceeding likeness was between them, though indeed it seemed that his lady was of the more pure and dainty complexion. She said it might very well be, having been many times taken one for another.

But as soon as she was brought into the house, before she would rest her, she desired to speak with Argalus publicly, who she heard was in the house. Argalus came in hastily, and as hastily thought as Kalander had done, with sudden changes of joy into sorrow. But when she had stayed their thoughts with telling them her name and quality, in this sort spake unto him: "My lord Argalus," said she, "being of late left in the court of Queen Helen of Corinth as chief in her absence (she being upon some occasion gone thence), there came unto me the Lady Parthenia, so disguised as I think Greece has nothing so ugly to behold. For my part, it was many days before, with vehement oaths and some good proofs, she could make me think she was Parthenia. Yet at last finding certainly it was she, and greatly pitying her misfortune, so much the more as that all men had ever told me (as now you do) of the great likeness between us, I took the best care I could of her, and of her understood the whole tragical history of her undeserved adventure and therewithal of that most noble constancy in you, my Lord Argalus, which whosoever loves not shows himself to be a hater of virtue and unworthy to live in the society of mankind. But no outward cherishing could salve the inward sore of her mind; but a few days since she died, before her death earnestly desiring and persuading me to think of no husband but of you, as of the only man in the world worthy to be loved. Withal, she gave me this ring to deliver you, desiring you and, by the authority of love, commanding you, that the affection you bare her you should turn to me, assuring you that nothing can please her soul more than to see you and me matched together. Now, my lord, though this office be not (perchance) suitable to my estate nor sex, who should rather look to be desired, yet an extraordinary desert requires an extraordinary proceeding; and therefore I am come, with faithful love built upon your worthiness, to offer myself and to beseech you to accept the offer. And if these noble gentlemen present will say it is great folly, let them withal say it is great love."

And then she stayed, earnestly attending Argalus' answer, who (first making most hearty sighs do such obsequies as he could to Parthenia) thus answered her: "Madame," said he, "infinitely bound am I unto you for this no more rare than noble courtesy, but most bound for the goodness I perceive you showed to the Lady Parthenia." With that, the tears ran down his eyes, but he followed on, "And as much as so unfortunate a man, fit to be the spectacle of misery, can do you service, determine you have made a purchase of a slave (while I live) never to fail you. But this great matter you propose unto me, wherein I am not so blind as not to see what happiness it should be unto me: excellent lady, know that if my heart were mine to give, you before all other should have it. But Parthenia's it is, though dead. There I began, there I end all matter of affection. I hope I shall not long tarry after her, with whose beauty if I had only been in love, I should be so with you who have the same beauty. But it was Parthenia's self I loved and love, which no likeness can make one, no commandment dissolve, no foulness defile, nor no death finish."

"And shall I receive," said she, "such disgrace as to be refused?"

"Noble lady," said he, "let not that hard word be used, who know your exceeding worthiness far beyond my desert; but it is only happiness I refuse, since of the only happiness I could and can desire I am refused."

He had scarce spoken those words when she ran to him, and embracing him, "Why then, Argalus," said she, "take thy Parthenia." And Parthenia it was indeed. But because sorrow forbade him too soon to believe, she told him the truth with all circumstances: how being parted alone, meaning to die in some solitary place, as she happened to make complaint the Queen Helen of Corinth (who likewise felt her part of miseries), being then walking also alone in that lovely place, heard her, and never left till she had known the whole discourse. Which the noble queen greatly pitying, she sent her to a physician of hers, the most excellent man in the world, in hope he could help her; which, in such sort as they saw, performed, and she taking with her of the Queen's servants, thought yet to make this trial whether he would quickly forget his true Parthenia or no.

Her speech was confirmed by the Corinthian gentlemen who before had kept her counsel, and Argalus easily persuaded to what more than ten thousand years of life he desired. And Kalander would needs have the marriage celebrated in his house, principally the longer to hold his dear guests, towards whom he was now (besides his own habit of hospitality) carried with love and duty; and therefore omitted no service that his wit could invent and his power minister.

Astrophil and Stella

> ⟶⟨ *"Here ... the tragicomedy of love is*
> *performed by starlight ... The argument cruel*
> *chastity, the prologue hope, the epilogue despair."*
> *The full text consists of 108 sonnets and 11 songs.*

Not at the first sight nor with a dribbed shot
Love gave the wound which while I breathe will bleed;
But known worth did in mine of time proceed
Till by degrees it had full conquest got.
I saw and liked. I liked but loved not.
I loved but straight did not what Love decreed.
At length to Love's decrees I, forced, agreed,
Yet with repining at so partial lot.
Now even that footstep of lost liberty
Is gone; and now, like slave-born Muscovite,
I call it praise to suffer tyranny;
And now employ the remnant of my wit
To make myself believe that all is well,
While with a feeling skill I paint my hell.

*   *   *

It is most true that eyes are formed to serve
The inward light, and that the heavenly part
Ought to be king, from whose rules who do swerve,
Rebels to Nature, strive for their own smart.
It is most true what we call Cupid's dart
An image is which for ourselves we carve
And, fools, adore in temple of our heart
Till that good god make church and churchmen starve.
True that true beauty virtue is indeed,
Whereof this beauty can be but a shade
Which elements with mortal mixture breed;

True that on earth we are but pilgrims made,
And should in soul up to our country move:
True, and yet true that I must Stella love.

*   *   *

Alas, have I not pain enough, my friend,
Upon whose breast a fiercer gripe doth tire
Than did on him who first stole down the fire,
While Love on me doth all his quiver spend,
But with your rhubarb words ye must contend
To grieve me worse, in saying that desire
Doth plunge my well-formed soul even in the mire
Of sinful thoughts which do in ruin end?
If that be sin which doth the manners frame,
Well-stayed with truth in word and faith of deed,
Ready of wit and fearing nought but shame;
If that be sin which in fixed heart doth breed
A loathing of all loose unchastity,
Then love is sin, and let me sinful be.

*   *   *

With what sharp checks I in myself am shent
When into Reason's audit I do go,
And by just counts myself a bankrupt know
Of all those goods which heaven to me hath lent:
Unable quite to pay even Nature's rent,
Which unto it by birthright I do owe;
And, which is worse, no good excuse can show
But that my wealth I have most idly spent.
My youth doth waste; my knowledge brings forth toys;
My wit doth strive those passions to defend
Which for reward spoil it with vain annoys.
I see my course to lose myself doth bend:
I see, and yet no greater sorrow take
Than that I lose no more for Stella's sake.

*   *   *

The curious wits, seeing dull pensiveness
Betray itself in my long-settled eyes
Whence those same fumes of melancholy rise,
With idle pains and missing aim do guess.
Some, that know how my spring I did address,
Deem that my Muse some fruit of knowledge plies;
Others, because the Prince my service tries,
Think that I think state errors to redress.
But harder judges judge ambition's rage
(Scourge of itself, still climbing slippery place)
Holds my young brain captived in golden cage.
O fools, or over-wise! alas, the race
Of all my thoughts hath neither stop nor start
But only Stella's eyes and Stella's heart.

*   *   *

I might—unhappy word—O me, I might,
And then would not or could not see my bliss,
Till now wrapped in a most infernal night
I find how heavenly day, wretch, I did miss.
Heart, rend thyself, thou dost thyself but right.
No lovely Paris made thy Helen his.
No force, no fraud robbed thee of thy delight,
Nor Fortune of thy fortune author is.
But to myself myself did give the blow,
While too much wit, forsooth, so troubled me
That I respects for both our sakes must show,
And yet could not by rising morn foresee
How fair a day was near. O punished eyes,
That I had been more foolish or more wise.

*   *   *

Come, let me write. *And to what end?* To ease
A burdened heart. *How can words ease, which are
The glasses of thy daily-vexing care?*

Oft cruel fights well pictured-forth do please.
Art not ashamed to publish thy disease?
Nay, that may breed my fame, it is so rare.
But will not wise men think thy words fond ware?
Then be they close, and so none shall displease.
What idler thing than speak and not be heard?
What harder thing than smart and not to speak?
Peace, foolish wit, with wit my wit is marred.
Thus write I while I doubt to write, and wreak
My harms on ink's poor loss. Perhaps some find
Stella's great powers that so confuse my mind.

* * *

What, have I thus betrayed my liberty?
Can those black beams such burning marks engrave
In my free side? Or am I born a slave
Whose neck becomes such yoke of tyranny?
Or want I sense to feel my misery,
Or spirit, disdain of such disdain to have—
Who for long faith, though daily help I crave,
May get no alms but scorn of beggary?
Virtue, awake: beauty but beauty is.
I may, I must, I can, I will, I do
Leave following that which it is gain to miss.
Let her go. Soft, but here she comes. *Go to,
Unkind, I love you not.* O me, that eye
Doth make my heart give to my tongue the lie.

* * *

No more, my dear, no more these counsels try.
O give my passions leave to run their race.
Let Fortune lay on me her worst disgrace,
Let folk o'ercharged with brain against me cry,
Let clouds bedim my face, break in mine eye,
Let me no steps but of lost labor trace,

Let all the earth with scorn recount my case,
But do not will me from my love to fly.
I do not envy Aristotle's wit,
Nor do aspire to Caesar's bleeding fame,
Nor ought do care though some above me sit,
Nor hope nor wish another course to frame
But that which once may win thy cruel heart:
Thou art my wit, and thou my virtue art.

*   *   *

And do I see some cause a hope to feed,
Or doth the tedious burden of long woe
In weakened minds quick apprehending breed
Of every image which may comfort show?
I cannot brag of word, much less of deed.
Fortune wheels still with me in one sort, slow.
My wealth no more and no whit less my need.
Desire still on the stilts of fear doth go.
And yet amid all fears a hope there is,
Stolen to my heart since last fair night—nay, day:
Stella's eyes sent to me the beams of bliss,
Looking on me while I looked other way.
But when mine eyes back to their heaven did move,
They fled with blush which guilty seemed of love.

*   *   *

Desire, though thou my old companion art
And oft so clings to my pure love that I
One from the other scarcely can descry
While each doth blow the fire of my heart,
Now from thy fellowship I needs must part.
Venus is taught with Dian's wings to fly.
I must no more in thy sweet passions lie;
Virtue's gold now must head my Cupid's dart.
Service and honor, wonder with delight,

Fear to offend, will worthy to appear,
Care shining in mine eyes, faith in my sprite:
These things are left me by my only Dear;
But thou, Desire, because thou wouldst have all,
Now banished art. But yet, alas, how shall?

* * *

Only joy, now here you are,
Fit to hear and ease my care,
Let my whispering voice obtain
Sweet reward for sharpest pain.
Take me to thee, and thee to me.
No no, no no, my dear, let be.

Night hath closed all in her cloak.
Twinkling stars love-thoughts provoke.
Danger hence good care doth keep.
Jealousy itself doth sleep.
Take me to thee, and thee to me.
No no, no no, my dear, let be.

Better place no wit can find
Cupid's yoke to loose or bind.
These sweet flowers on fine bed, too,
Us in their best language woo.
Take me to thee, and thee to me.
No no, no no, my dear, let be.

This small light the moon bestows
Serves thy beams but to disclose,
So to raise my hap more high.
Fear not else; none can us spy.
Take me to thee, and thee to me.
No no, no no, my dear, let be.

That you heard was but a mouse.
Dumb sleep holdeth all the house.
Yet, asleep, methinks they say,
"Young folks, take time while you may."
Take me to thee, and thee to me.
No no, no no, my dear, let be.

Niggard Time threats, if we miss
This large offer of our bliss,
Long stay ere he grant the same.
Sweet, then, while each thing doth frame,
Take me to thee, and thee to me.
No no, no no, my dear, let be.

Your fair mother is a-bed,
Candles out and curtain spread.
She thinks you do letters write.
Write, but let me first indite:
"Take me to thee, and thee to me."
No no, no no, my dear, let be.

Sweet, alas, why strive you thus?
Concord better fitteth us.
Leave to Mars the force of hands;
Your power in your beauty stands.
Take thee to me, and me to thee.
No no, no no, my dear, let be.

Woe to me and do you swear
Me to hate? But I forbear.
Cursed be my destinies all
That brought me so high to fall.
Soon with my death I will please thee.
No no, no no, my dear, let be.

*   *   *

Alas, whence came this change of looks? If I
Have changed desert, let mine own conscience be
A still-felt plague to self-condemning me.
Let woe gripe on my heart, shame load mine eye.
But if all faith like spotless ermine lie
Safe in my soul, which only doth to thee
(As his sole object of felicity)
With wings of love in air of wonder fly,
O ease your hand, treat not so hard your slave.
In justice, pains come not till faults do call.
Or if I needs (sweet judge) must torments have,
Use something else to chasten me withal
Than those blest eyes where all my hopes do dwell.
No doom should make one's heaven become his hell.

    *   *   *

Stella, while now by honor's cruel might
I am from you, light of my life, misled,
And that (fair you, my sun, thus overspread
With absence' veil) I live in sorrow's night;
If this dark place yet show like candlelight
Some beauty's piece, as amber-colored head,
Milk hands, rose cheeks, or lips more sweet, more red,
Or seeing jets, black, but in blackness bright—
They please, I do confess, they please mine eyes.
But why? Because of you they models be.
Models such be wood-globes of glistering skies.
Dear, therefore be not jealous over me
If you hear that they seem my heart to move:
Not them, O no, but you in them I love.

    *   *   *

Be your words made, good sir, of Indian ware
That you allow me them by so small rate?

Or do you cutted Spartans imitate?
Or do you mean my tender ears to spare
That to my questions you so total are?
When I demand of Phoenix Stella's state,
You say, forsooth, you left her well of late.
O God, think you that satisfies my care?
I would know whether she sit or walk;
How clothed, how waited on, sighed she or smiled;
Whereof, with whom, how often did she talk;
With what pastime time's journey she beguiled;
If her lips deigned to sweeten my poor name.
Say all and, all well-said, still say the same.

*   *   *

Stella, since thou so right a princess art
Of all the powers which life bestows on me
That ere by them aught undertaken be
They first resort unto that sovereign part,
Sweet, for a while give respite to my heart
Which pants as though it still should leap to thee,
And on my thoughts give thy lieutenancy
To this great cause which needs both use and art.
And, as a queen who from her presence sends
Whom she employs, dismiss from thee my wit
Till it have wrought what thy own will attends.
On servants' shame oft master's blame doth sit.
O let not fools in me thy works reprove,
And scorning say, "See what it is to love."

FULKE GREVILLE

—⟨ *Sir Fulke Greville (1554–1628), Lord Brooke,*
"Servant to Queen Elizabeth, Councillor to King
James, and Friend to Sir Philip Sidney.
Trophaeum Peccati."

Absence

Absence, the noble truce
Of Cupid's war,
Where though desires want use,
They honored are:
Thou art the just protection
Of prodigal affection;
Have thou the praise.
When bankrupt Cupid braveth,
Thy mines his credit saveth
With sweet delays.

Of wounds which presence makes
With beauty's shot,
Absence the anguish slakes
But healeth not.
Absence records the stories
Wherein desire glories
Although she burn;
She cherisheth the spirits
Where constancy inherits
And passions mourn.

[171]

Absence, like dainty clouds
On glorious-bright,
Nature's weak senses shrouds
From harming light.
Absence maintains the treasure
Of pleasure unto pleasure,
Sparing with praise;
Absence doth nurse the fire
Which starves and feeds desire
With sweet delays.

Presence to every part
Of beauty ties;
Where wonder rules the heart,
There pleasure dies.
Presence plagues mind and senses
With modesty's defenses;
Absence is free.
Thoughts do in absence venture
On Cupid's shadowed center;
They wink and see.

But thoughts be not so brave
With absent joy;
For you with that you have
Yourself destroy.
The absence which you glory
Is that which makes you sorry
And burn in vain;
For thought is not the weapon
Wherewith thought's ease men cheapen.
Absence is pain.

Scoggin

Scoggin's wife by chance mistook her bed.
Such chances oft befall poor womenkind.
Alas poor souls, for when they miss their head,
What marvel it is though the rest be blind?

This bed it was a lord's bed where she light,
Who nobly pitying this poor woman's hap,
Gave alms both to relieve and to delight,
And made the golden shower fall on her lap.

Then in a freedom asks her, as they lay,
Whose were her lips and breasts, and she sware, his—
For hearts are open when thoughts fall to play.
At last he asks her whose her backside is;
    She vowed that it was Scoggin's only part,
    Who never yet came nearer to her heart.

Scoggin o'erheard; but taught by common use
That he who sees all those which do him harm,
Or will in marriage boast such small abuse,
Shall never have his nightgown furred warm,
    And was content, since all was done in play,
    To know his luck and bear his arms away.

Yet when his wife should to the market go,
Her breast and belly he in canvas dressed,
And on her backside fine silk did bestow,
Joying to see it braver than the rest.

His neighbors asked him why, and Scoggin sware
That part of all his wife was only his;
The lord should deck the rest, to whom they are,

For he knew not what lordly fashion is.
   If husbands now should only deck their own,
   Silk would make many by their backs be known.

Down in the Depth

Down in the depth of mine iniquity,
That ugly center of infernal spirits
Where each sin feels her own deformity
In these peculiar torments she inherits,
Deprived of human graces and divine,
Even there appears this saving God of mine.

And in this fatal mirror of transgression
Shows man, as fruit of his degeneration,
The error's ugly infinite impression
Which bears the faithless down to desperation,
Deprived of human graces and divine,
Even there appears this saving God of mine.

In power and truth, almighty and eternal,
Which on the sin reflects strange desolation,
With glory scourging all the spirits infernal,
And uncreated hell with unprivation,
Deprived of human graces, not divine,
Even there appears this saving God of mine.

For on this spiritual cross condemned lying
To pains infernal by eternal doom,
I see my Savior for the same sins dying,
And from that hell I feared, to free me, come;
Deprived of human graces, not divine,
Thus hath His death raised up this soul of mine.

CHIDIOCK TICHBOURNE

*1558–1586. "Written with his own hand in the
Tower before his execution" for complicity in
the Babington plot to assassinate Queen Elizabeth.
This furnished the occasion for the trial and
execution of Mary Stuart.*

Tichbourne's Elegy

My prime of youth is but a frost of cares.
My feast of joy is but a dish of pain.
My crop of corn is but a field of tares,
And all my good is but vain hope of gain.
The day is past, and yet I saw no sun,
And now I live, and now my life is done.

My tale was heard, and yet it was not told.
My fruit is fallen, and yet my leaves are green.
My youth is spent, and yet I am not old.
I saw the world, and yet I was not seen.
My thread is cut, and yet it is not spun,
And now I live, and now my life is done.

I sought my death and found it in my womb.
I looked for life and saw it was a shade.
I trod the earth and knew it was my tomb,
And now I die, and now I was but made.
My glass is full, and now my glass is run,
And now I live, and now my life is done.

—⁕ *The Ocean is Sir Walter Ralegh (d. 1618): the Queen called him "Water," i.e. Walter. Cynthia is Queen Elizabeth. "My heart was never broken till this day that I hear the Queen goes away so far off, whom I have followed so many years with so great love and desire, in so many journeys, and am now left behind her in a dark prison all alone."*

The Ocean to Cynthia

Sufficeth it to you, my joys interred,
In simple words that I my woes complain,
You that then died when first my fancy erred,
Joys under dust that never live again.

If to the living were my muse addressed,
Or did my mind her own spirit still inhold,
Were not my living passion so repressed
As to the dead the dead did these unfold,

Some sweeter words, some more becoming verse,
Should witness my mishap in higher kind;
But my love's wounds, my fancy in the hearse,
The idea, but resting, of a wasted mind,

The blossoms fallen, the sap gone from the tree,
The broken monuments of my great desires:
From these so lost what may the affections be?
What heat in cinders of extinguished fires?

But as a body violently slain
Retaineth warmth although the spirit be gone,
And by a power in nature moves again
Till it be laid below the fatal stone;

Or as the earth even in cold winter days,
Left for a time by her life-giving sun,
Doth by the power remaining of his rays
Produce some green, though not as it hath done;

Or as a wheel forced by the falling stream,
Although the course be turned some other way,
Doth for a time go round upon the beam,
Till wanting strength to move, it stands at stay;

So my forsaken heart, my withered mind,
Widow of all the joys it once possessed,
My hopes clean out of sight, with forced wind
To kingdoms strange, to lands far off addressed,

Alone, forsaken, friendless on the shore,
With many wounds, with death's cold pangs embraced,
Writes in the dust as one that could no more,
Whom love, and time, and fortune had defaced.

*   *   *

Twelve years entire I wasted in this war,
Twelve years of my most happy younger days;
But I in them, and they now wasted are,
Of all which past the sorrow only stays.

So wrote I once, and my mishap foretold,
My mind still feeling sorrowful success,
Even as before a storm the marble cold
Doth by moist tears tempestuous times express.

And though strong reason hold before mine eyes
The images and forms of world's past,
Teaching the cause why all those flames that rise
From forms external can no longer last

Than that those seeming beauties hold in prime
Love's ground, his essence, and his empery:
All slaves to age and vassals unto time,
Of which repentance writes the tragedy.

But this my heart's desire could not conceive,
Whose love outflew the fastest flying time:
A beauty that can easily deceive
The arrest of years, and creeping age outclimb;

A spring of beauties which time ripeth not,
Time that but works on frail mortality;
A sweetness which woe's wrongs outwipeth not,
Whom love hath chose for his divinity;

A vestal fire that burns but never wasteth,
That loseth nought by giving light to all,
That endless shines eachwhere and endless lasteth;
Blossoms of pride that can nor fade nor fall.

            *   *   *

Yet have these wonders want which want compassion,
Yet hath her mind some marks of human race,
Yet will she be a woman for a fashion,
So doth she please her virtues to deface.

And like as that immortal power doth seat
An element of waters to allay
The fiery sunbeams that on earth do beat,
And temper by cold night the heat of day,

So hath perfection, which begat her mind,
Added thereto a change of fantasy,
And left her the affections of her kind,
Yet free from every evil but cruelty.

*   *   *

With youth is dead the hope of love's return,
Who looks not back to hear our after-cries.
Where he is not, he laughs at those that mourn;
Whence he is gone, he scorns the mind that dies,

When he is absent, he believes no words;
When reason speaks, he careless stops his ears;
Whom he hath left he never grace affords,
But bathes his wings in our lamenting tears.

*   *   *

But what of those or these, or what of ought
Of that which was, or that which is, to treat?
What I possess is but the same I sought;
My love was false, my labors were deceit.

Nor less than such they are esteemed to be:
A fraud bought at the price of many woes,
A guile, whereof the profits unto me—
Could it be thought premeditate for those?

Witness those withered leaves left on the tree,
The sorrow-worn face, the pensive mind;
The external shows what may the internal be:
Cold care hath bitten both the root and vine.

*   *   *

Thus home I draw, as death's long night draws on.
Yet every foot, old thoughts turn back mine eyes;

Constraint me guides as old age draws a stone
Against the hill which over-weighty lies

For feeble arms or wasted strength to move.
My steps are backward, gazing on my loss:
My mind's affection, and my soul's sole love,
Not mixed with fancy's chaff or fortune's dross.

To God I leave it who first gave it me,
And I her gave, and she returned again
As it was hers. So let his mercies be
Of my last comforts the essential mean.
  But be it so or not, the effects are past.
  Her love hath end; my woe must ever last.

FRANCIS BACON

–◦◖ *Sir Francis Bacon (1561–1626), Viscount St.
Albans. Ben Jonson wrote: "My conceit of his
person was never increased toward him by his place
or honors. But I have and do reverence him for the
greatness that was only proper to himself, in that he
seemed to me ever, by his work, one of the greatest
men and most worthy of admiration that had been
in many ages. In his adversity I ever prayed that
God would give him strength, for greatness he
could not want."*

Of Love

The stage is more beholding to love than the life of man. For
as to the stage, love is ever matter of comedies, and now and
then of tragedies: but in life it doth much mischief; sometimes
like a siren, sometimes like a fury. You may observe that
amongst all the great and worthy persons (whereof the memory
remaineth, either ancient or recent) there is not one that hath
been transported to the mad degree of love; which shows that
great spirits and great business do keep out this weak passion.
You must except, nevertheless, Marcus Antonius, the half part-
ner of the empire of Rome, and Appius Claudius, the decemvir
and lawgiver: whereof the former was indeed a voluptuous man
and inordinate; but the latter was an austere and wise man: and
therefore it seems (though rarely) that love can find entrance
not only into an open heart but also into a heart well fortified,
if watch be not well kept. It is a poor saying of Epicurus, *Satis
magnum alter alteri theatrum sumus:* as if man, made for the
contemplation of heaven and all noble objects, should do nothing but kneel before a little idol and make himself subject,
though not of the mouth (as beasts are) yet of the eye, which

was given them for higher purposes. It is a strange thing to note the excess of this passion and how it braves the nature and value of things by this, that the speaking in a perpetual hyperbole is comely in nothing but in love. Neither is it merely in the phrase; for whereas it hath been well said that the arch-flatterer, with whom all the petty flatterers have intelligence, is a man's self, certainly the lover is more. For there was never proud man thought so absurdly well of himself as the lover doth of the person loved: and therefore it was well said, *That it is impossible to love and to be wise.* Neither doth this weakness appear to others only, and not to the party loved, but to the loved most of all, except the love be reciproque. For it is a true rule, that love is ever rewarded either with the reciproque or with an inward and secret contempt. By how much the more men ought to beware of this passion, which loseth not only other things but itself. As for the other losses, the poet's relation doth well figure them: that he that preferred Helena quitted the gifts of Juno and Pallas. For whosoever esteemeth too much of amorous affection, quitteth both riches and wisdom. This passion hath his floods in the very times of weakness; which are great prosperity and great adversity (though this latter hath been less observed): both which times kindle love and make it more fervent, and therefore show it to be the child of folly. They do best who, if they cannot but admit love, yet make it keep quarter, and sever it wholly from their serious affairs and actions of life; for if it check once with business, it troubleth men's fortunes and maketh men that they can no ways be true to their own ends. I know not how, but martial men are given to love: I think it is but as they are given to wine, for perils commonly ask to be paid in pleasures. There is in man's nature a secret inclination and motion towards love of others, which, if it be not spent upon some one or a few, doth naturally spread itself towards many and maketh men become humane and charitable, as it is seen sometime in friars. Nuptial love maketh mankind; friendly love perfecteth it; but wanton love corrupteth and embaseth it.

Of Great Place

Men in great places are thrice servants: servants of the sovereign or state; servants of fame; and servants of business. So as they have no freedom, neither in their persons, nor in their actions, nor in their times. It is a strange desire, to seek power and to lose liberty; or to seek power over others and to lose power over a man's self. The rising unto place is laborious, and by pains men come to greater pains; and it is sometimes base, and by indignities men come to dignities. The standing is slippery; and the regress is either a downfall, or at least an eclipse, which is a melancholy thing. *Cum non sis qui fueris, non esse cur velis vivere.* Nay, retire men cannot when they would; neither will they when it were reason; but are impatient of privateness, even in age and sickness, which require the shadow, like old townsmen that will be still sitting at their street door though thereby they offer age to scorn. Certainly, great persons had need to borrow other men's opinions to think themselves happy, for if they judge by their own feeling they cannot find it: but if they think with themselves what other men think of them, and that other men would fain be as they are, then they are happy as it were by report, when perhaps they find the contrary within. For they are the first that find their own griefs, though they be the last that find their own faults. Certainly, men in great fortunes are strangers to themselves, and while they are in the puzzle of business they have no time to tend their health, either of body or mind. *Illi mors gravis incubat, qui notus nimis omnibus, ignotus moritur sibi.* In place there is licence to do good and evil; whereof the latter is a curse: for in evil the best condition is not to will, the second not to can. But power to do good is the true and lawful end of aspiring. For good thoughts (though God accept them) yet towards men are little better than good dreams, except they be put in act; and that cannot be without power and place, as the vantage and commanding ground. Merit

and good works is the end of man's motion; and conscience of
the same is the accomplishment of man's rest. For if a man can
be partaker of God's theatre, he shall likewise be partaker of
God's rest. *Et conversus Deus, ut aspiceret opera quæ fecerunt
manus suæ, vidit quod omnia essent bona nimis;* and then the
Sabbath. In the discharge of thy place set before thee the best
examples, for imitation is a globe of precepts. And after a time
set before thee thine own example; and examine thyself strictly,
whether thou didst not best at first. Neglect not also the examples of those that have carried themselves ill in the same place;
not to set off thyself by taxing their memory, but to direct thyself what to avoid. Reform, therefore, without bravery or scan-
dal of former times and persons; but yet set it down to thyself
as well to create good precedents as to follow them. Reduce
things to the first institution, and observe wherein and how
they have degenerate; but yet ask counsel of both times: of the
ancient time, what is best, and of the latter time, what is fittest.
Seek to make thy course regular that men may know beforehand what they may expect; but be not too positive and per-
emptory; and express thyself well when thou digressest from
thy rule. Preserve the right of thy place, but stir not questions
of jurisdiction, and rather assume thy right in silence and *de
facto* than voice it with claims and challenges. Preserve likewise
the rights of inferior places; and think it more honour to direct
in chief than to be busy in all. Embrace and invite helps and
advices touching the execution of thy place; and do not drive
away such as bring thee information as meddlers, but accept of
them in good part. The vices of authority are chiefly four: delays, corruption, roughness, and facility. For delays; give easy
access; keep times appointed; go through with that which is in
hand; and interlace not business but of necessity. For corruption;
do not only bind thine own hands or thy servants' hands from
taking, but bind the hands of suitors also from offering. For
integrity used doth the one; but integrity professed, and with a
manifest detestation of bribery, doth the other. And avoid not

only the fault, but the suspicion. Whosoever is found variable and changeth manifestly without manifest cause giveth suspicion of corruption. Therefore always when thou changest thine opinion or course, profess it plainly and declare it, together with the reasons that move thee to change; and do not think to steal it. A servant or a favourite, if he be inward, and no other apparent cause of esteem, is commonly thought but a by-way to close corruption. For roughness, it is a needless cause of discontent: severity breedeth fear, but roughness breedeth hate. Even reproofs from authority ought to be grave and not taunting. As for facility, it is worse than bribery. For bribes come but now and then, but if importunity or idle respects lead a man, he shall never be without. As Salomon saith: *To respect persons is not good; for such a man will transgress for a piece of bread.* It is most true that was anciently spoken, *A place sheweth the man:* and it sheweth some to the better and some to the worse. *Omnium consensu capax imperii, nisi imperasset,* saith Tacitus of Galba; but of Vespasian he saith, *Solus imperantium Vespasianus mutatus in melius,* though the one was meant of sufficiency, the other of manners and affection. It is an assured sign of a worthy and generous spirit, whom honour amends. For honour is, or should be, the place of virtue; and as in nature things move violently to their place, and calmly in their place, so virtue in ambition is violent, in authority settled and calm. All rising to great place is by a winding stair; and if there be factions, it is good to side a man's self whilst he is in the rising, and to balance himself when he is placed. Use the memory of thy predecessor fairly and tenderly, for if thou dost not, it is a debt will sure be paid when thou art gone. If thou have colleagues, respect them, and rather call them when they look not for it than exclude them when they have reason to look to be called. Be not too sensible or too remembering of thy place in conversation and private answers to suitors; but let it rather be said, *When he sits in place he is another man.*

Of Life

The world's a bubble, and the life of man
   Less than a span;
In his conception wretched, from the womb
   So to the tomb;
Cursed from the cradle, and brought up to years
   With cares and fears.
Who then to frail mortality shall trust
But limns on water, or but writes in dust.

Yet since with sorrow here we live oppressed,
   What life is best?
Courts are but only superficial schools
   To dandle fools;
The rural parts are turned into a den
   Of savage men;
And where's a city from all vice so free
But may be termed the worst of all the three?

Domestic cares afflict the husband's bed
   Or pains his head;
Those that live single take it for a curse,
   Or do things worse;
Some would have children, those that have them none,
   Or wish them gone;
What is it, then, to have or have no wife
But single thraldom or a double strife?

Our own affections still at home to please
   Is a disease;
To cross the sea to any foreign soil,
   Perils and toil;

Wars with their noise affright us; when they cease,
   We're worse in peace.
What then remains but that we still should cry
Not to be born, or being born, to die?

WILLIAM SHAKESPEARE

One of "divers poetical essays on the former subject, viz., the Turtle and Phoenix, done by the best and chiefest of our modern writers, with their names subscribed to their particular works, never before extant." The other names are Jonson, Chapman, Marston, Vatum Chorus, and Ignoto.

The Phoenix and the Turtle

Let the bird of loudest lay
  On the sole Arabian tree
  Herald sad and trumpet be,
To whose sound chaste wings obey.

But thou, shrieking harbinger,
  Foul precurrer of the fiend,
  Augur of the fever's end,
To this troop come thou not near.

From this session interdict
  Every fowl of tyrant wing
  Save the eagle, feathered king.
Keep the obsequy so strict.

Let the priest in surplice white
  That defunctive music can
  Be the death-divining swan,
Lest the requiem lack his right.

And thou, treble-dated crow,
  That thy sable gender mak'st

  With the breath thou giv'st and tak'st,
'Mongst our mourners shalt thou go.

Here the anthem doth commence:
    Love and constancy is dead;
    Phoenix and the turtle fled
In a mutual flame from hence.

So they loved as love in twain
    Had the essence but in one;
    Two distincts, division none;
Number there in love was slain.

Hearts remote, yet not asunder;
    Distance, and no space was seen
    'Twixt the turtle and his queen:
But in them it were a wonder.

So between them love did shine
    That the turtle saw his right
    Flaming in the phoenix' sight;
Either was the other's mine.

Property was thus appalled
    That the self was not the same;
    Single nature's double name
Neither two nor one was called.

Reason, in itself confounded,
    Saw division grow together,
    To themselves yet either neither,
Simple were so well compounded;

That it cried, "How true a twain
    Seemeth this concordant one!

Love hath reason, reason none
If what parts can so remain."

Whereupon it made this threne
　　To the phoenix and the dove,
　　Co-supremes and stars of love,
As chorus to their tragic scene.

THRENOS

Beauty, truth, and rarity,
Grace in all simplicity,
Here enclosed in cinders lie.

Death is now the phoenix' nest;
And the turtle's loyal breast
To eternity doth rest,

Leaving no posterity:
'Twas not their infirmity,
It was married chastity.

Truth may seem, but cannot be;
Beauty brag, but 'tis not she;
Truth and beauty buried be.

To this urn let those repair
That are either true or fair;
For these dead birds sigh a prayer.

WILLIAM SHAKESPEARE (?)

An additional scene, dealing with the riot on May Morning, 1517, against foreign craftsmen in London, from the manuscript play of Sir Thomas More. The play had been rejected by the censor for political reasons; five different handwritings have been distinguished in the revisions and additions. Many scholars believe this scene is in the handwriting of William Shakespeare (1564–1616) and in his style.

Evil May Day
Dramatis Personae

Earl of SHREWSBURY	WILLIAMSON
Earl of SURREY	A SERGEANT at arms
Thomas MORE	A CLOWN, brother of George BETTS
LORD MAYOR of London	DOLL, wife of WILLIAMSON
George BETTS ⎱ Citizens of London	A Crowd of London Citizens, etc.
John LINCOLN ⎰	

Scene: London

Enter Lincoln, Doll, Clown, Betts, Williamson, others, and a Sergeant at arms.

LINCOLN: Peace! Hear me! He that will not see a red herring at a Harry groat, butter at eleven pence a pound, meal at nine shillings a bushel, and beef at four nobles a stone, list to me.

BETTS: It will come to that pass if strangers be suffered. Mark him.

LINCOLN: Our country is a great eating country; ergo, they eat more in our country than they do in their own.

CLOWN: By a halfpenny loaf a day, troy weight.

[191]

LINCOLN: They bring in strange roots, which is merely to the undoing of poor prentices; for what's a sorry parsnip to a good heart?

WILLIAMSON: Trash, trash. They breed sore eyes, and 'tis enough to infect the city with the palsy.

LINCOLN: Nay, it has infected it with the palsy; for these bastards of dung (as you know, they grow in dung) have infected us, and it is our infection will make the city shake, which partly comes through the eating of parsnips.

CLOWN, BETTS: True, and pumpkins together.

Enter Sergeant at arms.

SERGEANT: What say ye to the mercy of the King? Do you refuse it?

LINCOLN: You would have us upon the hip, would you? No, marry, do we not. We accept of the King's mercy, but we will show no mercy upon the strangers.

SERGEANT: You are the simplest things that ever stood in such a question.

LINCOLN: How say you now, prentices? Prentices simple? Down with him!

ALL: Prentices simple! Prentices simple!

Enter the Lord Mayor, Surrey, Shrewsbury, More.

LORD MAYOR: Hold! In the King's name, hold!

SURREY: Friends, masters, countrymen—

LORD MAYOR: Peace, ho! Peace! I charge you, keep the peace!

SHREWSBURY: My masters, countrymen—

WILLIAMSON: The noble Earl of Shrewsbury, let's hear him.

BETTS: We'll hear the Earl of Surrey.

LINCOLN: The Earl of Shrewsbury!

BETTS: We'll hear both.

ALL: Both, both, both, both!

LINCOLN: Peace, I say! Peace! Are you men of wisdom, or what are you?

SURREY: What you will have them, but not men of wisdom.

ALL: We'll not hear my Lord of Surrey. No, no, no, no! Shrewsbury, Shrewsbury!

MORE: Whiles they are o'er the bank of their obedience,
Thus will they bear down all things.

LINCOLN: Sheriff More speaks. Shall we hear Sheriff More speak?

DOLL: Let's hear him. He keeps a plentiful shrievalty, and he made my brother, Arthur Watchins, Sergeant Safe's yeoman. Let's hear Sheriff More.

ALL: Sheriff More! More, More! Sheriff More!

MORE: Even by the rule you have among yourselves,
Command still audience.

ALL: Surrey, Surrey! More, More!

LINCOLN, BETTS: Peace, peace! Silence! Peace!

MORE: You that have voice and credit with the number,
Command them to a stillness.

LINCOLN: A plague on them; they will not hold their peace.
The devil cannot rule them.

MORE: Then what a rough and riotous charge have you,
To lead those that the devil cannot rule.—
Good masters, hear me speak.

DOLL: Aye, by th' mass will we, More: th'art a good housekeeper, and I thank thy good worship for my brother, Arthur Watchins.

ALL: Peace, peace!

MORE: Look, what you do offend you cry upon:
That is, the peace. Not one of you here present,
Had there such fellows lived when you were babes,
That could have topped the peace as now you would.
The peace wherein you have till now grown up
Had been ta'en from you, and the bloody times
Could not have brought you to the state of men.
Alas, poor things, what is it you have got
Although we grant you get the thing you seek?

BETTS: Marry, the removing of strangers, which cannot choose
but much advantage the poor handicrafts of the city.

MORE: Grant them removed, and grant that this your noise
Hath chid down all the majesty of England;
Imagine that you see the wretched strangers,
Their babies at their backs, and their poor luggage,
Plodding to th' ports and coasts for transportation,
And that you sit as kings in your desires,
Authority quite silenced by your brawl,
And you in ruff of your opinions clothed,
What had you got? I'll tell you: you had taught
How insolence and strong hand should prevail,
How order should be quelled, and by this pattern
Not one of you should live an aged man:
For other ruffians, as their fancies wrought,
With self-same hand, self reasons, and self right,
Would shark on you, and men, like ravenous fishes,
Would feed on one another.

DOLL: Before God, that's as true as the gospel.

LINCOLN: Nay, this a sound fellow, I tell you. Let's mark him.

MORE: Let me set up before your thoughts, good friends,
One supposition which, if you will mark,

You shall perceive how horrible a shape
Your innovation bears. First, 'tis a sin
Which oft the apostle did forewarn us of,
Urging obedience to authority;
And 'twere no error if I told you all
You were in arms 'gainst God.

ALL: Marry, God forbid that!

MORE: Nay, certainly you are;
For to the King God hath his office lent
Of dread, of justice, power, and command,
Hath bid him rule and willed you to obey;
And to add ampler majesty to this,
He hath not only lent the King his figure,
His throne and sword, but given him His own name,
Calls him a God on earth. What do you then,
Rising 'gainst him that God himself installs,
But rise 'gainst God? What do you to your souls
In doing this, oh desparate as you are?
Wash your foul minds with tears; and those same hands
That you, like rebels, lift against the peace,
Lift up for peace; and your unreverent knees,
Make them your feet to kneel to be forgiven.
Tell me but this: what rebel captain,
As mutinies are incident, by his name
Can still the rout? Who will obey a traitor?
Or how can well that proclamation sound
When there is no addition but a rebel
To qualify a rebel? You'll put down strangers,
Kill them, cut their throats, possess their houses,
And lead the majesty of law in lyam
To slip him like a hound. Say now the King,
As he is clement if the offender mourn,
Should so much come too short of your great trespass
As but to banish you, whither would you go?

What country, by the nature of your error,
Should give you harbor? Go you to France or Flanders,
To any German province, Spain or Portugal,
Nay, anywhere that not adheres to England,
Why, you must needs be strangers. Would you be pleased
To find a nation of such barbarous temper
That, breaking out in hideous violence,
Would not afford you an abode on earth,
Whet their detested knives against your throats,
Spurn you like dogs, and like as if that God
Owed not nor made not you, nor that the elements
Were not all appropriate to your comforts,
But chartered unto them? What would you think
To be thus used? This is the strangers' case,
And this your momtanish inhumanity.

ALL: Faith, he says true. Let's us do as we may be done by.

LINCOLN: We'll be ruled by you, Mr. More, if you'll stand our
friend to procure our pardon.

MORE: Submit you to these noble gentlemen,
Entreat their mediation to the King,
Give up yourself to form, obey the magistrate,
And there's no doubt but mercy may be found
If you so seek it.

JOHN HOSKYNS

"Ben Jonson called him father" (*1566–1638*).
"Sir Benet told me that one time desiring Mr. Jonson
to adopt him for his son, 'No,' said he, 'I dare not;
'tis honor enough for me to be your brother. I was
your father's son, and 'twas he that polished me.'"

An Epigram on a Man for Doing Nothing

Here lies the man was born and cried,
Lived three score years, fell sick, and died.

On a Young Gentlewoman

Nature in this small volume was about
To perfect what in woman was left out,
Yet careful lest a piece so well begun
Should want preservatives when she had done,
Ere she could finish what she undertook,
Threw dust upon it, and shut up the book.

To his Son, Benedict Hoskyns

Sweet Benedict, whilst thou art young
And knowst not yet the use of tongue,
Keep it in thrall whilst thou art free:
Imprison it or it will thee.

Cabalistical Verses

*"Which by transposition of words, syllables,
and letters make excellent sense, otherwise none.
In lauden authoris," Thomas Coryate.*

Even as the waves of brainless buttered fish,
With bugle horn writ in the Hebrew tongue,
Fuming up flounders like a chafing dish
That looks asquint upon a three-man's song;
Or as your equinoctial pasty-crust,
Projecting out a purple chariot wheel,
Doth squeeze the spheres and intimate the dust,
The dust which force of argument doth feel;
Even so this author, this gymnosophist,
Whom no delight of travel's toil dismays,
Shall sympathize (think, reader, what you list),
Crowned with a quinsil tipped with marble praise.

THOMAS CAMPIAN

Campian (1567–1620), of Gray's Inn, Doctor of Physic, Latin elegist and epigrammatist, composer.

The Writer to His Book

Whither thus hastes my little book so fast?
To Paul's Churchyard. What? in those cells to stand,
With one leaf like a rider's cloak put up
To catch a termer? Or lie musty there
With rhymes a term set out, or two, before?
Some will redeem me. Few. *Yes, read me too.*
Fewer. *Nay, love me.* Now thou dotest, I see.
Will not our English Athens art defend?
Perhaps. *Will lofty courtly wits not aim
Still at perfection?* If I grant? *I fly.*
Whither? *To Paul's.* Alas, poor book, I rue
Thy rash self-love. Go, spread thy papery wings:
Thy lightness cannot help or hurt my fame.

Epigram

Kate can fancy only beardless husbands.
That's the cause she shakes off every suitor,
That's the cause she lives so stale a virgin;
For, before her heart can heat her answer,
Her smooth youths she finds all hugely bearded.

"It fell on a summer's day"

It fell on a summer's day,
While sweet Bessie sleeping lay
In her bower on her bed,
Light with curtains shadowed,
Jamie came; she him spies,
Opening half her heavy eyes.

Jamie stole in through the door;
She lay slumbering as before.
Softly to her he drew near;
She heard him, yet would not hear.
Bessie vowed not to speak;
He resolved that dump to break.

First a soft kiss he doth take;
She lay still and would not wake.
Then his hands learned to woo;
She dreamt not what he would do
But still slept while he smiled
To see love by sleep beguiled.

Jamie then began to play;
Bessie as one buried lay,
Gladly still, through this sleight
Deceived in her own deceit.
And since this trance begun,
She sleeps every afternoon.

"Now winter nights enlarge"

Now winter nights enlarge
The number of their hours,

And clouds their storms discharge
Upon the airy towers.
Let now the chimneys blaze
And cups o'erflow with wine;
Let well-tuned words amaze
With harmony divine.
Now yellow waxen lights
Shall wait on honey love,
While youthful revels, masks, and courtly sights
Sleep's leaden spells remove.

This time doth well dispense
With lovers' long discourse;
Much speech hath some defense,
Though beauty no remorse.
All do not all things well:
Some measures comely tread;
Some knotted riddles tell;
Some poems smoothly read.
The summer hath his joys,
And winter his delights;
Though Love and all his pleasures are but toys,
They shorten tedious nights.

"The author," (*1570–1638*), *"of these ensuing poems did not affect the name of a poet, having neither published in print nor kept copies of anything he writ, either in Latin or English."*

Upon Love

I loved thee once, I'll love no more.
Thine be the grief as is the blame.
Thou art not what thou wast before
What reason I should be the same?
He that can love unloved again
Hath better store of love than brain.
God send me love my debts to pay,
While unthrifts fool their love away.

Nothing could have my love o'erthrown
If thou hadst still continued mine.
Nay, if thou hadst remained thine own
I might perchance have yet been thine.
But thou thy freedom did recall
That it thou might elsewhere enthrall,
And then how could I but disdain
A captive's captive to remain?

When new desires had conquered thee
And changed the object of thy will,
It had been lethargy in me,
Not constancy, to love thee still;

Yea, it had been a sin to go
And prostitute affection so,
Since we are taught no prayers to say
To such as must to others pray.

Yet do thou glory in thy choice,
Thy choice of his good fortune boast;
I'll neither grieve nor yet rejoice
To see him gain what I have lost.
The height of my disdain shall be
To laugh at him, to blush for thee,
To love thee still but go no more
A-begging at a beggar's door.

JOHN DONNE

--◦◦{ *Donne (1572–1631), D.D., Dean of St. Paul's.
Jonson "affirmeth Donne to have written all his
best pieces ere he was twenty-five years old."
Thomas Carew: "Verse" was "refined by thee in
this last age." A valediction is a good-by poem on
the theme of absence.*

A Valediction: Of my Name in the Window

I

My name engraved herein
Doth contribute my firmness to this glass,
Which ever since that charm hath been
As hard as that which graved it was.
Thine eye will give it price enough to mock
The diamonds of either rock.

II

'Tis much that glass should be
As all-confessing and through-shine as I;
'Tis more that it shows thee to thee
And clear reflects thee to thine eye.
But all such rules love's magic can undo:
Here you see me, and I am you.

III

As no one point nor dash,
Which are but accessories to this name,
The showers and tempests can outwash,
So shall all times find me the same.

You this entireness better may fulfil
Who have the pattern with you still.

IV

Or, if too hard and deep
This learning be for a scratched name to teach,
It as a given death's head keep,
Lovers' mortality to preach;
Or think this ragged bony name to be
My ruinous anatomy.

V

Then, as all my souls be
Imparadised in you—in whom alone
I understand and grow and see—
The rafters of my body (bone)
Being still with you, the muscle, sinew and vein
Which tile this house will come again.

VI

Till my return, repair
And recompact my scattered body so.
As all the virtuous powers which are
Fixed in the stars are said to flow
Into such characters as graved be
When these stars have supremacy,

VII

So, since this name was cut
When love and grief their exaltation had,
No door 'gainst this name's influence shut!
As much more loving as more sad
'Twill make thee. And thou shouldst till I return,
Since I die daily, daily mourn.

VIII

When thy inconsiderate hand
Flings ope this casement, with my trembling name,
To look on one whose wit, or land,
New battery to thy heart may frame,
Then think this name alive, and that thou thus
In it offendst my Genius.

IX

And when thy melted maid,
Corrupted by thy lover's gold, and page,
His letter at thy pillow hath laid,
Disputed it, and tamed thy rage,
And thou beginst to thaw towards him for this,
May my name step in and hide his.

X

And if this treason go
To an overt act, and that thou write again,
In superscribing, this name flow
Into thy fancy from the pane.
So, in forgetting thou rememberst right,
And unaware to me shalt write.

XI

But glass and lines must be
No means our firm, substantial love to keep.
Near death inflicts this lethargy,
And this I murmur in my sleep.
Impute this idle talk to that I go,
For dying men talk often so.

A Nocturnal upon St. Lucy's Day,
Being the Shortest Day

'Tis the year's midnight and it is the day's,
Lucy's, who scarce seven hours herself unmasks.
The sun is spent, and now his flasks
Send forth light squibs, no constant rays.
The world's whole sap is sunk;
The general balm the hydroptic earth hath drunk,
Whither as to the bed's feet life is shrunk,
Dead and interred. Yet all these seem to laugh
Compared with me who am their epitaph.

Study me, then, you who shall lovers be
At the next world, that is, at the next Spring,
For I am every dead thing
In whom love wrought new alchemy.
For his art did express
A quintessence even from nothingness,
From dull privations and lean emptiness.
He ruined me, and I am re-begot
Of absence, darkness, death—things that are not.

All others from all things draw all that's good—
Life, soul, form, spirit, whence they being have;
I by love's limbeck am the grave
Of all that's nothing. Oft a flood
Have we two wept, and so
Drowned the whole world, us two; oft did we grow
To be two chaoses when we did show.
Care to aught else; and often absences
Withdrew our souls and made us carcases.

But I am by her death (which word wrongs her)
Of the first nothing the elixir grown.

Were I a man, that I were one
I needs must know. I should prefer
If I were any beast
Some ends, some means. Yea, plants, yea, stones detest
And love. All, all, some properties invest.
If I an ordinary nothing were,
As shadow, a light and body must be there.

But I am none, nor will my sun renew.
You lovers, for whose sake the lesser sun
At this time to the Goat is run
To fetch new lust and give it you,
Enjoy your summer all.
Since she enjoys her long night's festival
Let me prepare towards her, and let me call
This hour her Vigil and her Eve, since this
Both the year's and the day's deep midnight is.

The Apparition

When by thy scorn, O murderess, I am dead
And that thou thinkst thee free
From all solicitation from me,
Then shall my ghost come to thy bed
And thee, feigned Vestal, in worse arms shall see.
Then thy sick taper will begin to wink,
And he, whose thou art then, being tired before,
Will, if thou stir or pinch to wake him, think
Thou callst for more,
And in false sleep will from thee shrink.
And then, poor aspen wretch, neglected thou
Bathed in cold quicksilver sweat will lie,
A verier ghost than I.
What I will say I will not tell thee now
Lest that preserve thee. And since my love is spent

I'd rather thou shouldst painfully repent
Than by my threatenings rest still innocent.

Hero and Leander

Both robbed of air, we both lie in one ground,
Both whom one fire had burnt, one water drowned.

Elegy

Nature's lay idiot, I taught thee to love,
And in that sophistry, Oh, thou dost prove
Too subtle. Fool, thou didst not understand
The mystic language of the eye nor hand;
Nor couldst thou judge the difference of the air
Of sighs, and say, this lies, this sounds despair;
Nor by the eye's water call a malady
Desperately hot or changing feverously.
I had not taught thee then the alphabet
Of flowers, how they, devisefully being set
And bound up, might with speechless secrecy
Deliver errands mutely and mutually.
Remember, since, all thy words used to be
To every suitor, *Aye, if my friends agree;*
Since, household charms thy husband's name to teach
Were all the love tricks that thy wit could reach;
And, since, an hour's discourse could scarce have made
One answer in thee, and that ill arrayed
In broken proverbs and torn sentences.
Thou art not by so many duties his
That from the world's common having severed thee,
Inlaid thee, neither to be seen nor see,
As mine who have with amorous delicacies
Refined thee into a blissful paradise.
Thy graces and good words my creatures be.

I planted knowledge and life's tree in thee,
Which, Oh, shall strangers taste? Must I, alas,
Frame and enamel plate, and drink in glass?
Chafe wax for others' seals? Break a colt's force
And leave him, then, being made a ready horse?

Satire: On Religion

—⊰ (The Third Satire, *line 43 to the end*.)

Seek true religion. O where? Mirreus
Thinking her unhoused here and fled from us,
Seeks her at Rome: there, because he doth know
That she was there a thousand years ago.
He loves her rags so, as we here obey
The statecloth where the prince sat yesterday.
Crantz to such brave loves will not be enthralled,
But loves her only who at Geneva is called
Religion, plain, simple, sullen, young,
Contemptuous yet unhandsome; as, among
Lecherous humors, there is one that judges
No wenches wholesome but coarse country drudges.
Graius stays still at home here, and because
Some preachers (vile ambitious bawds) and laws,
Still new like fashions, bid him think that she
Which dwells with us is only perfect, he
Embraceth her whom his godfathers will
Tender to him, being tender, as wards still
Take such wives as their guardians offer or
Pay values. Careless Phrygius doth abhor
All because all cannot be good, as one
Knowing some women whores dares marry none.
Graccus loves all as one, and thinks that so

As women do in diverse countries go
In diverse habits, yet are still one kind,
So doth, so is religion. And this blind-
ness too much light breeds. But, unmoved, thou
Of force must one and, forced, but one allow.
And the right. Ask thy father which is she,
Let him ask his. Though truth and falsehood be
Near twins, yet truth a little elder is.
Be busy to seek her. Believe me this,
He's not of none nor worst that seeks the best.
To adore or scorn an image, or protest,
May all be bad. Doubt wisely. In strange way
To stand inquiring right is not to stray:
To sleep, or run wrong, is. On a huge hill,
Cragged and steep, Truth stands, and he that will
Reach her about must and about must go,
And what the hill's suddenness resists win so.
Yet strive so, that before age, death's twilight,
Thy soul rest, for none can work in that night.
To will implies delay; therefore now do.
Hard deeds the body's pains, hard knowledge, too,
The mind's endeavors reach; and mysteries
Are like the sun, dazzling yet plain to all eyes.
Keep the truth which thou hast found. Men do not stand
In so ill case here that God hath with his hand
Signed Kings blank charters to kill whom they hate,
Nor are they Vicars but Hangmen to Fate.
Fool and wretch, wilt thou let thy soul be tied
To man's laws, by which she shall not be tried
At the last day? Oh, will it then boot thee
To say a Philip or a Gregory,
A Harry or a Martin taught thee this?
Is not this excuse for mere contraries,
Equally strong? Cannot both sides say so?
That thou mayst rightly obey power, her bounds know;

Those past, her nature and name is changed. To be
Then humble to her is idolatry.
As streams are, power is: those blest flowers that dwell
At the rough stream's calm head thrive and do well;
But, having left their roots and themselves given
To the stream's tyrannous rage, alas, are driven
Through mills and rocks and woods, and at last, almost
Consumed in going, in the sea are lost.
So perish souls which more choose men's unjust
Power from God claimed than God himself to trust.

The Calm

--•≪| *The calm succeeded "a fierce and tempestuous
storm full in our teeth, continuing for four days,"
during the Islands Voyage against Spain in midsummer of 1597. The lanthorns mentioned are ship's
ventilators. Jonson told Drummond in 1619, "he hath
by heart . . . that passage of* The Calm *that dust
and feathers do not stir, all is so quiet."*

Our storm is past, and that storm's tyrannous rage,
A stupid calm, but nothing it, doth 'suage.
The fable is inverted, and far more
A block afflicts, now, than a stork before.
Storms chafe, and soon wear out themselves, or us;
In calms, Heaven laughs to see us languish thus.
As steady as I can wish that my thoughts were,
Smooth as thy mistress' glass, or what shines there,
The sea is now. And as the isles which we
Seek when we can move, our ships rooted be.
As water did in storms, now pitch runs out:
As lead, when a fired church becomes one spout;
And all our beauty, and our trim, decays,

Like courts removing or like ended plays.
The fighting place now seamen's rags supply,
And all the tackling is a frippery.
No use of lanthorns, and in one place lay
Feathers and dust, today and yesterday.
Earth's hollownesses, which the world's lungs are,
Have no more wind than the upper vault of air.
We can nor lost friends nor sought foes recover,
But meteor-like, save that we move not, hover.
Only the calenture together draws
Dear friends, which meet dead in great fishes' jaws;
And on the hatches as on altars lies
Each one, his own priest and own sacrifice.
Who live, that miracle do multiply
Where walkers in hot ovens do not die.
If, in despite of these, we swim, that hath
No more refreshing than our brimstone bath,
But from the sea into the ship we turn,
Like parboiled wretches, on the coals to burn.
Like Bajazet encaged, the shepherd's scoff,
Or like slack-sinewed Samson, his hair off,
Languish our ships. Now, as a myriad
Of ants durst the emperor's loved snake invade,
The crawling galleys, sea jails, finny chips,
Might brave our pinnaces, now bedrid ships.
Whether a rotten state and hope of gain,
Or to disuse me from the queasy pain
Of being beloved and loving, or the thirst
Of honor or fair death out-pushed me first,
I lose my end, for here as well as I
A desperate may live and a coward die.
Stag, dog, and all which from or toward flies
Is paid with life or prey, or doing dies.
Fate grudges us all, and doth subtly lay
A scourge 'gainst which we all forget to pray:

He that at sea prays for more wind as well
Under the poles may beg cold, heat in hell.
What are we then? How little more, alas,
Is man now than before he was. He was
Nothing. For us, we are for nothing fit;
Chance or ourselves still disproportion it.
We have no power, no will, no sense. I lie.
I should not then thus feel this misery.

To Mr. Rowland Woodward

Like one who in her third widowhood doth profess
Herself a nun tied to retiredness,
So affects my muse now a chaste fallowness

Since she to few, yet to too many, hath shown
How love-song weeds and satiric thorns are grown
Where seeds of better arts were early sown.

Though to use and love poetry to me,
Betrothed to no one art, be no adultery,
Omissions of good, ill as ill deeds be.

For though to us it seem and be light and thin,
Yet in those faithful scales where God throws in
Men's works, vanity weighs as much as sin.

If our souls have stained their first white, yet we
May clothe them with faith and dear honesty,
Which God imputes as native purity.

There is no virtue but religion:
Wise, valiant, sober, just are names which none
Want which want not vice-covering discretion.

Seek we then ourselves in our selves. For as
Men force the sun with much more force to pass
By gathering his beams with a chrystal glass,

So we, if we into our selves will turn,
Blowing our sparks of virtue, may outburn
The straw which doth about our hearts sojourn.

You know physicians, when they would infuse
Into any oil the souls of simples, use
Places where they may lie still warm to choose;

So works retiredness in us. To roam
Giddily and be everywhere but at home,
Such freedom doth a banishment become.

We are but farmers of ourselves, yet may,
If we can stock ourselves and thrive, up-lay
Much, much dear treasure for the great rent day.

Manure thyself then, to thyself be approved,
And with vain outward things be no more moved,
But to know that I love thee and would be loved.

An Epithalamion, or Marriage Song

On the Lady Elizabeth and Count Palatine Being Married on St. Valentine's Day, 1613

1

Hail, Bishop Valentine, whose day this is.
   All the air is thy diocese,
   And all the chirping choristers
And other birds are thy parishioners.
   Thou marriest every year
The lyric lark and the grave whispering dove,

The sparrow, that neglects his life for love,
The household bird with the red stomacher;
   Thou mak'st the blackbird speed as soon
As doth the goldfinch or the halcyon;
The husband cock looks out and straight is sped,
And meets his wife, which brings her feather-bed.
This day more cheerfully than ever shine,
This day, which might inflame thyself, old Valentine.

   2

Till now thou warm'dst with multiplying loves
   Two larks, two sparrows, or two doves.
   All that is nothing unto this,
For thou this day couplest two phoenixes.
   Thou mak'st a taper see
What the sun never saw; and what the ark
(Which was of fowls and beasts the cage and park)
Did not contain, one bed contains through thee:
   Two phoenixes, whose joined breasts
Are unto one another mutual nests
Where motion kindles such fires as shall give
Young phoenixes. And yet the old shall live,
Whose love and courage never shall decline,
But make the whole year through, thy day, O Valentine.

   3

Up then, fair phoenix bride, frustrate the sun!
   Thyself from thine affection
   Tak'st warmth enough, and from thine eye
All lesser birds will take their jollity.
   Up, up, fair bride, and call
Thy stars from out their several boxes, take
Thy rubies, pearls, and diamonds forth, and make
Thyself a constellation of them all,
   And by their blazing signify
That a great princess falls, but doth not die.

Be thou a new star that to us portends
Ends of much wonder, and be thou those ends.
Since thou dost this day in new glory shine,
May all men date records from this thy valentine.

4

Come forth, come forth, and as one glorious flame
  Meeting another grows the same,
  So meet thy Frederick, and so
To an inseparable union grow.
  Since separation
Falls not on such things as are infinite,
Nor things which are but one can disunite,
You're twice inseparable, great, and one.
  Go then to where the bishop stays
To make you one, his way, which divers ways
Must be effected; and when all is past,
And that you're one, by hearts and hands made fast,
You two have one way left, yourselves t' entwine,
Besides this bishop's knot or Bishop Valentine.

5

But O, what ails the sun, that here he stays
  Longer today than other days?
  Stays he new light from these to get?
And finding here such store, is loath to set?
  And why do you two walk
So slowly pac'd in this procession?
Is all your care but to be look'd upon
And be to others spectacle and talk?
  The feast with gluttonous delays
Is eaten, and too long their meat they praise;
The maskers come late, and I think will stay
Like fairies till the cock crow them away.
  Alas, did not antiquity assign
A night as well as day to thee, O Valentine?

6

They did, and night is come; and yet we see
   Formalities retarding thee.
   What mean these ladies, which, as though
They were to take a clock in pieces, go
   So nicely about the bride?
A bride, before a good-night could be said,
Should vanish from her clothes into her bed,
As souls from bodies steal and are not spied.
   But now she's laid. What though she be?
Yet there are more delays. For where is he?
He comes, and passes through sphere after sphere,
First her sheets, then her arms, then anywhere.
   Let not this day, then, but this night be thine;
Thy day was but the eve to this, O Valentine.

7

Here lies a she-sun, and a he-moon here;
   She gives the best light to his sphere,
   Or each is both, and all, and so
They unto one another nothing owe;
   And yet they do, but are
So just and rich in that coin which they pay
That neither would, nor needs forbear nor stay.
Neither desires to be spar'd nor to spare;
   They quickly pay their debt, and then
Take no acquittances, but pay again;
They pay, they give, they lend, and so let fall
No such occasion to be liberal.
   More truth, more courage in these two do shine
Than all thy turtles have, and sparrows, Valentine.

8

And by this act of these two phoenixes
   Nature again restored is,
   For since these two are two no more,

There's but one phoenix still, as was before.
   Rest now at last, and we
(As satyrs watch the sun's uprise) will stay,
Waiting when your eyes open'd let out day,
Only desir'd because your face we see.
   Others near you shall whispering speak,
And wagers lay at which side day will break,
And win by observing then whose hand it is
That opens first a curtain, hers or his.
   This will be tried tomorrow after nine;
Till which hour we thy day enlarge, O Valentine.

Three Holy Sonnets

At the round earth's imagined corners, blow
Your trumpets, angels, and arise, arise
From death, you numberless infinities
Of souls, and to your scattered bodies go;
All whom the flood did, and fire shall o'erthrow;
All whom war, dearth, age, agues, tyrannies,
Despair, law, chance, hath slain, and you whose eyes
Shall behold God, and never taste death's woe.

But let them sleep, Lord, and me mourn a space,
For, if above all these, my sins abound,
'Tis late to ask abundance of Thy grace,
When we are there; here on this lowly ground,
Teach me how to repent, for that's as good
As if Thou hadst sealed my pardon with Thy blood.

    *   *   *

If poisonous minerals, and if that tree
Whose fruit threw death on else immortal us,
If lecherous goats, if serpents envious
Cannot be damned, alas, why should I be?

Why should intent or reason, born in me,
Make sins, else equal, in me more heinous?
And mercy being easy and glorious
To God, in his stern wrath why threatens he?

But who am I, that dare dispute with thee,
O God? O! of thine only worthy blood
And my tears, make a heavenly Lethean flood,
And drown in it my sin's black memory.
That thou remember them, some claim as debt,
I think it mercy, if thou wilt forget.

*   *   *

Death, be not proud, though some have callèd thee
Mighty and dreadful, for thou art not so;
For those whom thou think'st thou dost overthrow
Die not, poor Death, nor yet canst thou kill me.
From rest and sleep, which but thy pictures be,
Much pleasure; then from thee much more must flow;
And soonest our best men with thee do go—
Rest of their bones and souls' delivery!

Thou'rt slave to fate, chance, kings, and desperate men,
And dost with poison, war, and sickness dwell;
And poppy or charms can make us sleep as well
And better than thy stroke. Why swell'st thou then?
One short sleep past, we wake eternally,
And Death shall be no more: Death, thou shalt die.

A Hymn: To God the Father

Izaak Walton: "Yea, even on his former sick-bed he wrote this heavenly hymn expressing the great joy that then possessed his soul in the assurance of God's favor to him when he composed it."

Wilt thou forgive that sin where I begun,
Which is my sin though it were done before?
Wilt thou forgive those sins through which I run
And do them still, though still I do deplore?
  When thou hast done thou hast not done,
    For I have more.

Wilt thou forgive that sin by which I've won
Others to sin and made my sin their door?
Wilt thou forgive that sin which I did shun
A year or two, but wallowed in a score?
  When thou hast done thou hast not done,
    For I have more.

I have a sin of fear that when I've spun
My last thread I shall perish on the shore.
Swear by thyself that at my death thy Sun
Shall shine as it shines now and heretofore.
  And having done that thou hast done;
    I have no more.

BEN JONSON

---✠ *Jonson (1572–1637). It was said in 1629: "And we, that Latin studied have so long, Shall now dispute and write in Jonson's tongue."*

On Old Colt

For all night-sins with others' wives, unknown,
Colt now doth daily penance in his own.

On My First Son

Farewell, thou child of my right hand, and joy;
My sin was too much hope of thee, loved boy.
Seven years thou wert lent to me, and I thee pay,
Exacted by thy fate, on the just day.
O, could I lose all father now. For why
Will man lament the state he should envy?
To have so soon 'scaped world's and flesh's rage,
And, if no other misery, yet age?
Rest in soft peace and, asked, say *Here doth lie
Ben Jonson his best piece of poetry;*
For whose sake, henceforth, all his vows be such
As what he loves may never like too much.

To Heaven

Good and great God, can I not think of thee
But it must straight my melancholy be?

[222]

Is it interpreted in me disease
That, laden with my sins, I seek for ease?
O be thou witness that the reins dost know
And hearts of all, if I be sad for show,
And judge me after if I dare pretend
To aught but grace, or aim at other end.
As thou art all, so be thou all to me,
First, midst, and last, converted one and three,
My faith, my hope, my love, and in this state
My judge, my witness, and my advocate.
Where have I been this while, exiled from thee,
And whither rapt now thou but stoopst to me?
Dwell, dwell here still! O, being everywhere,
How can I doubt to find thee ever here?
I know my state, both full of shame and scorn,
Conceived in sin and unto labor born,
Standing with fear, and must with horror fall,
And destined unto judgement after all.
I feel my griefs too, and there scarce is ground
Upon my flesh to inflict another wound,
Yet dare I not complain, or wish for death
With holy Paul, lest it be thought the breath
Of discontent, or that these prayers be
For weariness of life, not love of thee.

A Nymph's Passion

I love and he loves me again,
Yet dare I not tell who;
For if the nymphs should know my swain,
I fear they'd love him too;
Yet if it be not known,
The pleasure is as good as none,
For that's a narrow joy is but our own.

I'll tell, that if they be not glad,
They yet may envy me;
But then if I grow jealous mad,
And of them pitied be,
It were a plague 'bove scorn;
And yet it cannot be forborne
Unless my heart would as my thought be torn.

He is, if they can find him, fair,
And fresh and fragrant, too,
As summer's sky or purged air,
And looks as lilies do
That were this morning blown;
Yet, yet I doubt he is not known,
And fear much more that more of him be shown.

But he has eyes so round and bright
As make away my doubt,
Where Love may all his torches light
Though hate had put them out;
But then to increase my fears,
What nymph soe'er his voice but hears
Will be my rival, though she have but ears.

I'll tell no more, and yet I love,
And he loves me; yet no
One unbecoming thought doth move
From either heart, I know;
But so exempt from blame
As it would be to each a fame
If love or fear would let me tell his name.

The Dream

Or scorn or pity on me take;
I must the true relation make:

I am undone tonight.
Love, in a subtle dream disguised,
Hath both my heart and me surprised,
Whom never yet he durst attempt awake.
Nor will he tell me for whose sake
He did me the delight
Or spite,
But leaves me to inquire,
In all my wild desire,
Of sleep again, who was his aid;
And sleep so guilty and afraid
As since he dares not come within my sight.

An Epistle to a Friend

--◆{ *"To persuade him to the wars," lines 31 to 58.*

The whole world here leavened with madness swells,
And being a thing blown out of nought, rebels
Against his Maker: high alone with weeds
And impious rankness of all sects and seeds,
Not to be checked or frighted now with fate,
But more licentious made and desperate!
Our delicacies are grown capital,
And even our sports are dangers. What we call
Friendship is now masked hatred; justice fled,
And shamefastness together; all laws dead
That kept men living; pleasures only sought;
Honor and honesty as poor things thought
As they are made; pride and stiff clownage mixed
To make up greatness; and man's whole good fixed
In bravery or gluttony or coin,
All which he makes the servants of the groin;

Thither it flows. How much did Stallion spend
To have his court-bred filly there commend
His lace and starch, and fall upon her back
In admiration, stretched upon the rack
Of lust, to his rich suit and title. Lord?
Aye, that's a charm and a half! She must afford
That all respect; she must lie down. Nay, more,
'Tis there civility to be a whore.
He's one of blood and fashion! And with these
The bravery makes, she can no honor lose:
To do it with cloth or stuffs, lust's name might merit;
With velvet, plush, and tissues, it is spirit.

The Mind of the Frontispiece to a Book

--•◖ *Printed opposite the frontispiece of Ralegh's*
History of the World (*1614*). *The poem exactly*
describes the frontispiece.

From death and dark oblivion, near the same,
The mistress of man's life, grave History,
Raising the world to good or evil fame,
Doth vindicate it to eternity.
Wise providence would so, that nor the good
Might be defrauded nor the great secured,
But both might know their ways were understood
When vice alike in time with virtue 'dured.
Which makes that (lighted by the beamy hand
Of Truth that searcheth the most hidden springs,
And guided by Experience, whose straight wand
Doth mete, whose line doth sound the depth of things)
She cheerfully supporteth what she rears,
Assisted by no strengths but are her own,
Some note of which each varied pillar bears,

By which, as proper titles, she is known:
Time's witness, herald of Antiquity,
The light of Truth and life of Memory.

An Elegy

Since you must go and I must bid farewell,
Hear, mistress, your departing servant tell
What it is like; and do not think they can
Be idle words, though of a parting man.
It is as if a night should shade noonday,
Or that the sun was here, but forced away,
And we were left under that hemisphere
Where we must feel it dark for half a year.
What fate is this, to change men's days and hours,
To shift their seasons and destroy their powers!
Alas, I have lost my heat, my blood, my prime;
Winter is come a quarter ere his time.
My health will leave me; and when you depart,
How shall I do, sweet mistress, for my heart?
You would restore it? No, that's worth a fear,
As if it were not worthy to be there.
O, keep it still, for it had rather be
Your sacrifice than here remain with me.
And so I spare it. Come what can become
Of me, I'll softly tread unto my tomb,
Or like a ghost walk silent amongst men
Till I may see both it and you again.

To the Right Honorable, the Lord High Treasurer of England
An Epistle Mendicant

My Lord:
Poor wretched states, pressed by extremities,

Are fain to seek for succors, and supplies
Of princes' aids or good men's charities.

Disease, the enemy, and his engineers,
Want, with the rest of his concealed compeers,
Have cast a trench about me, now, five years,

And made those strong approaches by false brayes,
Reduits, half-moons, horn-works, and such close ways
The Muse not peeps out one of hundred days,

But lies blocked up and straightened, narrowed in,
Fixed to the bed and boards, unlike to win
Health or scarce breath, as she had never been,

Unless some saving honor of the Crown
Dare think it, to relieve, no less renown,
A bed-rid wit, than a besieged town.

A Spectacle of Strangeness

From The Masque of Queens (*1609*).

It increasing, now, to the third time of my being used in these
services to Her Majesty's personal presentations with the ladies
whom she pleaseth to honor, it was my first and special regard
to see that the nobility of the invention should be answerable
to the dignity of their persons. For which reason, I chose the
argument to be a celebration of honorable and true fame bred
out of virtue, observing that rule of the best artist, to suffer
no object of delight to pass without his mixture of profit and
example.

And because Her Majesty (best knowing that a principal part of life in these spectacles lay in their variety) had commanded me to think on some dance or show that might precede hers, and have the place of a foil or false-masque, I was careful to decline not only from others', but mine own steps in that kind, since the last year I had an anti-masque of boys; and therefore now devised that twelve women, in the habit of hags or witches, sustaining the persons of Ignorance, Suspicion, Credulity, etc. (the opposites to good Fame), should fill that part—not as a masque, but a spectacle of strangeness, producing multiplicity of gesture and not unaptly sorting with the current and whole fall of the device.

First, then, His Majesty being set and the whole company in full expectation, that which presented itself was an ugly Hell which, flaming beneath, smoked unto the top of the roof. And, in respect all evils are (morally) said to come from Hell (as also from that observation of Torrentius upon Horace's *Canidia:* "*Quae tot instructa venenis, ex Orci faucibus profecta videri possit*"), these witches, with a kind of hollow and infernal music, came forth from thence: first one, then two and three and more, till their number increased to eleven; all differently attired, some with rats on their heads, some on their shoulders, others with ointment-pots at their girdles; all with spindles, timbrels, rattles, or other veneficall instruments, making a confused noise with strange gestures. (The device of their attire was Mr. Jones', with the invention and architecture of the whole scene. Only I prescribed them their properties of vipers, snakes, bones, herbs, roots, and other engines of their magic, out of the authority of ancient and late writers; wherein the faults are mine, if there be any found, and for that cause I confess them.)

These eleven witches beginning to dance (which is an usual ceremony at their convents or meetings, where sometimes also they are vizarded and masked), on the sudden one of them missed their chief, and interrupted the rest with this speech:

Sisters, stay; we want our Dame.
Call upon her by her name,
And the charm we use to say,
That she quickly anoint and come away.

1. Charm

Dame, Dame, the watch is set.
Quickly come, we all are met.
From the lakes and from the fens,
From the rocks and from the dens,
From the woods and from the caves,
From the church yards, from the graves,
From the dungeon, from the tree
That they die on, here are we.
Comes she not yet?
Strike another heat.

2. Charm

The weather is fair, the wind is good;
Up, Dame, on your horse of wood.
Or else tuck up your gray frock,
And saddle your goat or your green cock,
And make his bridle a bottom of thread
To roll up how many miles you have rid.
Quickly come away;
For we all stay.

Nor yet? Nay, then,
We'll try her again.

3. Charm

The owl is abroad, the bat and the toad,
And so is the cat-a-mountain;
The ant and the mole sit both in a hole,

And frog peeps out of the fountain;
The dogs they do bay, and the timbrels play,
The spindle is now a-turning;
The moon it is red, and the stars are fled,
But all the sky is a-burning.
The ditch is made, and our nails the spade,
With pictures full of wax and of wool.
Their livers I stick with needles quick;
There lacks but the blood to make up the flood.
Quickly, Dame, then; bring your part in.
Spur, spur upon little Martin.
Merely, merely, make him sail:
A worm in his mouth and a thorn in his tail,
Fire above and fire below,
With a whip in your hand to make him go.

O, now she's come!
Let all be dumb.

At this, the Dame entered to them, naked-armed, barefooted,
her frock tucked, her hair knotted and folded with vipers; in
her hand, a torch made of a dead man's arm, lighted; girded
with a snake. To whom they all did reverence; and she spake,
uttering by way of question the end wherefore they came.
(Which, if it had been done either before or otherwise, had
not been so natural. For to have made themselves their own
decipherers, and each one to have told, upon their entrance,
what they were and whither they would, had been a most
piteous hearing and utterly unworthy any quality of a poem:
wherein a writer should always trust somewhat to the capacity
of the spectator, especially at these spectacles, where men, beside inquiring eyes, are understood to bring quick ears, and
not those sluggish ones of porters and mechanics that must be
bored through at every act with narrations.)

DAME: Well done, my hags. And come we, fraught with spite,
To overthrow the glory of this night?
Holds our great purpose?

HAGS: Yes.

DAME: But wants there none
Of our just number?

HAGS: Call us, one by one,
And then our Dame shall see.

DAME: First, then, advance
My drowsy servant, stupid Ignorance,
Known by thy scaly vesture; and bring on
Thy fearful sister, wild Suspicion,
Whose eyes do never sleep. Let her knit hands
With quick Credulity that next her stands,
Who hath but one ear, and that always ope.
Two-faced Falsehood follow in the rope,
And lead on Murmur with the cheeks deep hung;
She, Malice, whetting of her forked tongue,
And Malice, Impudence, whose forehead's lost.
Let Impudence lead Slander on, to boast
Her oblique look; and to her subtle side,
Thou, black-mouthed Execration, stand applied.
Draw to thee Bitterness, whose pores sweat gall;
She, flame-eyed Rage; Rage, Mischief.

HAGS: Here we are all.

DAME: Join now our hearts, we faithful opposites
To Fame and Glory. Let not these bright nights
Of Honor blaze thus to offend our eyes.
Show ourselves truly envious, and let rise
Our wonted rages. Do what may beseem
Such names and natures. Virtue, else, will deem
Our powers decreased, and think us banished earth

No less than heaven. All her antique birth,
As Justice, Faith, she will restore; and, bold
Upon our sloth, retrieve her Age of Gold.
We must not let our native manners, thus,
Corrupt with ease. Ill lives not but in us.
I hate to see these fruits of a soft peace,
And curse the piety gives it such increase.
Let us disturb it, then, and blast the light,
Mix Hell with Heaven and make Nature fight
Within herself, loose the whole hinge of things,
And cause the ends run back into their springs.

HAGS: What our Dame bids us do,
We are ready for.

DAME: Then fall to.
But first relate me what you have sought,
Where you have been, and what you have brought.

HAGS:

1.

I have been all day looking after
A raven feeding upon a quarter;
And soon as she turned her beak to the south,
I snatched this morsel out of her mouth.

2.

I have been gathering wolves' hairs,
The mad dog's foam, and the adder's ears,
The spurging of a dead man's eyes:
And all since the Evening Star did rise.

3.

I, last night, lay all alone
On the ground to hear the Mandrake groan,
And plucked him up though he grew full low,
And, as I had done, the cock did crow.

4.

And I have been choosing out this skull
From charnel houses that were full,
From private grots and public pits,
And frightened a sexton out of his wits.

5.

Under a cradle I did creep
By day; and when the child was asleep
At night, I sucked the breath, and rose
And plucked the nodding nurse by the nose.

6.

I had a dagger. What did I with that?
Killed an infant to have his fat.
A piper it got at a church-ale;
I bade him again blow wind in the tail.

7.

A murderer yonder was hung in chains;
The sun and the wind had shrunk his veins.
I bit off a sinew; I clipped his hair;
I brought off his rags that danced in the air.

8.

The screech-owl's eggs and the feathers black,
The blood of the frog and the bone in his back,
I have been getting, and made of his skin
A purset to keep Sir Cranion in.

9.

And I have been plucking plants among:
Hemlock, henbane, adder's-tongue,
Nightshade, moonwort, leopard's-bane;
And twice by the dogs was like to be ta'en.

10.

I, from the jaws of a gardener's bitch,
Did snatch these bones and then leaped the ditch;
Yet went I back to the house again,
Killed the black cat—and here's the brain.

11.

I went to the toad breeds under the wall;
I charmed him out and he came at my call;
I scratched out the eyes of the owl before;
I tore the bat's wing. What would you have more?

DAME.

12.

Yes, I have brought (to help our vows)
Horned poppy, cypress boughs,
The fig-tree wild, that grows on tombs,
And juice that from the larch-tree comes,
The basilisk's blood, and the viper's skin.
And now our orgies let's begin.

Here the Dame put herself into the midst of them, and began her following invocation wherein she took occasion to boast all the power attributed to witches by the ancients, of which every poet (or the most) doth give some. . . .

DAME: You fiends and furies (if yet any be
Worse than ourselves), you that have quaked to see
These knots untied, and shrunk when we have charmed;
You, that to arm us have yourselves disarmed,
And to our powers resigned your whips and brands
When we went forth, the scourge of men and lands;
You, that have seen me ride when Hecate
Durst not take chariot, when the boisterous sea,
Without a breath of wind, hath knocked the sky,

And that hath thundered, Jove not knowing why:
When we have set the elements at wars,
Made midnight see the sun, the day the stars;
When the winged lightning in the course hath stayed,
And swiftest rivers have run back, afraid
To see the corn remove, the groves to range,
Whole places alter, and the seasons change;
When the pale moon, at the first voice, down fell
Poisoned, and durst not stay the second spell:
You, that have oft been conscious of these sights,
And thou, three-formed star, that on these nights
Art only powerful, to whose triple name
Thus we incline—once, twice, and thrice-the-same:
If now with rites profane and foul enough
We do invoke thee, darken all this roof
With present fogs. Exhale earth's rottenest vapors,
And strike a blindness through these blazing tapers.

> Come, let a murmuring charm resound
> The whilst we bury all in the ground;
> But first, see every foot be bare,
> And every knee.

HAGS: Yes, Dame; they are.

4. Charm
> Deep, O deep, we lay thee to sleep;
> We leave thee drink by, if thou chance to be dry:
> Both milk and blood, the dew and the flood.
> We breathe in thy bed, at the foot and the head.
> We cover thee warm, that thou take no harm.
> And, when thou dost wake,
> Dame Earth shall quake,
> And the houses shake,
> And her belly shall ache
> As her back were brake,

  Such a birth to make
  As is the blue Drake
  Whose form thou shalt take.

DAME: Never a star yet shot?
  Where be the ashes?

HAGS: Here, in the pot.

DAME: Cast them up, and the flint stone
  Over the left shoulder bone
  Into the west.

HAGS: It will be best.

5. Charm

The sticks are across; there can be no loss;
The sage is rotten; the sulphur is gotten
Up to the sky, that was in the ground.
Follow it, then, with our rattles, round.
Under the bramble, over the briar;
A little more heat will set it on fire.
Put it in mind to do it kind;
Flow water and blow wind.
Rouncy is over, Robble is under;
A flash of light and a clap of thunder;
A storm of rain, another of hail;
We all must home in the egg-shell sail.
The mast is made of a great pin,
The tackle of cobweb, the sail as thin;
And if we go through, and not fall in—

DAME: Stay! All our charms do nothing win
Upon the night. Our labor dies!
Our magic feature will not rise,
Nor yet the storm! We must repeat
More direful voices far, and beat
The ground with vipers till it sweat.

6. *Charm*

HAGS: Bark dogs, wolves howl,
   Seas roar, woods roll,
   Clouds crack; all be black
   But the light our charms do make.

DAME: Not yet? My rage begins to swell.
Darkness, Devils, Night and Hell,
Do not thus delay my spell.
I call you once, I call you twice;
I beat you again if you stay me thrice.
Through these crannies where I peep,
I'll let in the light to see your sleep;
And all the secrets of your sway
Shall lie as open to the day
As unto me. Still are you deaf?
Reach me a bough that ne'er bare leaf,
To strike the air; and aconite,
To hurl upon this glaring light;
A rusty knife, to wound mine arm;
And as it drops I'll speak a charm
Shall cleave the ground as low as lies
Old shrunk-up Chaos, and let rise
Once more his dark and reeking head,
To strike the world and Nature dead
Until my magic birth be bred.

7. *Charm*

HAGS: Black go in and blacker come out;
   At thy going down, we give thee a shout:
   Hoo!
   At thy rising again, thou shalt have two;
   And if thou dost what we would have thee do,
   Thou shalt have three, thou shalt have four,
   Thou shalt have ten, thou shalt have a score.
   Hoo, Har, Har, Hoo.

8. *Charm*

A cloud of pitch, a spur and a switch,
To haste him away; and a whirlwind play
Before and after, with thunder for laughter,
And storms for joy of the roaring boy:
His head of a Drake, his tail of a snake.

9. *Charm*

About, about, and about,
Till the mist arise and the lights fly out;
The images neither be seen nor felt;
The woolen burn and the waxen melt;
Sprinkle your liquors upon the ground
And into the air. Around, around,
Around, around,
Around, around,
Till a music sound,
And a pace be found
To which we may dance
And our charms advance.

At which, with a strange and sudden music, they fell into a
magical dance, full of preposterous change and gesticulation,
but most applying to their property; who, at their meetings, do
all things contrary to the custom of men, dancing back to back,
hip to hip, their hands joined, and making their circles backward
to the left hand, with strange fantastic motions of their heads
and bodies. (All which were excellently imitated by the maker
of the dance, Mr. Jerome Herne, whose right it is here to be
named.)

In the heat of their dance, on the sudden was heard a sound
of loud music, as if many instruments had given one blast. With
which, not only the hags themselves, but their Hell into which
they ran, quite vanished; and the whole face of the scene altered,
scarce suffering the memory of any such thing. But in the place

of it appeared a glorious and magnificent building, figuring the House of Fame, in the upper part of which were discovered twelve masquers sitting upon a throne triumphal, erected in form of a pyramid and circled with all store of light.

Lovers Made Men [1617]

The front before the scene was an arch-triumphal, on the top of which Humanity, placed in figure, sat with her lap full of flowers— scattering them with her right hand and holding a golden chain in her left hand, to show both the freedom and the bond of Courtesy —with this inscription: SUPER OMNIA VULTUS. On the two sides of the arch, Cheerfulness and Readiness, her servants: Cheerfulness in a loose flowing garment, filling out wine from an antique piece of plate, with this word, ADSIT LAETITIAE DATOR; Readiness, a winged maid with two flaming bright lights in her hands, and her word, AMOR ADDIDIT ALAS.

The scene discovered is, on the one side, the head of a boat, and in it Charon putting off from the shore, having landed certain imaginary ghosts, whom Mercury there receives and encourageth to come on towards the river Lethe, who appears lying in the person of an old man: the Fates sitting beside him on his bank, a grove of myrtles behind them presented in perspective and growing thicker to the outer side of the scene. Mercury, perceiving them to faint, calls them on and shows them his golden rod.

MERCURY: Nay, faint not now, so near the fields of rest.
Here no more Furies, no more torments dwell,
Than each hath felt already in his breast.
Who hath been once in love hath proved his Hell.
Up then, and follow this, my golden rod,
That points you next to aged Lethe's shore,
Who pours his waters from his urn abroad,
Of which, but tasting, you shall faint no more.

LETHE: Stay! Who or what fantastic shades are these
That Hermes leads?

MER.:   They are the gentle forms
Of lovers, tossed upon those frantic seas
Whence Venus sprung.

LETHE: And have rid out her storms?

MER.: No.

LETHE: Did they perish?

MER.:   Yes.

LETHE: How?

MER.:   Drowned by Love,
That drew them forth with hopes as smooth as were
The unfaithful waters he desired them prove.

LETHE: And turned a tempest when he had them there?

MER.: He did. And on the billow would he roll,
And laugh to see one throw his heart away,
Another, sighing, vapor forth his soul,
A third to melt himself in tears and say,

"O Love, I now to salter water turn
Than that I die in;" then a fourth to cry
Amid the surges, "Oh! I burn, I burn!"
A fifth laugh out, "It is my ghost, not I."

And thus in pairs I found them. Only one
There is that walks and stops and shakes his head,
And shuns the rest as glad to be alone,
And whispers to himself he is not dead.

FATES: No more are all the rest.

MER.:   No?

I. FATE: No.

MER.:   But why
Proceeds this doubtful voice from destiny?

FATES: It is too sure.

MER.:   Sure?

2. FATE: Aye. Thinks Mercury
That any things or names on earth do die
That are obscured from knowledge of the Fates,
Who keep all rolls?

3. FATE: And know all natures' dates.

MER.: They say, themselves, they are dead.

1. FATE: It not appears:
Or by our rock,

2. FATE: Our spindle,

3. FATE: Or our shears.

FATES: Here all their threads are growing yet—none cut.

MER.: I begin to doubt that Love, with charms, hath put
This fancy in them, and they only think
That they are ghosts.

1. FATE: If so, then let them drink
Of Lethe's stream.

2. FATE: 'Twill make them to forget
Love's name.

3. FATE: And so, they may recover yet!

MER: Do bow unto the reverend lake,
And having touched there, up, and shake
The shadows off, which yet do make
Us you, and you yourselves, mistake.

*Here they all stoop to the water, and dance forth their Anti-
masque in several gestures, as they lived in love. And retiring
into the grove, before the last person be off the stage the first*

couple appear in their posture between the trees, ready to come forth changed.

MER.: See! See! They are themselves again!

1. FATE: Yes, now they are substances, and men.

2. FATE: Love at the name of Lethe flies.

LETHE: For in oblivion drowned he dies.

3. FATE: He must not hope, though other states
He oft subdue, he can the Fates.

FATES: 'Twere insolence to think his powers
Can work on us or equal ours.

CHORUS: Return, return,
Like lights to burn
On earth
For others' good.
Your second birth
Will fame old Lethe's flood,
And warn a world,
That now are hurled
About in tempest, how they prove
Shadows for Love.
Leap forth. Your light it is the nobler made
By being struck out of a shade.

Here they dance forth their entry, or first dance, after which Cupid, appearing, meets them.

CUPID: Why, now you take me! These are rites
That grace Love's days and crown his nights!
These are the motions I would see
And praise in them that follow me.
Not sighs, nor tears, nor wounded hearts,
Nor flames, nor ghosts, but airy parts

Tried and refined as yours have been;
And such they are I glory in!

MER.: Look, look unto this snaky rod,
And stop your ears against the charming god.
His every word falls from him is a snare,
Who have so lately known him should beware.

Here they dance their main dance, which ended—

CUPID: Come, do not call it Cupid's crime
You were thought dead before your time.
If thus you move to Hermes' will
Alone, you will be thought so still.
Go, take the ladies forth, and talk,
And touch, and taste too. Ghosts can walk.
'Twixt eyes, tongues, hands, the mutual strife
Is bred that tries the truth of life.
They do, indeed, like dead men move
That think they live, and not in love!

Here they take forth the Ladies,
and the revels follow. After which—

MER.: Nay, you should never have left off,
But stayed and heard your Cupid scoff
To find you in the line you were.

CUPID: Your too much wit breeds too much fear.

MER.: Good Fly, good night.

CUPID: But will you go?
Can you leave Love, and he entreat you so?
Here, take my quiver and my bow,
My torches too, that you, by all, may know
I mean no danger to your stay.
This night I will create my holiday,
And be yours, naked and entire.

MER.: As if that Love disarmed were less a fire?
Away, away!

They dance their going out, which done—

MER.: Yet lest that Venus' wanton son
Should with the world be quite undone,
For your fair sakes (you brighter stars,
Who have beheld these civil wars),
Fate is content these lovers here
Remain still such, so Love will swear
Never to force them act to do
But what he will call Hermes, too.

CUPID: I swear, and with like cause thank **Mercury**,
As these have, to thank him and destiny.

CHORUS: All then take cause of joy, for who hath not?
Old Lethe, that their follies are forgot;
We, that their lives unto their fates they fit;
They, that they still shall love, and love with wit.

ANONYMOUS

"A Yorkshire Tragedy. Not so New as Lamentable and true. Acted by his Maiesties Players at the Globe. Written by W. Shakespeare." "All's One, or, One of the foure plaies in one, called A York-shire Tragedy." London, 1608. The gentleman, Walter Calverley, was executed for murder, August 5, 1605. Most scholars believe this is not Shakespeare's work.

A Yorkshire Tragedy

Enter Oliver and Ralph, two servingmen.

OLIVER: Sirrah Ralph, my young mistress is in such a pitiful passionate humor for the long absence of her love—

RALPH: Why, can you blame her? Why, apples, hanging longer on the tree than when they are ripe, makes so many fallings; viz., mad wenches, because they are not gathered in time, are fain to drop of themselves. And then 'tis common, you know, for every man to take them up.

OLIVER: Mass, thou sayest true. 'Tis common, indeed. But, sirrah, is neither our young master returned, nor our fellow Sam come from London?

RALPH: Neither of either, as the Puritan bawd says. 'Slid, I hear Sam. Sam's come! Here's! Tarry! Come, i' faith; now my nose itches for news.

OLIVER: And so does mine elbow.

SAM *calls within.* Where are you there? Boy, look you walk my horse with discretion; I have rid him simply. I warrant his skin sticks to his back with very heat. If he should catch cold, and get the cough of the lungs, I were well served, were I not?

Enter Sam, furnished with things from London.

SAM: What, Ralph and Oliver!

BOTH: Honest fellow Sam, welcome, i' faith! What tricks hast thou brought from London?

SAM: You see I am hanged after the truest fashion: three hats, and two glasses bobbing upon 'em, two rebato wires upon my breast, a cap case by my side, a brush at my back, an almanac in my pocket and three ballads in my codpiece. Nay, I am the true picture of a common servingman.

OLIVER: I'll swear thou art. Thou mayest set up when thou wilt. There's many a one begins with less, I can tell thee, that proves a rich man ere he dies. But what's the news from London, Sam?

RALPH: Aye, that's well said. What's the news from London, sirrah? My young mistress keeps such a puling for her love.

SAM: Why, the more fool she; aye, the more ninny-hammer she.

OLIVER: Why, Sam, why?

SAM: Why, he's married to another long ago.

BOTH: I' faith, ye jest.

SAM: Why, did you not know that till now? Why, he's married, beats his wife, and has two or three children by her. For you must note that any woman bears the more when she is beaten.

RALPH: Aye, that's true, for she bears the blows.

OLIVER: Sirrah Sam, I would not, for two years' wages, my young mistress knew so much. She'd run upon the left hand of her wit, and ne'er be her own woman again.

SAM: And I think she was blessed in her cradle that he never came in her bed. Why, he has consumed all, pawned his lands, and made his university brother stand in wax for him. (There's a fine phrase for a scrivener!) Puh, he owes more than his skin's worth.

OLIVER: Is't possible?

SAM: Nay, I'll tell you, moreover, he calls his wife "whore" as familiarly as one would call Moll and Doll, and his children "bastards" as naturally as can be.—But what have we here? I thought 'twas somewhat pulled down my breeches: I quite forgot my two poting-sticks. These came from London. Now, anything is good here that comes from London.

OLIVER: Aye, far-fetched, you know.

SAM: But speak in your conscience, i' faith: have not we as good poting sticks i' th' country as need to be put i' th' fire? The mind of a thing's all, and as thou saidst e'en now, far-fetched is the best things for ladies.

OLIVER: Aye, and for waiting-gentlewomen, too.

SAM: But, Ralph, what, is our beer sour this thunder?

OLIVER: No, no. It holds countenance yet.

SAM: Why, then, follow me. I'll teach you the finest humor to be drunk in. I learned it at London last week.

BOTH: I' faith, let's hear it, let's hear it.

SAM: The bravest humor! 'Twould do a man good to be drunk in't; they call it "knighting" in London, when they drink upon their knees.

BOTH: Faith, that's excellent. Come, follow me. I'll give you all the degrees on't in order.   *Exeunt.*

Enter Wife.

WIFE: What will become of us? All will away.
My husband never ceases in expense,

Both to consume his credit and his house;
And 'tis set down by Heaven's just decree
That Riot's child must needs be Beggary.
Are these the virtues that his youth did promise?
Dice, and voluptuous meetings, midnight revels,
Taking his bed with surfeits: ill beseeming
The ancient honor of his house and name!
And this not all, but that which kills me most:
When he recounts his losses and false fortunes,
The weakness of his state so much dejected,
Not as a man repentant, but half mad
His fortunes cannot answer his expense,
He sits and sullenly locks up his arms,
Forgetting Heaven looks downward, which makes him
Appear so dreadful that he frights my heart;
Walks heavily, as if his soul were earth,
Not penitent for those his sins are past,
But vexed his money cannot make them last:
A fearful melancholy, ungodly sorrow.
Oh, yonder he comes. Now, in despite of ills,
I'll speak to him, and I will hear him speak,
And do my best to drive it from his heart.

Enter Husband.

HUSBAND: Pox o' th' last throw! It made
Five hundred angels vanish from my sight.
I'm damned, I'm damned: the angels have forsook me.
Nay, 'tis certainly true; for he that has
No coin is damned in this world: he's gone, he's gone!

WIFE: Dear husband!

HUSBAND: Oh! most punishment of all: I have a wife.

WIFE: I do entreat you, as you love your soul,
Tell me the cause of this your discontent.

HUSBAND: A vengeance strip thee naked! thou art cause,
Effect, quality, property, thou, thou, thou!   *Exit.*

WIFE: Bad, turned to worse! Both beggary of the soul
As of the body; and so much unlike
Himself at first, as if some vexed spirit
Had got his form upon him.—   *Enter Husband again.*
                    He comes again.
He says I am the cause; I never yet
Spoke less than words of duty and of love.

HUSBAND: If marriage be honorable, then cuckolds are honorable;
for they cannot be made without marriage. Fool! What meant I
to marry to get beggars? Now must my eldest son be a knave or
a nothing. He cannot live upon the fool, for he will have no
land to maintain him: that mortgage sits like a snaffle upon mine
inheritance, and makes me chaw upon iron. My second son must
be a promoter, and my third a thief or an underputter, a slave-
pander. Oh, beggary, beggary, to what base uses thou dost put
a man! I think the Devil scorns to be a bawd; he bears himself
more proudly, has more care on's credit. Base, slavish, abject,
filthy poverty!

WIFE: Good sir, by all our vows I do beseech you,
Show me the true cause of your discontent.

HUSBAND: Money, money, money; and thou must supply me.

WIFE: Alas, I am the least cause of your discontent,
Yet what is mine, either in rings or jewels,
Use to your own desire. But I beseech you,
As you're a gentleman by many bloods,
Though I myself be out of your respect,
Think on the state of these three lovely boys
You have been father to.

HUSBAND: Puh! Bastards, bastards, bastards; begot in tricks, begot
in tricks.

WIFE: Heaven knows how those words wrong me, but I may
Endure these griefs among a thousand more.
Oh, call to mind your lands already mortgaged,
Yourself wound into debts, your hopeful brother
At the university in bonds for you,
Like to be seized upon. And—

HUSBAND: Ha' done, thou harlot,
Whom, though for fashion's sake I married,
I never could abide. Thinkst thou thy words
Shall kill my pleasures? Fall off to thy friends;
Thou and thy bastards beg. I will not bate
A whit in humor! Midnight, still I love you
And revel in your company. Curbed in,
Shall it be said in all societies
That I broke custom, that I flagged in money?
No, those thy jewels I will play as freely
As when my state was fullest.

WIFE: Be it so.

HUSBAND: Nay, I protest (and take that for an earnest)
                                        Spurns her.

I will forever hold thee in contempt,
And never touch the sheets that cover thee,
But be divorced in bed till thou consent
Thy dowry shall be sold to give new life
Unto those pleasures which I most affect.

WIFE: Sir, do but turn a gentle eye on me,
And what the law shall give me leave to do
You shall command.

HUSBAND: Look it be done. Shall I want dust and, like a slave,
Wear nothing in my pockets but my hands,
To fill them up with nails?   *Holding his hands in his pockets.*
Oh, much against my blood! Let it be done.
I was never made to be a looker-on,

A bawd to dice. I'll shake the drabs myself
And make 'em yield. I say, look it be done.

WIFE: I take my leave. It shall.   *Exit.*

HUSBAND: Speedily, speedily. I hate the very hour I chose a wife.
A trouble, trouble! Three children, like three evils, hang upon
me. Fie, fie, fie, strumpet and bastards!

Enter three gentlemen, hearing him.

1 GENT.: Still do those loathsome thoughts jar on your tongue?
Yourself to stain the honor of your wife,
Nobly descended! Those whom men call mad
Endanger others; but he's more than mad
That wounds himself, whose own words do proclaim
Scandals unjust, to soil his better name.
It is not fit; I pray, forsake it.

2 GENT.: Good sir, let modesty reprove you.

3 GENT.: Let honest kindness sway so much with you.

HUSBAND: Good e'en, I thank you, sir! How do you? Adieu! I'm
glad to see you. Farewell. Instructions! Admonitions!

Exeunt gentlemen.

Enter a servant.

HUSBAND: How now, sirrah, what would you?

SERVANT: Only to certify you, sir, that my mistress was met by
the way by them who were sent for her up to London by her
honorable uncle, your worship's late guardian.

HUSBAND: So, sir, then she is gone and so may you be. But let
her look that the thing be done she wots of, or hell will stand
more pleasant than her house at home.   *Exit Servant.*

Enter a gentleman.

GENT.: Well or ill met, I care not.

HUSBAND: No, nor I.

GENT.: I am come with confidence to chide you.

HUSBAND: Who? me?
Chide me? Do't finely then. Let it not move me,
For if thou chid'st me angry, I shall strike.

GENT.: Strike thine own follies, for it is they deserve
To be well beaten. We are now in private;
There's none but thou and I. Thou'rt fond and peevish,
An unclean rioter; thy lands and credit
Lie now both sick of a consumption.
I am sorry for thee. That man spends with shame
That with his riches does consume his name,
And such art thou.

HUSBAND: Peace!

GENT.: No, thou shalt hear me further.
Thy father's and forefathers' worthy honors,
Which were our country monuments, our grace,
Follies in thee begin now to deface.
The spring time of thy youth did fairly promise
Such a most fruitful summer to thy friends,
It scarce can enter into men's beliefs
Such dearth can hang on thee. We that see it
Are sorry to believe it. In thy change
This voice into all places will be hurled:
Thou and the devil has deceived the world.

HUSBAND: I'll not endure thee.

GENT.: But of all, the worst:
Thy virtuous wife, right honorably allied,
Thou hast proclaimed a strumpet.

HUSBAND: Nay, then, I know thee.
Thou art her private champion, thou, her private friend,
The party you wot on.

GENT.:   Oh, ignoble thought!
I am past my patient blood. Shall I stand idle
And see my reputation touched to death?

HUSBAND: It has galled you, this, has it?

GENT.:   No, monster, I will prove
My thoughts did only tend to virtuous love.

HUSBAND: Love of her virtues? There it goes.

GENT.:   Base spirit,
To lay thy hate upon the fruitful honor
Of thine own bed!

                              They fight, and the Husband is hurt.

HUSBAND: Oh!

GENT.: Wilt thou yield it yet?

HUSBAND: Sir, sir, I have not done with you.

GENT.: I hope nor ne'er shall do.   *Fight again.*

HUSBAND: Have you got tricks? Are you in cunning with me?

GENT.: No, plain and right.
He needs no cunning that for truth doth fight.

                                          Husband falls down.

HUSBAND: Hard fortune! Am I levelled with the ground?

GENT.: Now, sir, you lie at mercy.

HUSBAND: Aye, you slave.

GENT.: Alas, that hate should bring us to our grave.
You see my sword's not thirsty for your life;
I am sorrier for your wound than yourself.
You're of a virtuous house, show virtuous deeds;
'Tis not your honor, 'tis your folly bleeds.
Much good has been expected in your life;

Cancel not all men's hopes. You have a wife
Kind and obedient: heap not wrongful shame
On her and your posterity, nor blame
Your overthrow; let only sin be sore,
And by this fall, rise never to fall more.
And so I leave you.   *Exit.*

HUSBAND: Has the dog left me, then,
After his tooth hath left me? Oh, my heart
Would fain leap after him. Revenge, I say,
I'm mad to be revenged, My strumpet wife,
It is thy quarrel that rips thus my flesh
And makes my breast spit blood, but thou shalt bleed.
Vanquished? Got down? Unable e'en to speak?
Surely 'tis want of money makes men weak.
Aye, 'twas that o'erthrew me; I'd ne'er been down else.   *Exit.*

Enter Wife in a riding suit, with a servingman.

SERV.: Faith, mistress, if it might not be presumption
In me to tell you so, for his excuse
You had small reason, knowing his abuse.

WIFE: I grant I had; but, alas,
Why should our faults at home be spread abroad?
'Tis grief enough within doors. At first sight
Mine uncle could run o'er his prodigal life
As perfectly as if his serious eye
Had numbered all his follies,
Knew of his mortgaged lands, his friends in bonds,
Himself withered with debts. And in that minute
Had I added his usage and unkindness,
'Twould have confounded every thought of good.
Where now, fathering his riots on his youth,
Which time and tame experience will shake off,
Guessing his kindness to me (as I smoothed him
With all the skill I had), though his deserts

Are in form uglier than an unshaped bear,
He's ready to prefer him to some office
And place at Court, a good and sure relief
To all his stooping fortunes. 'Twill be a means, I hope,
To make new league between us, and redeem
His virtues with his lands.

SERV.: I should think so, mistress. If he should not now be kind
to you and love you, and cherish you up, I should think the devil
himself kept open house in him.

WIFE: I doubt not but he will now. Prithee, leave me; I think I
hear him coming.

SERV.: I am gone.   *Exit.*

WIFE: By this good means I shall preserve my lands
And free my husband out of usurers' hands.
Now there is no need of sale; my uncle's kind.
I hope, if ought, this will content his mind.—
Here comes my husband.   *Enter Husband.*

HUSBAND: Now, are you come? Where's the money? Let's see
the money! Is the rubbish sold, those wiseacres, your lands?
Why, when? The money! Where is't? Pour't down, down with
it, down with it. I say pour't o' th' ground! Let's see it, let's see
it!

WIFE: Good sir, keep but in patience and I hope my words shall
like you well. I bring you better comfort than the sale of my
dowry.

HUSBAND: Hah, what's that?

WIFE: Pray, do not fright me, sir, but vouchsafe me hearing. My
uncle, glad of your kindness to me and mild usage—for so I
made it to him—has, in pity of your declining fortunes, provided a place for you at Court of worth and credit, which so
much overjoyed me—

HUSBAND: Out on thee, filth! Over and overjoyed, [*spurns her*] when I'm in torments? Thou politic whore, subtler than nine devils, was this thy journey to Nunck? To set down the history of me, of my state and fortunes? Shall I, that dedicated myself to pleasure, be now confined in service, to crouch and stand like an old man i' th' hams, my hat off? I that never could abide to uncover my head i' th' church? Base slut! This fruit bears thy complaints.

WIFE: Oh, heaven knows
That my complaints were praises and best words
Of you and your estate, only my friends
Knew of our mortgaged lands, and were possessed
Of every accident before I came.
If thou suspect it but a plot in me
To keep my dowry, or for mine own good
Or my poor children's (though it suits a mother
To show a natural care in their reliefs),
Yet I'll forget myself to calm your blood.
Consume it as your pleasure counsels you,
And all I wish e'en clemency affords:
Give me but comely looks and modest words.

HUSBAND: Money, whore, money, or I'll—   *Draws his dagger.*

Enters a servant very hastily.

What the devil? How now, thy hasty news?   *To his man*

SERV.: May it please you, sir—   *Servant in a fear.*

HUSBAND: What? May I not look upon my dagger? Speak, villain, or I will execute the point on thee. Quick, short.

SERV.: Why, sir, a gentleman from the University stays below to speak with you.

HUSBAND: From the University? So! University—that long word runs through me.   *Exeunt.*

WIFE: Was ever wife so wretchedly beset?   *Wife alone.*
Had not this news stepped in between, the point
Had offered violence unto my breast.
That which some women call great misery
Would show but little here, would scarce be seen
Amongst my miseries. I may compare
For wretched fortune with all wives that are.
Nothing will please him until all be nothing.
He calls it slavery to be preferred,
A place of credit a base servitude.
What shall become of me, and my poor children,
Two here and one at nurse, my pretty beggars?
I see how ruin with a palsy hand
Begins to shake the ancient seat to dust.
The heavy weight of sorrow draws my lids
Over my dankish eyes; I scarce can see.
Thus grief will last: it wakes and sleeps with me.   *Exit Wife.*

Enter the Husband with the Master of the College.

HUSBAND: Please you draw near, sir, you're exceeding welcome.

MASTER: That's my doubt. I fear I come not to be welcome.

HUSBAND: Yes, howsoever.

MASTER: 'Tis not my fashion, sir, to dwell in long circumstance, but to be plain and effectual; therefore, to the purpose. The cause of my setting forth was piteous and lamentable. That hopeful young gentleman, your brother, whose virtues we all love dearly, through your default and unnatural negligence lies in bond executed for your debt, a prisoner, all his studies amazed, his hope struck dead, and the pride of his youth muffled in these dark clouds of oppression.

HUSBAND: Hm, hm, hm!

MASTER: Oh, you have killed the towardest hope of all our university. Wherefore, without repentance and amends, expect ponderous and sudden judgements to fall grievously upon you. Your brother, a man who, profited in his divine employments, might have made ten thousand souls fit for heaven, now by your careless courses cast in prison, which you must answer for; and assure your spirit it will come home at length.

HUSBAND: Oh, God! Oh!

MASTER: Wise men think ill of you; others speak ill of you; no man loves you; nay, even those whom honesty condemns, condemn you. And take this from the virtuous affection I bear your brother: never look for prosperous hour, good thought, quiet sleeps, contented walks, nor anything that makes man perfect till you redeem him. What is your answer? How will you bestow him? Upon desperate misery or better hopes? I suffer till I hear your answer.

HUSBAND: Sir, you have much wrought with me. I feel you in my soul; you are your art's master. I never had sense till now; your syllables have cleft me. Both for your words and pains I thank you. I cannot but acknowledge grievous wrongs done to my brother, mighty, mighty, mighty wrongs.—Within there!

Enter a servingman.

HUSBAND: Sir, fill me a bowl of wine.—Alas, poor brother,
Bruised with an execution for my sake.   *Exit servant for wine.*

MASTER: A bruise indeed makes many a mortal sore
Till the grave cure 'em.

Enter with wine.

HUSBAND: Sir, I begin to you. You've chid your welcome.

MASTER: I could have wished it better for your sake.
I pledge you, sir, to the kind man in prison.

HUSBAND: Let it be so. Now, sir, if you so please   [*Drink both.*]
to spend but a few minutes in a walk about my grounds below,

my man here shall attend you. I doubt not but by that time to
be furnished of a sufficient answer, and therein my brother fully
satisfied.

MASTER: Good sir, in that the angels would be pleased,
And the world's murmurs calmed, and I should say
I set forth then upon a lucky day.   *Exit.*

HUSBAND: Oh, thou confused man! Thy pleasant sins have undone thee, thy damnation has beggared thee! That heaven
should say we must not sin, and yet made women! gives our
senses way to find pleasure which, being found, confounds us.
Why should we know those things so much misuse us? Oh,
would virtue had been forbidden! We should then have proved
all virtuous, for 'tis our blood to love what were forbidden. Had
not drunkenness been forbidden, what man would have been
fool to a beast and zany to a swine, to show tricks in the mire?
What is there in three dice to make a man draw thrice three
thousand acres into the compass of a round little table and, with
the gentleman's palsy in the hand, shake out his posterity thieves
or beggars? 'Tis done! I have done it, i' faith, terrible, horrible
misery.—How well was I left! Very well, very well. My lands
showed like a full moon about me, but now the moon's in the
last quarter, waning, waning. And I am mad to think that moon
was mine, mine and my father's and my forefathers'—generations, generations. Down goes the house of us, down, down it
sinks. Now is the name a beggar; begs in me that name which
hundreds of years has made this shire famous. In me and my
posterity runs out. In my seed five are made miserable besides
myself: my riot is now my brother's jailer, my wife's sighing,
my three boys' penury, and mine own confusion. *Tears his hair.*
Why sit my hairs upon my cursed head?
Will not this poison scatter them? Oh, my brother's in execution
among devils that stretch him and make him give. And I in
want, not able for to live nor to redeem him.
Divines and dying men may talk of hell,

But in my heart her several torments dwell.
Slavery and misery! Who in this case
Would not take up money upon his soul,
Pawn his salvation, live at interest?
I, that did ever in abundance dwell,
For me to want exceeds the throes of hell.

Enter his little son with a top and a scourge.

SON: What ail you, father? Are you not well? I cannot scourge
my top as long as you stand so. You take up all the room with
your wide legs. Pooh, you cannot make me afeared with this;
I fear no vizards nor bugbears.

*Husband takes up the child by the skirts of his long coat in one
hand, and draws his dagger with th' other.*

HUSBAND: Up, sir, for here thou hast no inheritance left.

SON: Oh, what will you do, father? I am your white boy.

HUSBAND: Thou shalt be my red boy. Take that.   *Strikes him.*

SON: Oh, you hurt me, father.

HUSBAND: My eldest beggar! Thou shalt not live to ask an
usurer bread, to cry at a great man's gate or follow "good
your honor" by a coach; no, nor your brother. 'Tis charity to
brain you.

SON: How shall I learn, now my head's broke?

HUSBAND: Bleed, bleed, rather than beg, beg!   *Stabs him.*
Be not thy name's disgrace:
Spurn thou thy fortunes first if they be base.
Come view thy second brother.—Fates,
My children's blood
Shall spin into your faces; you shall see
How confidently we scorn beggary!   *Exit with his son.*

Enter a maid with a child in her arms; the mother by her, asleep.

MAID: Sleep, sweet babe; sorrow makes thy mother sleep:
It bodes small good when heaviness falls so deep.
Hush, pretty boy, thy hopes might have been better.
'Tis all lost at dice what ancient honor won.
Hard when the father plays away the son!
Nothing but misery serves in this house.
Ruin and desolation, oh!

Enter Husband with the boy bleeding.

HUSBAND: Whore, give me that boy.

> *Strives with her for the child.*

MAID: Oh, help, help! Out, alas, murder, murder!

HUSBAND: Are you gossiping, prating, sturdy quean?
I'll break your clamor with your neck! Down stairs
Tumble, tumble, headlong! So!   *Throws her down.*
The surest way to charm a woman's tongue
Is break her neck: a politician did it.

SON: Mother, mother; I am killed, mother.

WIFE *wakes.* Ha, who's that cried? Oh me, my children!
Both, both, both, bloody, bloody.   *Catches up the youngest.*

HUSBAND: Strumpet, let go the boy; let go the beggar.

WIFE: Oh, my sweet husband!

HUSBAND: Filth, harlot.

WIFE: Oh, what will you do, dear husband?

HUSBAND: Give me the bastard.

WIFE: Your own sweet boy!

HUSBAND: There are too many beggars.

WIFE: Good my husband—

HUSBAND: Dost thou prevent me still?

WIFE: Oh, God!

HUSBAND: Have at his heart!   *Stabs at the child in her arms.*

WIFE: Oh, my dear boy!   *Gets it from her.*

HUSBAND: Brat, thou shalt not live to shame thy house!

WIFE: Oh, heaven!   *She's hurt and sinks down.*

HUSBAND: And perish! Now begone:
There's whores enough, and want would make thee one.

Enter a lusty servant.

SERV.: Oh, sir, what deeds are these?

HUSBAND: Base slave, my vassal,
Comest thou between my fury to question me?

SERV.: Were you the devil, I would hold you, sir.

HUSBAND: Hold me? Presumption! I'll undo thee for 't.

SERV.: 'Sblood, you have undone us all, sir.

HUSBAND: Tug at thy master?

SERV.: Tug at a monster.

HUSBAND: Have I no power? Shall my slave fetter me?

SERV.: Nay then, the devil wrestles; I am thrown.

HUSBAND: Oh, villain, now I'll tug thee [*overcomes him*], now
I'll tear thee;
Set quick spurs to my vassal, bruise him, trample him.
So! I think thou wilt not follow me in haste.
My horse stands ready saddled. Away, away;
Now to my brat at nurse, my sucking beggar.
Fates, I'll not leave you one to trample on.

The Master meets him.

MASTER: How is 't with you, sir? Methinks you look
Of a distracted color.

HUSBAND: Who? I, sir? 'Tis but your fancy.
Please you walk in, sir, and I'll soon resolve you.
I want one small part to make up the sum,
And then my brother shall rest satisfied.

MASTER: I shall be glad to see it; sir, I'll attend you.   *Exeunt.*

SERV.: Oh, I am scarce able to heave up myself,
He's so bruised me with his devilish weight,
And torn my flesh with his blood-hasty spur.
A man before of easy constitution,
Till now hell's power supplied to his soul's wrong.
Oh, how damnation can make weak men strong.

Enter Master and two servants.

SERV.: Oh, the most piteous deed, sir, since you came.

MASTER: A deadly greeting! Has he summed up these
To satisfy his brother? Here's another,
And by the bleeding infants, the dead mother.

WIFE: Oh, oh.

MASTER: Surgeons, surgeons! She recovers life.
One of his men all faint and bloodied!

I SERV.: Follow! our murderous master has took horse
To kill his child at nurse. Oh, follow quickly.

MASTER: I am the readiest. It shall be my charge
To raise the town upon him.   *Exit Master and servants.*

I SERV.: Good sir, do follow him.

WIFE: Oh, my children.

I SERV.: How is it with my most afflicted mistress?

WIFE: Why do I now recover? why half live?
To see my children bleed before my eyes?
A sight able to kill a mother's breast
Without an executioner! What, art thou mangled too?

I SERV.: I, thinking to prevent what his quick mischiefs
Had so soon acted, came and rushed upon him.
We struggled, but a fouler strength than his
O'erthrew me with his arms; then did he bruise me
And rent my flesh, and robbed me of my hair,
Like a man mad in execution;
Made me unfit to rise and follow him.

WIFE: What is it has beguiled him of all grace
And stole away humanity from his breast?
To slay his children, purposed to kill his wife
And spoil his servants.

Enter two servants.

BOTH: Please you leave this most accursed place;
A surgeon waits within.

WIFE: Willing to leave it!
'Tis guilty of sweet blood, innocent blood.
Murder has took this chamber with full hands,
And will ne'er out as long as the house stands. *Exeunt.*

Enter Husband as being thrown off his horse, and falls.

HUSBAND: Oh, stumbling jade, the spavin overtake thee, the fifty diseases stop thee! Oh, I am sorely bruised; plague founder thee! Thou runnest at ease and pleasure, heart, of chance to throw me now within a flight of the town in such plain even ground. 'Sfoot, a man may dice upon 't and throw away the meadows! Filthy beast!

CRY WITHIN: Follow, follow, follow!

HUSBAND: Ha! I hear sounds of men, like hue and cry.
Up, up, and struggle to thy horse, make on;
Dispatch that little beggar and all's done.

CRY WITHIN: Here, this way, this way!

HUSBAND: At my back? Oh,
What fate have I? My limbs deny me go,
My will is bated, beggary claims a part.
Oh, could I here reach to the infant's heart!

Enter Master of the College, three gentlemen, and others with halberds.

ALL: Here, here. Yonder, yonder.   *Find him.*

MASTER: Unnatural, flinty, more than barbarous:
The Scythians in their marble-hearted feats
Could not have acted more remorseless deeds
In their relentless natures than these of thine.
Was this the answer I long waited on,
The satisfaction for thy 'prisoned brother?

HUSBAND: Why, he can have no more on us than our skins, and some of 'em want but flaying.

I GENT.: Great sins have made him impudent.

MASTER: He's shed so much blood that he cannot blush.

2 GENT.: Away with him; bear him along to the Justices.
A gentleman of worship dwells at hand;
There shall his deeds be blazed.

HUSBAND: Why, all the better.
My glory 'tis to have my action known:
I grieve for nothing but I missed of one.

MASTER: There's little of a father in that grief.
Bear him away.   *Exeunt.*

Enters a knight with two or three gentlemen.

KNIGHT: Endangered so his wife? murdered his children?

I GENT.: So the cry comes.

KNIGHT: I am sorry I e'er knew him,

That ever he took life and natural being
From such an honored stock and fair descent:
Till this black minute without stain or blemish.

I GENT.: Here come the men.

Enter the Master of the College and the rest, with the prisoner.

KNIGHT: The serpent of his house! I'm sorry for this time that I am in place of justice.

MASTER: Please you, sir.

KNIGHT: Do not repeat it twice; I know too much. Would it had ne'er been thought on. Sir, I bleed for you.

I GENT.: Your father's sorrows are alive in me.
What made you show such monstrous cruelty?

HUSBAND: In a word, sir, I have consumed all, played away long acre, and I thought it the charitablest deed I could do to cozen beggary and knock my house o' th' head.

KNIGHT: Oh, in a cooler blood you will repent it.

HUSBAND: I repent now that one's left unkilled,
My brat at nurse. Oh, I would full fain have weaned him.

KNIGHT: Well, I do not think but in tomorrow's judgement
The terror will sit closer to your soul
When the dread thought of death remembers you;
To further which, take this sad voice from me:
Never was act played more unnaturally.

HUSBAND: I thank you, sir.

KNIGHT: Go, lead him to the jail:
Where justice claims all, there must pity fail.

HUSBAND: Come, come, away with me.   *Exit prisoner.*

MASTER: Sir, you deserve the worship of your place.
Would all did so: in you the law is grace.

KNIGHT: It is my wish it should be so.—Ruinous man,
The desolation of his house, the blot
Upon his predecessors' honored name!
That man is nearest shame that is past shame.   *Exeunt.*

*Enter Husband with the officers, the Master and gentlemen, as
going by his house.*

HUSBAND: I am right against my own house, seat of my ancestors. I hear my wife's alive but much endangered. Let me entreat to speak with her before the prison grip me.

Enter his Wife, brought in a chair.

GENT: See, here she comes of herself.

WIFE: Oh, my sweet husband, my dear distressed husband,
Now in the hands of unrelenting laws!
My greatest sorrow, my extremest bleeding;
Now my soul bleeds.

HUSBAND: How now? kind to me? Did I not wound thee, left
thee for dead?

WIFE: Tut, far greater wounds did my breast feel:
Unkindness strikes a deeper wound than steel;
You have been still unkind to me.

HUSBAND: Faith, and so I think I have.
I did my murders roughly, out of hand,
Desperate and sudden; but thou hast devised
A fine way now to kill me: thou hast given mine eyes
Seven wounds apiece. Now glides the devil from me,
Departs at every joint, heaves up my nails.
Oh, catch him new torments that were ne'er invented;
Bind him one thousand more, you blessed angels,
In that pit bottomless; let him not rise
To make men act unnatural tragedies,
To spread into a father and, in fury,

Make him his children's executioners,
Murder his wife, his servants, and who not?
For that man's dark, where heaven is quite forgot.

WIFE: Oh, my repentant husband!

HUSBAND: My dear soul, whom I too much have wronged,
For death I die, and for this have I longed.

WIFE: Thou shouldst not, be assured, for these faults die,
If the law could forgive as soon as I.

HUSBAND: What sight is yonder?   *Children laid out.*

WIFE: Oh, our two bleeding boys
Laid forth upon the threshold.

HUSBAND: Here's weight enough to make a heart-string crack.
Oh, were it lawful that your pretty souls
Might look from heaven into your father's eyes,
Then should you see the penitent glasses melt
And both your murders shoot upon my cheeks;
But you are playing in the angels laps
And will not look on me,
Who, void of grace, killed you in beggary.
Oh, that I might my wishes now attain,
I should then wish you living were again,
Though I did beg with you, which thing I feared.
Oh, 'twas the enemy my eyes so bleared.
Oh, would you could pray heaven me to forgive,
That will unto my end repentant live.

WIFE: It makes me e'en forget all other sorrows
And leave part with this.

OFFICER: Come, will you go?

HUSBAND: I'll kiss the blood I spilled and then I go;
My soul is bloodied, well may my lips be so.

Farewell, dear wife, now thou and I must part;
I of thy wrongs repent me with my heart.

WIFE: Oh, stay! Thou shalt not go.

HUSBAND: That's but in vain; you see it must be so.
Farewell, ye bloody ashes of my boys!
My punishments are their eternal joys.
Let every father look into my deeds,
And then their heirs may prosper while mine bleeds.

WIFE: More wretched am I now in this distress

Exit Husband with halberds.

Than former sorrows made me.

MASTER: Oh, kind wife,
Be comforted. One joy is yet unmurdered:
You have a boy at nurse; your joy's in him.

WIFE: Dearer than all is my poor husband's life.
Heaven give my body strength, which yet is faint
With much expense of blood, and I will kneel,
Sue for his life, number up all my friends
To plead for pardon for my poor husband's life.

MASTER: Was it in man to wound so kind a creature?
I'll ever praise a woman for thy sake.
I must return with grief; my answer's set:
I shall bring news weighs heavier than the debt.—
Two brothers: one in bond lies overthrown,
This on a deadlier execution.

Lord Herbert of Cherbury (1583–1648), son of Donne's patron and friend, Mrs. Magdalen Herbert, and elder brother of George Herbert.

To his Watch when he could not Sleep

Uncessant minutes, whilst you move you tell
The time that tells our life, which, though it run
Never so fast or far, your new begun,
Short steps shall overtake; for, though life well

May scape his own account, it shall not yours.
You are Death's auditors that both divide
And sum whate'er that life inspired endures
Past a beginning; and through you we bide

The doom of Fate, whose unrecalled decree
You date, bring, execute, making what's new
(Ill and good) old; for as we die in you,
You die in Time, Time in Eternity.

"Lord, thus I sin"

Lord, thus I sin, repent, and sin again,
As if repentance only were in me
Leave for new sin. Thus do I entertain
My short time, and Thy grace, abusing Thee
And Thy long-suffering, which, though it be

Ne'er overcome by sin, yet were in vain
If tempted oft. Thus we our errors see

Before our punishment, and so remain
Without excuse. And, Lord, in them 'tis true
Thy laws are just, but why dost Thou distrain
Ought else for life save life? That is Thy due;
The rest Thou makst us owe and mayst to us
As well forgive. But oh, my sins renew
Whilst I do talk with my Creator thus.

"Thus ends my love"

Thus ends my love. But this doth grieve me most,
That so it ends. But that ends too. This yet,
Besides the wishes, hopes, and time I lost,
Troubles my mind a while, that I am set
Free, worse than denied. I can neither boast
Choice nor success, as my case is, nor get
Pardon from myself that I loved not
A better mistress or a worse. This debt
Only's her due, still, that she be forgot
Ere changed, lest I love none. This done, the taint
Of foul inconstancy is cleared, at least
In me. There only rests but to unpaint
Her form in my mind that so, dispossessed,
It be a temple but without a saint.

In a Glass Window: For Inconstancy

Love, of this clearest, frailest glass,
Divide the properties so as
In the division may appear
Clearness for me, frailty for her.

Bibliography

PERCY S. ALLEN. *The Age of Erasmus.* 1914.

S. T. BINDHOFF. *Tudor England.* 1950.

DOUGLAS BUSH. *English Literature in the Earlier Seventeenth Century.* 1945; 2nd ed. 1962.

MURIEL ST. C. BYRNE. *Elizabethan Life in Town and Country.* 2nd ed. 1934.

R. W. CHAMBERS. *Thomas More.* 1935.

E. P. CHEYNEY. *History of England from the Defeat of the Armada to the Death of Elizabeth.* 2 vols. 1914–26.

MARCHETTE CHUTE. *Ben Jonson of Westminster.* 1953.

———. *Shakespeare of London.* 1949.

HARDIN CRAIG. *The Enchanted Glass.* 1936.

G. R. ELTON. *England under the Tudors.* 1955.

S. R. GARDINER. *History of England from the Accession of James I to the Outbreak of the Civil War.* 10 vols. 1884.

JOHN GERARD, S.J. *The Autobiography of a Hunted Priest.* Tr. Philip Caraman, S.J. 1952.

ALLAN H. GILBERT. *Literary Criticism: Plato to Dryden.* 1940.

JAN HUIZINGA. *The Waning of the Middle Ages.* 1924.

SIDNEY LEE and C. T. ONIONS, EDS. *Shakespeare's England.* 2 vols. 1916.

C. S. LEWIS. *English Literature in the Sixteenth Century, Excluding Drama.* 1954.

ROBERT NAUNTON. *Fragmenta Regalia.* 1870.

J. E. NEALE. *The Elizabethan House of Commons.* 1950.

J. E. NEALE. "The Elizabethan Age," "The Elizabethan Political Scene," in *Essays in Elizabethan History*. 1958.

——. *Queen Elizabeth*. 1934.

WALLACE NOTESTEIN. *The English People on the Eve of Colonization: 1603–1630*. 1954.

CONYERS READ. *The Tudors*. 1936.

A. L. ROWSE. *The England of Elizabeth*. 1950.

G. GREGORY SMITH, ED. *Elizabethan Critical Essays*. 2 vols. 1904.

JOHN SPEED. *An Atlas of Tudor England and Wales*. Ed. E. G. R. Taylor. 1951.

E. M. W. TILLYARD. *The Elizabethan World Picture*. 1943.

F. P. WILSON. *Elizabethan and Jacobean*. 1945.

YVOR WINTERS. "The 16th Century Lyric in England," *Poetry* LIII (February and March, 1939), 258–72 and 320–35; and LIV (April, 1939), 35–51.